ARCO

Air Conditioning
& Refrigeration
Toolbox Manual

2nd Edition

David J. Tenenbaum

PETERSON'S

A nelnet. COMPANY

PETERSON'S

A ⓝelnet. COMPANY

About Peterson's, a Nelnet company

Peterson's (www.petersons.com) is a leading provider of education information and advice, with books and online resources focusing on education search, test preparation, and financial aid. Its Web site offers searchable databases and interactive tools for contacting educational institutions, online practice tests and instruction, and planning tools for securing financial aid. Peterson's serves 110 million education consumers annually.

For more information, contact Peterson's, 2000 Lenox Drive, Lawrenceville, NJ 08648; 800-338-3282; or find us on the World Wide Web at www.petersons.com/about.

Editor: Joe Krasowski; Production Editor: Bret Bollmann; Manufacturing Manager: Ray Golaszewski; Composition Manager and Interior Design: Michele Able

ISBN-13: 978-0-7689-2235-6
ISBN-10: 0-7689-2235-6

Printed in Canada

10 9 8 7 6 5 4 3 2   08 07 06

Second Edition

Acknowledgments

I am grateful to Jim McDonald, a veteran steamfitter and instructor of apprentices in Madison, Wisconsin, who contributed immensely to the scope and quality of this manual. Equally creditworthy is Kenneth Brodzik, a journeyman steamfitter who teaches air conditioning and refrigeration at Milwaukee Area Technical College and Steamfitters Local 601, and has been servicing HVAC systems since 1984. Ken played a crucial role in ensuring high quality and relevance in this second edition.

CONTENTS

Introduction

Much has changed in the air conditioning and refrigeration field since this manual was first published nearly twenty years ago. Computers and electronic controls are everywhere. New environmental regulations have ushered in new equipment, new procedures, and new ozone-friendly refrigerants. Although the second edition has been updated to include the latest technological advances, refrigerants, and regulations, what remains the same is the utility and comprehensiveness of a manual that has both served and been lauded by the air conditioning and refrigeration industry for twenty years.

This manual describes the installation, troubleshooting, and repair of hermetic, semihermetic, and open refrigeration systems using the vapor-compression or absorption cycle. The manual is intended to help apprentice and journeyman cooling-system technicians work safely and efficiently.

This manual covers central comfort-cooling systems for residences and larger buildings, and refrigeration systems used in commercial and small industrial settings. Although the installation and repair of auto air conditioners and domestic refrigerators and freezers is not described, the operating principles and many repair techniques described here would apply to these smaller systems.

Any cooling system must meet certain basic operating conditions, including:

- The system must be dry and uncontaminated.
- The compressor (in a vapor-compression system) or generator (in an absorption system) must remain within safe and efficient temperature, pressure, and electrical limits.
- All moving parts that require lubrication must receive enough oil under the proper pressure.
- No liquid refrigerant can enter the compressor through the suction line.
- The evaporator must receive enough liquid refrigerant.
- The piping cannot cause excessive pressure reduction.
- The devices for disposing of heat must function well.

How to Use This Book

This manual will help you install, diagnose, and service cooling systems in accordance with the basic requirements outlined above. The logical arrangement and index will help you quickly find the information you need. Illustrations, graphics, charts, and tables are included for various systems, components, devices, and procedures.

Chapter 1 describes the trade's tools, equipment, and materials, with a focus on choosing the best device for the task and using it safely.

Chapter 2 explains the scientific principles of heat, electricity, and magnetism that every cooling-system technician must understand. The absorption and vapor-compression cooling cycles are described in detail, in terms of both mechanical and physical principles.

Chapter 3 describes the various types of compressors—centrifugal, helical, rotary, scroll, and reciprocatingùthat a technician will encounter.

Chapter 4 explains the principles of controls and the operation and servicing of capacity, operating, refrigerant, and safety controls, with a special emphasis on metering devices.

Chapter 5 covers other essential components—condensers, evaporators, fans, filters, and pumps found in cooling systems.

Chapter 6 details the various types of motors and drives that power compressors, fans, and pumps, along with suggestions for troubleshooting motors.

Chapter 7 covers tubing and fittings and the numerous valves used in cooling systems, such as the condenser pressure regulator, evaporator pressure regulator, and heat-pump four-way valve.

Chapter 8 describes various complete comfort-cooling, refrigeration, and defrost systems, using the absorption and vapor-compression cycles. Suggestions are given for choosing and installing complete systems.

Chapter 9 describes refrigerants and the requirements for handling and recovering refrigerants to preserve the stratospheric ozone layer. Also discussed are pressure-temperature charts for many common azeotropic and zeotropic refrigerants, including the ozone-friendly refrigerants.

Chapter 10 provides troubleshooting information on compressors, condensers, metering devices, oil-control systems, absorption systems, motors, and pumps.

Chapter 11 covers the basic procedures of comfort-cooling and refrigeration maintenance: using the gauge manifold, removing and adding oil, checking the charge, charging with refrigerant, servicing drive systems, and performing periodic maintenance.

The Appendixes cover mathematics, fundamental formulas, measurement conversions, and basic rules of thumb. Also included are a list of abbreviations, a glossary, and the complete addresses of unions, manufacturers, and trade associations.

1

Tools, Equipment, and Materials

The basic hand and power tools needed to install and repair comfort-cooling and refrigeration systems are covered in this chapter. Specifically, this chapter covers soldering, brazing, cutting, bending, and flaring. Also covered are the many meters and gauges needed on the job as well as refrigerant recovery equipment.

HAND AND POWER TOOLS

Many of the tools used for installing and repairing cooling systems inside any good tool kit, but others are unique to the trade, especially those used for tubing.

Tubing Tools

Much of the work of an air-conditioning/refrigeration (ACR) technician involves bending, cutting, flaring, and joining tubing. Let's start with cutters.

Tubing Cutters and Hacksaw

A wheeled tubing cutter is best for cutting small and soft tubing, while a hacksaw is best for hard and large tubing. Some tubing cutters allow one to slide the cutting wheel against the tube without turning the feed screw. During the cut, do not advance the cutting wheel too fast, or the tube will be squashed. Worn cutter parts may cause the cutter wheel to travel along the tube instead of cutting squarely. A three-wheel cutter is handy for cutting in tight places, as it only requires 120° of rotation. Most tubing cutters have a reamer to clean out burrs and ensure full flow.

A hacksaw should have a wave-set blade with 32 teeth per inch (13 teeth per cm). Use a cutting fixture to get a straight, square cut. Prevent chips or filings from entering the tubing. For a fixed tube, insert a coat hanger with a rag on the end before sawing; remove it afterwards. Hold a detached tube upside down and tap it to remove chips.

To prevent dirt and moisture from entering idle tubes, insert a cap or plug in the ends.

1

Pipe Machine

A pipe machine will cut, ream, and thread steel pipe. Simple machines merely rotate the pipe and fit the cutter and die to it. More elaborate machines have a reamer, cutter, and adjustable die that can easily be applied to the pipe. An adjustable die is manually adjusted to the pipe size. Many machines also automatically pump oil onto the die while the motor runs.

> **TIP:** Keep all clothing clear of rotating parts. Maintain a supply of cutting oil in the reservoir. Oil the die manually if necessary. Always ground the machine.

Measuring Pipe and Tube

One can determine pipe lengths by laying out the pipes and fittings and marking the pipe, or by taking dimensions from plans, which are more accurate. Plans show the centerline of each tube and fitting, and list center-to-center measurements. Convert center-to-center dimensions to actual pipe lengths before cutting, usually by calculating one end at a time. Figure 1-A illustrates how to find the deduction for the left end when given a center-to-center measurement AB (6'0") between the fittings.

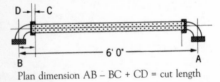

Plan dimension AB – BC + CD = cut length

Figure 1-A: Calculating actual pipe length (repeat for right end)

Then make a similar calculation for the other end. If the other end has the same type of fitting, double the cut-off amount just calculated. Otherwise, subtract the second calculation from the shortened length (not the plan's center-to-center measurement).

To find the cut length based on the calculated length, for threaded fittings on pipe up to 2" in diameter, use this rule of thumb:

center-to-center plan dimension – (diameter of pipe x number of fittings) = cut length.

For a 2" (5.08 cm) pipe with center-to-center plan length of 48" (122 cm) ending in two elbows:

48" – (2" × 2) = 44"
122 cm – (5.08 cm × 2) = 111.84 cm
For a 90° welded elbow: center-to-center plan length –
  (1.5 × pipe ID) = cut length (calculate again for other end)
For a 45° welded elbow: center-to-center plan length –
  (0.625 × pipe ID) = cut length (calculate again for other end)

Figuring Offsets

An offset is a change of direction to pass a tube around an obstruction. The offset typically terminates in pipes that run parallel to each other. We call the angled piece the "offset."

Here's how to calculate the length of a 45° offset to bypass the obstruction shown in Figure 1-B.

1. Measure distance A between the centerlines of pipes B and C (Example: 15" [38.1 cm]).

2. Plan dimension of offset
   E = 1.41 × A
   21.15" = 1.41 × 15" (53.72 cm = 1.41 × 38.1cm)

3. Now, subtract for the elbows to find the cut length of the offset.

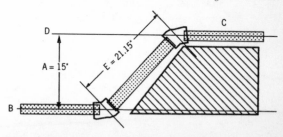

Figure 1-B: Calculating offset length with 45° elbows

Benders

Benders are used to bend soft tubing without flattening or kinking, which reduces flow capacity or causes weakness or leaks. All bends must be accurate so the finished assembly is not under strain. When bending tube, avoid pinching, kinking, and "too-sharp" bends. A good guideline is to make the minimum radius 5 to 10 times the tube diameter. Tighter changes in direction require fittings. Hard tube resists bending and needs fittings. The best tool for a particular bend depends on tubing size and whether flares and fittings are installed before or after bending.

Lever Benders

Lever benders can be slipped over the tube for fast, accurate bends. The bender forces a lever against a fixed pin. Some units intensify the bending force with gears. If the bender does not have replaceable parts to accommodate various tubing sizes, a separate tool for each tubing size will be required. The bender may have a scale showing how much the bending will stretch the tube. A second scale may measure the bend in degrees.

Spring Benders

Spring benders are coil springs that slip over (external spring) or inside (internal spring) the tubing. An internal spring must be used on a flared tube because the flare would prevent removal of an external spring. An external spring must be used to bend the middle of a tube, where an internal spring could not be extracted. For an especially tight bend, try using internal and external bending springs in combination. A spring bender fits a single size of tubing, so a set will be required. Keep internal springs clean so they don't contaminate the tubing. Twist an external spring to remove it after bending, or take the bend slightly beyond the desired angle, then relax the bend slightly as the spring is removed.

Flaring Block

Refrigeration systems often use flared joints between copper tubes and fittings or valves. Flares offer an easy-to-make connection that can be separated much easier than a soldered or brazed joint. The flare must have the correct angle (45°) and a full seat to seal. Because steel tubing is less malleable, it is usually flared to 37°. A separate tool is needed for each angle.

Flares may be either single- or double-thickness, also called a "double-flare." Double-flares are stronger and more reliable when properly constructed, and are used with tubing 5/16" (7.9 mm) and larger. Some flaring blocks have adaptors for single and double flares.

Soft tubing is easier to flare. To flare hard (or old, brittle copper) tubing, anneal it first to prevent cracking.

To make a single flare:

1. Cut the tube to the proper length and square the end with a file. Prevent filings from entering the tube.

2. Remove the burr left by the file with a reamer (this is essential for a good contact between the flare and the fitting).

3. Slip the coupling nut onto the tube.

4. Clamp the tube in the flaring block with about one-third of the height of the flare protruding. If too much protrudes, the flare will be too large. If too little protrudes, the seating surface will be too small.

5. Place the yoke of the flaring tool around the shoulders of the block and insert the cone into the tube. Add a few drops of refrigerant oil where the flaring cone meets the tube to prevent the flare from being thin and brittle.

6. Screw the cone to make contact, then screw 1/2 turn further, unscrew 1/4 turn, then screw 3/4 turn and unscrew 1/4 turn. Repeat this sequence until the flare is done. Do not overtighten the tool. (The back-and-forth motion limits work-hardening of the tube, which could weaken the flare.)

7. Remove the tool, clean the flare, and assemble the joint.

To make a double flare:

1. Clamp the tubing in the block.

2. Insert the female punch into the tubing and hammer it down. This will start the double flare.

3. Remove the female punch and insert the male punch.

4. Hammer down the male punch to give the flare its final shape.

Pinch-off Tool

This tool is used to temporarily close off a process tube after completing work on a system. Place the tool on the tube, screw it tight to pinch the tube, solder or braze the end of the tube, then remove the pinch-off tool.

Line Piercing Tool

This tool installs a tee in a line so one can charge or recover refrigerant in a small hermetic system that has no service valves. Clamp the tool to the line and connect the gauge manifold or refrigerant tank to the valve on the line-piercing tool. Then force the valve stem into the line until it pierces the wall. When the repair is completed, leave the valve in position to plug the line and allow service in the future. (See Chapter 7, "Pipe, Tube, Fittings, and Valves.")

Hermetic Adjustment Kit

Many small hermetic systems are not designed to be serviced, primarily because they lack service valves. A hermetic adjustment kit contains a set of valves to overcome this difficulty. The kit allows one to install a gauge manifold for system diagnosis or charging with oil or refrigerant. The kit includes adaptors, a line piercing tool, wrenches, a gauge, and other tools.

Capillary Tube Cleaner

A "cap tube" cleaner creates pressure inside the tube to force out wax and debris. Disconnect the tube at both ends and connect the front end of the cleaner to the tube. Turning the handle can create up to 20,000 pounds per square inch (psi) pressure in the tube. Finally, the tube needs to be purged using the system refrigerant.

Soldering and Brazing

Soldering and brazing are methods used to join copper and brass tubing and fittings by applying a "filler material" to a hot (but not molten) base metal. Capillary action draws the brazing or soldering filler material into the joint. Welding, in contrast, melts and fuses similar metals. Welding is also a hotter, more localized operation that proceeds from one end of a joint to the other, while soldering and brazing usually affect the whole joint at once. Welding is more likely to cause heat damage (warping or burn-through) than brazing and soldering.

Soldering occurs below 800°F (426°C). Soldered joints are less heat-tolerant than brazed joints, and soldering is widely used for water lines and drains. However, soldering can be used for refrigerant lines as long as the refrigerant does not exceed the solder's maximum operating temperature. Soldering makes the joint with silver-bearing solder using heat from an air-acetylene or propane torch.

The strength of soldering depends greatly on the solder chosen (the strength of brazing depends more on joint design). 95/5 tin-antimony soft solder contains 95% tin and 5% antimony, melts at 450°F (232°C), and becomes fluid at 465°F (241°C). Silver solders (containing 5%, 15%, or 45% silver) are sometimes recommended for high-pressure or high-temperature joints. However, brazing takes no more time and makes a stronger joint.

Brazing is used for operating temperatures above 250°F (121.1°C) and also for steel pipe. Brazing makes a joint with molten bronze, with heat from an oxyacetylene (oxygen-acetylene) torch. Select the filler metal according to the manufacturer's recommendations for the fitting and tubing metals and system operating temperature. The two categories of filler material are:

1. Copper-silver alloys (the BAg series)
2. Copper-phosphorus alloys (BCuP series)

Orifice size determines the amount of fuel gas and oxygen fed to the flame and therefore the amount of heat produced. If the orifice is too small, not enough heat will be available to heat the metal to brazing or soldering temperature. If the orifice is too large, it will overheat the pipe and fittings. Torch tip and orifice size are designated by a number stamped on the tip. Each manufacturer uses its own numbering system for torch tip size. In this manual, the orifice size is given as the number drill size. Number drills consist of a series of eighty drills, numbered 1 (0.2280 inch) through 80 (0.0135 inch). Once one learns a specific manufacturer's torch numbering system, it becomes unnecessary to refer to orifice number drill size. The mixing action of a "turbo" torch creates a flame that is hotter than that particular orifice size would otherwise produce.

The following tip sizes are a good starting point for brazing:

Table 1-A: Suggested Oxyacetylene Tip Sizes for Brazing

Tubing size	Drill size
3/4" and smaller (1.90 cm)	54
1" to 1 1/2" (2.54 to 3.8 cm)	51
2" to 2 1/2" (5 to 6.4 cm)	48–44
3" (7.6 cm)	44–42
4" (10 cm) and up	42 or multiple orifice

CAUTION: When making the last joint in a closed system, heat will cause a pressure buildup that can force molten solder out of the joint. Be sure to open a service valve to vent the system.

Preparing the Joint

The most important step in soldering and brazing is to remove oxides and contaminants from the metal beforehand and to set up a clean, tight joint by:

- cutting the tube square and clean so it reaches the bottom of the fitting. If necessary, throw out any damaged tubing;
- squaring the end with a file and reaming the inside to remove burrs; and
- cleaning the joint. Degrease first if necessary. Remove exterior oxide with sandpaper. Clean only the tubing that will be in or near the joint. Use a steel brush to clean interiors of valves and fittings. Prevent filings and dirt from entering the tubing or fitting. Do not touch a cleaned area, as skin acid causes oxidation that will impair bonding. Do not blow on the clean area; this will moisten it.

Soldering Procedure

Soldering starts with a good, clean (see above), and tight mechanical joint. After cleaning:

1. Immediately apply flux to the tube exterior and the fitting interior with a clean rag or brush. Remove the excess flux with a rag. Do not use acid flux or acid-core solder; these degrade metal.

2. Assemble the joint with a slight twist to spread the flux. The parts must fit tightly with some clearance for the solder to flow. Line up the parts on supports if necessary.

3. Heat the joint evenly with an air-acetylene or propane torch. Test the joint with solder. When the joint is hot enough, solder will melt on contact with the joint. Do not overheat, which will ruin the flux and oxidize the metal. If you overheat the joint, take it apart, clean it, reapply flux, and resolder.

4. Remove the flame and apply solder to the joint. Solder should flow towards the hottest spot. Reapply the flame to the far side of the joint, and let the heat draw the solder into the joint. Then remove the torch and add more solder. A clean, well-fluxed joint at the right temperature will quickly fill with solder. Use extra care when soldering large fittings. Tap the fitting occasionally with a hammer to break surface tension that can inhibit solder flow.

5. Wipe the joint with a rag to smooth the molten solder and allow the joint to cool.

6. Remove excess flux, which can corrode the tube over time.

Brazing Procedure

Start with a neutral or slightly reducing flame, never an oxidizing one, on an air-acetylene or oxyacetylene torch. A blue cone with a reddish-purple fringe indicates a neutral flame. A large torch tip will create a large, hot flame with mild gas pressure. Smaller torches running near maximum heat output make an extremely hot point that can burn through the metal. For large fittings, try a multiple-tip torch. Flux will turn from a milky liquid to a clear liquid around 1100°F (593°C), which is near brazing temperature. Brazing alloys melt at about 1120°F (604°C) and flow at about 1145°F (618°C).

Filler will flow inside a joint by capillary action as long as the clearance is at least .003" (.072 mm). Large clearances weaken a joint.

Be careful not to overheat the fittings and components. Some valves can be disassembled to protect the delicate parts from heat. Otherwise, drape the fitting with a wet rag to keep it cool. Do not ignite anything with the torch. When in doubt, put sheet metal or another shield over any flammable area.

Before brazing, purge air from the system with a nonreactive gas, like nitrogen or carbon dioxide, to reduce oxidation and prevent oil inside the piping from vaporizing and exploding. A nitrogen tank feeding 20 cubic feet (557 liters) per hour should be enough for most systems. Purging is especially important when using the higher-temperature silver-bearing filler metals. Do not fill the system with refrigerant or compressed air before brazing; they are reactive at brazing temperature. Never introduce oxygen into any system to clean, purge, or pressurize it; heated oil can explode when only slightly pressurized with oxygen.

Follow this general procedure for brazing:

1. Start with a clean joint. (See Figure 1-C.)

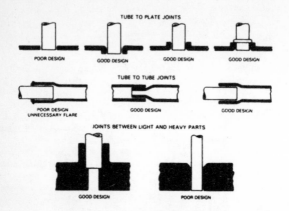

TUBE TO PLATE JOINTS

POOR DESIGN　GOOD DESIGN　GOOD DESIGN　GOOD DESIGN

TUBE TO TUBE JOINTS

POOR DESIGN
UNNECESSARY FLARE　GOOD DESIGN　GOOD DESIGN

JOINTS BETWEEN LIGHT AND HEAVY PARTS

GOOD DESIGN　POOR DESIGN

Figure 1-C: Good and bad brazing joints
Courtesy of Handy & Harman

2. If necessary, prop up the tube and fittings so they stay in perfect alignment.

3. Select flux to match the filler material and follow the manufacturer's directions. Some brazing rods come precoated with flux. Others require that the rod be heated with the torch and pushed into the can of flux to pick up flux. Do not use too much flux. This could contaminate the system.

4. Evenly heat the joint to the correct temperature. Using a sweeping motion to avoid overheating, move the torch around to heat all parts evenly. Keep in mind that filler will flow toward the heat. When brazing a small mass to a larger one, concentrate the heat on the larger one. When brazing copper to steel, concentrate on the copper, which will conduct more heat away from the joint. Note that the flame should be slightly green at brazing temperature.

5. Move the torch tip to another part of the joint and apply filler. Do not heat the filler with the torch; the alloy should flow freely.

Continue heating by waving the torch across the joint. When finished, look for a continuous fillet of filler around the edge of the joint.

6. Cool the joint. After brief air cooling, wet the joint with warm (120°F or 50°C) water to break up the flux. Wrought fittings can be cooled quickly, but cast fittings need more cooling time before wetting.

7. Brush off flux from the outside. If left, it could cause corrosion or hide flaws in the joint. Difficulty removing flux could be the result of not having used enough or having overheated the joint. Check the color. Overheated flux is saturated with oxides and generally turns green or black.

8. Inspect the cold joint for dark, cup-shaped areas, which can mark poor adhesion of the braze alloy. If major problems are discovered, take the joint apart under heat and redo it.

Table 1-B: Brazing Troubleshooting

Problem	Cause	Remedy
Filler does not flow or balls up.	Oxidation on the base metal or insufficient heat	Disassemble and clean the joint or add more heat.
Oxide forms on joint during heating.	Inadequate flux	Cool, clean, add flux, and reheat.
Filler does not enter the joint but flows on the outside.	One part was underheated	Add heat to the cooler part.

Soldering and Brazing Safety

Acetylene burns fiercely, oxygen accelerates the combustion of other materials, and the mixture is explosive. Oxygen tanks are green; acetylene tanks are usually black. Below is a summary of OSHA's extensive standards for general torch safety:

• Ship and move tanks with protective caps screwed over the valve.
• Secure tanks upright during use.
• Check that the tanks, hoses, and fittings have no leaks.
• Do not damage the gauges.
• Move tanks by rolling on bottom edges.
• Protect tanks from damage, heat, improper filling, and abuse.

- Do not oil the regulator.
- Never mix oxygen and oil, as the oil may spontaneously combust.

Oxyacetylene torch operators should follow proper safety procedures, such as:

- Always wear proper eye protection and gloves.
- Never solder or braze piping that is under pressure.

Fumes, fire, and explosion are the major hazards of soldering and brazing. Follow these safety guidelines:

- Use adequate ventilation in confined areas. A respirator with an air supply might be required. Do not breathe or allow fumes to contact eyes. Use caution with lines that have held halocarbon refrigerant, which breaks down into a toxic gas.
- Do not use brazing filler metal containing cadmium, which makes poisonous fumes when heated.
- Flux is particularly harmful to the eyes. Do not apply it with fingers, as it can damage the skin.
- Clean the base materials. This is necessary for a tight joint, and also removes unknown contaminants that can cause hazardous fumes.
- Use enough flux to prevent oxidation of the base metals, which releases fumes.
- Heat the joint broadly to prevent hot spots, flux burnout, and fumes. Do not heat filler directly, which can cause fumes.
- Learn to recognize coatings of galvanized zinc and cadmium. These metals produce dangerous fumes. Remove the coating before heating.
- Never use oxygen to pressure-test piping: Oxygen and oil are an explosive mix.

Drills

Drills are used for many purposes in installation and repair. Twist drills are measured in fractions of an inch or millimeters and are labeled with numbers or letters. Number and letter drills are closer together in size than fractional drills, so they are used for drilling precision holes, such as before tapping.

Number drills sizes: No. 1 = 0.0135" . . . No. 80 = 0.228"

Letter drill sizes: A = 0.234" . . . Z = 0.413"

Drills must be carefully chosen for tapping applications. They must be sharp and operated at the correct speed. Sharp drills run smoother and cooler than dull ones and are less likely to break. Smaller drills should run faster than large ones. Make sure the object being drilled is secured since steady force will be applied. Ground a plug-in electric drill and do not operate it if the grounding plug has been removed. For safety, always wear goggles while drilling.

Hoses

Hoses connect the gauge manifold, service tanks, recycling apparatus, and other equipment to a system for many diagnostic and repair operations. Hoses have a neoprene interior and a braided cotton exterior; the brass fittings have a neoprene gasket to meet the flare of the connecting valve. Hoses are made in lengths from 3' to 6'. The most common use for hoses is to connect the gauge manifold. Gauge manifold hoses have OD flare fittings. Use different hoses to drain crankcase oil, hook up a vacuum pump, or pressure test a system with nitrogen.

Pump, Oil

Hand or electric oil pumps are used to force oil into the crankcase in a pressurized system, which is useful when adding oil without tearing apart a system. One hose connects the pump to an oil container; the second connects the pump to the crankcase oil port.

Never try to pump against a closed valve in the pump discharge, especially with an electric pump. Be sure to empty one type of oil from the pump before adding a different type. Keep the pump clean, with all openings plugged, when not in use. Never allow air into the refrigeration system.

Pump, Vacuum

Vacuum pumps are used to evacuate air, moisture, and other contaminants from a system before charging or recharging. Once the vacuum has been established, the system must be checked for leaks before adding refrigerant.

A single-stage pump, capable of pulling a vacuum of 50 microns, is used for a simple evacuation or a triple-evacuation. (See Chapter 11, "Standard ACR Procedures.") Use a two-stage (high-vacuum) pump to do high (deep) vacuum charging. A very good two-stage pump should pull down to an extremely high vacuum of 1 micron.

Reciprocating vacuum pumps are built like reciprocating compressors, but high-vacuum pumps have one or two rotors in series and slots to guide the vanes as the rotor spins. The rotors enlarge and then shrink the pumping chamber as they rotate. Gas is pushed into the chamber by the pressure differential between the chamber and the piping system. The vanes on the revolving rotor force the gas out the exhaust port.

As gas is removed from the cooling system pipes and equipment, system pressure drops and the remaining gas expands. Over time, the pump draws in less gas, so the last stages of an evacuation take longer than the first stages.

Use copper tubing or special metal hose for most evacuation work. Charging hoses (used with gauge manifolds) may collapse under the vacuum or release gas under prolonged vacuum. When drawing a deep vacuum, a large line will greatly shorten the pumping time. Changing from a 1/4" (0.635 cm) ID line to a 1/2" (1.27 cm) ID line may speed the pumping more than switching from a 1 cubic foot per minute (28 liters/minute) pump to a 5 cf/m (142 l/min.) pump.

The oil in a vacuum pump can be contaminated by water and solvents in the system, creating sludge that will wear the pump and cut efficiency. Dirty or watery oil looks white and foamy. Change the pump oil before each pump-down when using either a single-stage or a two-stage pump.

Make sure to release the vacuum before storing the pump; otherwise, the pump cylinder might become filled with oil and resistant to turning.

Grabbing and Turning Tools

To assemble ACR systems, a good selection of pliers; wrenches; and specialized keys for holding, tightening, and turning is required.

Pliers

Pliers are used for general tightening and holding purposes and are especially handy for holding hot pipes and fittings. Arc-joint pliers have opposing jaws that adjust to different sizes. Insulated handles are an excellent safety measure when working near electricity. Note: Do not use pliers handles as pry bars.

Pipe Wrench

Pipe wrenches are used for assembling and disassembling threaded pipe and fittings. Wrenches between 12" and 24" are most common. A pair of each size is handy. A 36" wrench is useful for pipes up to 4" in diameter. Aluminum wrenches are great because they are much lighter than steel wrenches. Keep the jaws sharp and free of rust. Replace jaws when needed. Oil the adjustment threads occasionally. Never put a piece of pipe on the handle for extra leverage; instead, get a larger wrench.

Valve Key

Because some system valves have no handles, technicians carry a set of valve keys in the toolbox. Also called tee wrenches, valve keys have a square opening on the bottom to fit the valve stem. Common sizes are 3/16", 7/32", 1/4", and 5/16".

Packing Key

A packing key is a cylindrical piece of steel with two studs on the bottom to turn internal packing nuts on valves. (An external packing nut can be turned with a conventional wrench, but the slot on an internal nut is on both sides of the valve stem, requiring this special key.)

Socket Wrench

Socket wrenches are used to tighten plugs and nuts and bolts. Socket sizes from 1/4" to 2" are ideal. Both 3/8" and 1/2" drive systems should be found in any basic tool kit; a 3/4" drive is useful for large systems. Carry both 8- and 12-point sockets for square and hexagonal nuts. Adaptors to drive one size socket from another size wrench are a useful addition. An extension and a universal joint will allow the sockets to reach into tight quarters. Never put a piece of pipe on the handle for extra leverage. Make sure the socket does not slip off the bolt when pulling on the wrench. Pulling the wrench is generally safer than pushing, but make sure you know where your knuckles will be when the wrench slips!

Impact Wrench

An electric or air-operated impact wrench is used to tighten or loosen nuts and bolts. Use with impact sockets, which are tougher than standard ratchet-wrench sockets. A 1/2"-drive impact wrench is the most useful size.

Torque Wrench

Torque wrenches connect to sockets to tighten a bolt with the right amount of force. Undertightening can cause leakage, while overtightening can warp fittings or strip threads. A steady force on the handle will improve accuracy.

METERS AND GAUGES

Meters and gauges are the hallmark of the ACR technician. To do this work, a technician needs a good set of electrical meters, and various gauges for dealing with pressure and vacuum.

Charging Cylinder or Board

A charging cylinder (or charging board) is used to charge refrigerant to a small system. Deluxe charging cylinders have a gauge manifold mounted alongside the cylinder so technicians do not have to hook up their own gauges. Newer charging boards have a digital gauge to measure the flow of refrigerant. Most charging cylinders allow for the installation of a vapor charge through the top valve, or a liquid charge through the bottom valve.

Some cylinders have a heating element to vaporize the refrigerant and speed up the transfer; other cylinders move the refrigerant with pressure in the storage cylinder. Before using a heating element, make sure the cylinder's pressure relief valve is operating properly.

Electric Meters

Cooling system technicians use a variety of meters to measure current, electromotive force (emf or voltage), and resistance in power and control circuits. Although many electric meters measure more than one quantity— frequently resistance and voltage—meters are described individually here in the interests of simplicity.

Many meters require that the technician manually set the range of the measurement before measuring. If unsure about the correct range, start with a high range and gradually reduce it until the proper range is found. Although a range need not be set on auto-ranging meters or most digital meters, a manual setting might work faster than automatic ranging. Digital meters have several other advantages over the older, analog types. They are smaller, easier to read, and have no moving parts.

Connect all meters properly, do not drop them, and routinely check their adjustment. Always make sure meter batteries are charged.

Ammeter

An ammeter measures the current flow past a certain point in a circuit. An ammeter measures direct and/or alternating current. Connect a conventional ammeter in series with the circuit. The circuit must be disconnected before hooking up the meter. To measure AC (but not DC), slip a convenient clamp-on ammeter around the conductor. AC will induce a current in the meter. If the current is too weak to get a good reading, wrap the wire once around one tong of the meter and divide the reading by 2.

A "current transformer" can help an ammeter measure large currents. Disconnect the wire being measured, feed it through the hole in the current transformer, and reconnect. Connect the leads from the current transformer to the ammeter. The current transformer reduces the amperage enough for safe measurement.

Circuit Tester

A light bulb connected to two probes in series can test for an electric current between two points. (See Figure 1-D.)

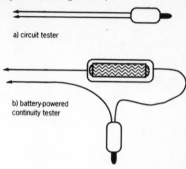

a) circuit tester

b) battery-powered continuity tester

Figure 1-D: Simple electrical testers

Continuity Tester

A continuity tester detects a complete circuit. Some ready-made continuity testers can either run on batteries. Others consist of a bulb (choose the correct voltage for the system) connected to a plug and two probes. (See Chapter 6, "Motors.") In any case, the circuit being tested must not be energized.

Voltmeter

A voltmeter measures the voltage, or *emf*, between two points in an energized circuit. Connect a voltmeter in parallel with the load being checked. A voltmeter can measure input voltage; determine whether a switch is open or closed; or find the voltage drop (and hence resistance) across a relay, motor, or other component. Do not use a 120V voltmeter on a 240V circuit, as this could burn out the voltmeter. (See Figure 1-E.)

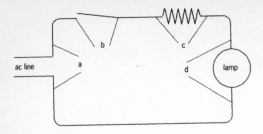

a = line voltage if power is on
b = voltage across switch: 0 if switch is closed (no potential difference), line voltage if switch is open
c = voltage drop across resistor
d = voltage drop across lamp: 0 if lamp is shorted, line voltage if lamp is broken

Figure 1-E: Using a voltmeter

Ohmmeter

An ohmmeter measures resistance (in ohms, or Ω) between two points in a circuit. The meter applies a small current from its battery and measures the drop in voltage caused by resistance in the circuit. The resistance depends on composition, cross-section, length, and temperature of the conductor.

Always shut off power before using an ohmmeter. (See Figure 1-F.) Do not connect an ohmmeter to a circuit that operates at a voltage below what the ohmmeter creates, or damage to low-voltage equipment, like sensors, can result.

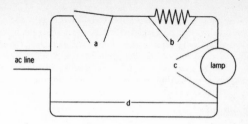

Turn power off before testing!
a = 0 if switch is closed and in good condition
b = resistance across heating coil
c = resistance across lamp
d = continuity of conductor. Resistance = 0 if all switches in line
are closed, conductor is in good condition, and no loads are present.

Figure 1-F: Using an ohmmeter

Megohmmeter

A megohmmeter tests the insulation between a motor winding and the motor frame. This device applies 250 to 10,000 volts DC to the circuit being tested—much higher than a standard ohmmeter. Use a megohmmeter carefully to prevent personal injury or damage to equipment. A megohmmeter can detect motor-insulation problems before the motor burns out. Motor manufacturers may set standards for the resistance of winding insulation—it should usually test at several-million ohms.

Do winding tests after the motor has been running for about an hour, as changing temperature may change the insulation. If a motor with marginal resistance is detected, test it repeatedly with a megohmmeter to see if the trend in resistance is up, down, or stable.

VOM or Multitester

A VOM (volt-ohm-meter) can read voltage or resistance. A VOM is now incorporated in some clamp-on ammeters, making it a very useful tool. The more elaborate models have several scales for greater accuracy. A VOM that includes an ammeter is commonly called a multitester.

Wattmeter

A wattmeter measures the power consumed by an electrical device in watts. Connect the meter in series and parallel with the device. The meter reads the true power consumption by measuring voltage and current and correcting automatically for power factor. (See Chapter 2, "Energy, Electricity, and Cooling Cycles.") One can also find the power draw by measuring with a power-factor meter or calculating the power factor. A clamp-on wattmeter is available.

Gauge Manifold

The gauge manifold is the most important instrument in the air conditioning and refrigeration service business, as it is used for diagnosing system trouble as well as evacuating, charging, and adding oil. The manifold has fittings for three hoses, taps for two gauges, and a valve at each end. The pressure gauge measures 0 to 500 lbs. pressure. The compound gauge measures pressure from 0 to 250 lbs. and vacuum from 0" to 30". The pressure gauge is usually on the right tap of the manifold. (See Figure 1-G.)

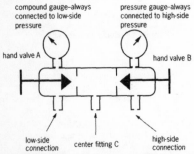

compound gauge-always connected to low-side pressure

pressure gauge-always connected to high-side pressure

hand valve A

hand valve B

low-side connection

center fitting C

high-side connection

To read pressures on each side, close A and B.
To connect low side to C, open A and close B.
To connect high side to C, close A and open B.
To connect high side to low side, open A and B, cap C.
To connect high side to low side and to C, open A and B.

Figure 1-G: Using the gauge manifold

The valve at each end controls whether that end hose connects to the center of the manifold. Both gauges are always connected to their respective sides of the system, so one can read high- and low-side pressures whenever the gauge manifold is connected. The valve can be backseated when introducing refrigerant through the center port, or when evacuating a system. Backseating removes the valve from the system, preventing the possibility of leaks through the gauge manifold.

The hoses should be colored to avoid confusion. Some technicians have their own scheme, but this is the conventional color scheme:

Red: connects the high side to the high-pressure gauge.

Blue: connects the low side to the compound gauge.

White or yellow: connects a charging cylinder, oil can, or other service device to the center outlet of the gauge manifold.

Hermetic Analyzer

A hermetic analyzer is an electric device used to analyze refrigeration systems and cure some of the electrical troubles it detects. The device generally contains an ohmmeter, voltmeter, and ammeter, and can be used to check for shorts, grounds, open windings, and continuity. Some hermetic analyzers can also test capacitors and relays. An analyzer has a bank of starting capacitors that can reverse motor rotation and rock a stuck compressor free.

Leak Detectors

Four methods can check for leaks in a new or established system: bubble solution, electronic detector, halide torch, and refrigerant dye.

Bubble Solution

A bubble solution is a primitive method of detecting leaks and should only be used when a better method is not available or cannot be used for some reason. Brush a solution of soap and water or a special solution (with longer-lasting bubbles) over the suspect area. Unfortunately, large leaks will blow right through the solution, slow leaks may be difficult to detect, and you may need to use an inspection mirror for hard-to-reach fittings.

In one instance—testing for leaks near urethane foam—bubble-solution is *better* than an electronic detector or halide torch. Because refrigerants were once used to "blow" foam in the factory, a halide torch and an electronic leak detector may register a false positive in the vicinity of old urethane foam.

Electronic Detector

Electronic detectors are the most sensitive type of detector, and some detect leaks as small as 1/2 oz. (14 grams) per year. Most electronic detectors use the dielectric principle, which compares the electrical conduction of surrounding air to the conduction of air near the suspected leak. Electronic detectors may be battery-operated or AC-powered. The device generally beeps; as refrigerant concentration increases, the beeping speeds up.

Some electronic leak detectors must be adjusted to ambient air before use, while others do this automatically. After (if necessary) adjusting the meter, pass the probe over the suspected leak. Molecules of air (and any halocarbon refrigerant present) are drawn into the probe and analyzed. Always place the inlet tube below the suspected leak, because refrigerant is heavier than air. Move the tip slowly across the surface, at about one inch per second. Shut off all fans to minimize air movement in the area, and observe operating temperature restrictions on the detector. In atmospheres heavily contaminated with refrigerant, the detector may be overwhelmed and inaccurate.

Halide Torch

A halide torch works because a green color is produced when refrigerant touches hot copper. Move the torch's hose around the suspected leak to draw in air (and any leaking refrigerant) toward the heated piece of copper. A faint green color indicates a small leak; green-to-purple indicates a large leak.

High system pressure (about 75 psi [620 kPa]) will help when using a halide torch. However, the torch is slower and less sensitive than an electronic detector. If it is difficult to read the torch in bright light, make a shield from an old tin can and paint the inside black. Cut a viewing slit on the side. Other contaminants may cause a change in flame color. The torch cannot be used near old urethane foam (which may contain halocarbons) or in areas with flammable vapors or other fire hazards.

Refrigerant Dye

Adding dye to refrigerant is a time-honored method of detecting leaks, especially when leak detectors fail or cannot isolate the leak. Although modern fluorescent dyes are easy to spot under a black light, dye:

- works best when the whole charge is replaced with dyed refrigerant, which is expensive;
- works slowly if oil does not circulate quickly in the system—leaks might take up to 24 hours to detect; and
- will cause some compressor manufacturers to void the warranty.

Manometer

A manometer measures the pressure of a fluid. Different manometers are required to measure air pressure in a duct or vacuum pressure in a system line. Flexible tubes are a handy feature because they make the tool easier to store.

A water manometer measures pressure in an air duct, including when static pressure or pressure drop across a filter must be measured. A water manometer has either a U-tube, with the top of one end connected by tube to the duct you are measuring (see Figure 1-H) and a scale graduated in fractions of an inch or millimeters, or an inclined tube with a sloping tube that allow pressure measurements accurate to hundredths of an inch.

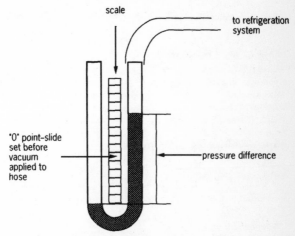

Figure 1-H: U-tube manometer

To measure pressure drop across an air filter, connect a probe to one tube of the manometer, place it in the duct, and open the other end of the manometer to the atmosphere. Then switch the probe to the other side of the filter and read again. Subtract the higher measurement from the lower one to find pressure drop. If the probe tube is long, allow a few minutes for pressure to stabilize before reading.

A *dial-type manometer* can also measure pressure differential. Insert one probe in each side of the filter and read the differential directly from the dial.

A *mercury manometer* can measure system vacuum, which can also be done with an electronic vacuum gauge. The mercury manometer looks and works much like a U-tube water manometer, except that the adjustable scale is calibrated in inches or millimeters of mercury.

To use a mercury manometer, connect the hose to the system being evacuated. Start the vacuum pump and watch the level of the mercury. When the vacuum stabilizes, slide the zero indicator on the adjustable scale opposite the level of the mercury in one leg of the U-tube, then read the pressure difference from the scale opposite the other leg.

When using a manometer:

1. Hold the manometer vertical;
2. Don't spill the mercury or the water (Mercury is toxic!); and
3. Keep caps tight in storage.

Sight Glass, Electronic

An electronic sight glass uses sonar to detect bubbles in the liquid-line refrigerant. The device can be used as a clamp-on sight glass for charging or analyzing a system that lacks a sight glass, or has one in a poor location. The electronic sight glass emits a sound when it detects no bubbles, so you needn't return to the sight glass while charging or diagnosing.

Temperature-Measuring Devices

Various devices are used in the trade to measure air or liquid temperatures in the system and the cooled air, water, or product. Thermometers, thermistors, and thermocouples all have their place. Never expose a measuring device to temperatures beyond its measuring range; this could ruin it.

Thermometer

Clip-on and dial-stem thermometers are both popular in cooling system work. Dial-stem thermometers may have a remote-reading bulb. A thermometer for measuring superheat should read fast and make good contact with the suction line or evaporator. A recording thermometer registers temperatures over a 24-hour period, for assessing system performance.

A wet-bulb thermometer determines the degree of evaporative cooling taking place. In combination with a normal, or "dry-bulb" thermometer, the device can measure relative humidity. (See below.) The bulb of this thermometer is, like a person, cooled by evaporation of water, so the thermometer registers colder in a dry environment. In short, the thermometer mimics what a person would feel in the environment.

To use a wet-bulb thermometer, fill the reservoir with water and leave the thermometer for a few minutes in the area you are measuring, preferably in a strong air flow. Keep the thermometer away from radiant heat, and take the reading before the bulb dries out.

Sling Psychrometer

A sling psychrometer combines dry-bulb and wet-bulb thermometers in an instrument that you whirl around on a sling. The movement makes enough air flow to get an accurate wet-bulb reading. For accuracy, use a clean white wick and distilled water on the wet bulb. For locations where the sling would be awkward, an aspiring thermometer has a fan that blows air across the wet bulb.

To find relative humidity with a sling psychrometer or aspiring thermometer, see Chapter 2, "Energy, Electricity, and Cooling Cycles."

Thermistor

A thermistor is a semiconductor whose resistance changes quickly when temperature changes. That quick response makes thermistors good for operating and safety controls, where they are used to send electric signals to system components.

Thermistors can measure temperature in motor windings, conditioned space, and compressor crankcases. Some thermistors change resistance gradually over the entire working range, which is useful in a sensor. Others change resistance rapidly at a specific temperature range, making them good thermally operated switches.

Thermocouple

A thermocouple measures temperature by reading the voltage created when a bimetallic strip is heated. The device can be used as a thermometer, or to signal an operating or safety control.

Vacuum Gauge, Electronic

This instrument is used to accurately measure the high vacuum that would be needed, for example, when evacuating a room-temperature system before charging. The sensing element is actually a thermocouple that measures the rate of heat transfer. As air is removed from the system, heat transfer slows, showing that the vacuum is increasing. Connect the gauge to the suction-service valve with lines that are as large in diameter and as short as possible.

After the vacuum pump is shut off, system pressure will rise for a certain time while trapped moisture evaporates. If the system is tight, the vacuum will stabilize after all moisture evaporates. If the pressure continues rising, there is a leak that must be fixed before charging. Follow the manufacturer's directions when using an electronic vacuum gauge.

REFRIGERANT RECOVERY

The ozone crisis has revolutionized the way we handle halocarbon refrigerants. While technicians once allowed great quantities to evaporate when emptying a system or testing it for leaks, this is no longer legal. There is no choice but to recover and reuse halocarbon refrigerants, which can save money and the ozone layer at the same time. With many of the most common refrigerants no longer being produced, they are only available as a recycled product.

The industry distinguishes recovery (the removal of refrigerant from a system) from recycling (the cleaning of moisture and contamination from recovered refrigerants in preparation for reuse). In general, ACR technicians handle the recovery phase, while recycling is done at specialized facilities. Technicians are required to own and use refrigerant-recovery equipment.

Here are some questions to ask to determine the effectiveness of recovery equipment:

1. Does it have vacuum and outlet-pressure gauges? If so, a gauge manifold will not have to be hooked up.

2. How portable is it?

3. Does it work with virgin (oil-free) refrigerant, or only with refrigerant containing oil?

4. Does it automatically shut down at the desired vacuum level, or when the recovery tank is full?

5. Does it recover to an internal or external tank?

6. How many types of refrigerant can it recover? Can it work with high-pressure refrigerants like R-410-A?

7. Is it self-purging? How easily and well does it clean itself out with a vacuum after recovery, to minimize refrigerant releases?

8. Can it recover vapor and/or liquid?

9. Do you need to connect a filter or filter-drier to the recovery hoses?

10. Can a push-pull recovery (see number 11) be used with virgin refrigerant?

11. Can it do "liquid push-pull" recovery? In this technology, the compressor "pulls" vapors from the recovery cylinder, which "pushes" the liquid from the system and into the recovery cylinder. At the end, a conventional recovery operation needs to be performed. Push-pull moves a lot of liquid while pumping only a small amount of vapor, and the liquid does not even go through the recovery unit. It does require a special hookup. For recovery techniques, see Chapter 11, "Standard ACR Procedures."

SAFETY RULES AND EQUIPMENT

Any form of construction can be dangerous, and workers and management are obliged to cooperate to ensure a safe workplace. The following material covers minimum requirements and is not intended to be a comprehensive guide to job safety.

Some conditions greatly increase the chance for accidents in any working environment, including crowded work areas, blocked passageways, overloaded platforms and hoists, inadequate support for scaffolds, elevators without proper guards, damaged tools or power cords, poor ventilation or lighting, defective or worn protective equipment and clothing, improper storage or use of chemicals, and unsafe use of flammable materials.

Some behaviors also boost the odds of accident and injury, such as inattention, creating sparks or flames near flammable materials, creating toxic fumes in unventilated areas, riding equipment not designed for personnel, removing guards from machinery, stacking materials poorly, and neglecting to wear protective clothing. Horsing around and working when tired are other common causes of accidents.

The American Society of Heating, Refrigeration and Air Conditioning Engineers (ASHRAE) sponsors an ACR safety code. Copies can be obtained at www.ashrae.org.

The Occupational Safety and Health Administration (OSHA) is responsible for establishing and enforcing workplace health and safety standards. Although the detailed regulations are complex, OSHA maintains a good clearinghouse of accident-avoidance standards on the Web at www.osha.gov/SLTC/smallbusiness/index.html. Most sections below contain more detailed references to relevant coverage at the OSHA Web site.

Accident Reporting

The employer must maintain a log and summary (OSHA Form 300 or equivalent) of all reportable injuries and illnesses for each work site. Reportable events are those that result in fatality, hospitalization, lost workdays, medical treatment, job transfer or termination, or loss of consciousness. Incidents must be entered in the log within six days of the date the employer learns of them.

Hand Tool Safety

First, always wear safety glasses or goggles when using any striking tools. Check that the handle is securely attached before using a hammer. Never pound one hammer with another. Use the correct sized hammer for the job. Throw out a hammer or chisel with dents, cracks, chips, or mushrooming.

Electric tools must have double insulation, proper grounding, or a ground-fault circuit interrupter. Dead-man switches, which require constant pressure on the trigger to operate, are required for electric tools at construction sites. Go to www.osha.gov/SLTC/handpowertools/index.html.

Housekeeping

Good housekeeping reduces hazards and increases efficiency by allowing work to flow smoothly and reducing searches for tools or materials. OSHA requires that job sites be orderly and clear of debris and recognized hazards. OSHA requires that:

- material storage and waste disposal yards are convenient but out of the way;
- traffic lanes permit efficient movement;
- hazardous materials are stored in proper containers and away from the work area;
- obstacles and uneven ground are clear of trash, piles of fill, and other obstacles; and
- ropes, electric cords, and tools from the working area are kept as clear as possible during construction.

Lifting and Carrying

Proper lifting and carrying procedures can prevent falls, back injuries, and hernias. Before carrying something heavy, make sure the route is clear of obstructions and has good footing. Wipe off oil or grease. Wear gloves if necessary. Get a firm grip on the object, being wary of splinters, nails, and other hazards. Then lift it with the knees, keeping the back straight and vertical. Set the object down the same way it was lifted, with the knees and not the back. Make sure fingers and toes are clear before setting down the object.

When carrying a long object on shoulders, lower the front end to get a clear view of the path. Use special care when turning. Ask for help when needed.

Railings and Floor Openings

Railings are required on all platforms that are 4' or more above adjacent surfaces. Railings are also required on exposed edges of stairs. On a standard railing, the top rail is 42" (107 cm) above the floor and the intermediate rail is 21" above the floor. A toe board at least 4" (10.2 cm) high is required at floor level.

Openings in floors may have standard railings or be covered with planks or steel plate. Do not cover floor openings with plastic as this will hide the danger. Ladderway openings require standard railings except at the entrance. Passage through the entrance must be guarded by a swinging gate or the path can be offset so a worker cannot walk directly into the opening. More detailed regulations on railings and floor openings is at www.osha.gov/SLTC/smallbusiness/sec15.html.

Safety Equipment

Installation and repair of comfort-cooling and refrigeration machinery can be hazardous, and employees must wear and use OSHA-approved safety equipment. Wear steel toes to prevent foot injury. Do not use lifelines or lanyards for any purpose except employee safeguarding.

Air Pack

Employees must be trained to use respiratory protective equipment. The protective devices must be appropriate to the danger and the nature of the work requirements and inspected daily before use.

One good protective measure is an air pack—a small, self-contained breathing apparatus for use in areas that may become contaminated with dangerous gas, such as ammonia and high concentrations of halocarbon refrigerants. The mask covers the head to protect the eyes, nose, and face, and receives bottled air through a hose. A common type of air pack—the mine safety apparatus—provides "pressure-demand" air supply. A positive pressure of about 1" of mercury (6.9 kPa above atmospheric pressure) inside the mask prevents entry of toxic gas. An exhaling valve allows easy exhalation. With a

45 cubic-foot (1275 liter) cylinder, the air pack is rated at 30 minutes of breathing time and weighs 25 lbs. (11.3 kg) to 33 lbs. (15 kg), depending on the cylinder.

Head, Eye, and Face Protection

Helmets must be worn in areas where head injuries are possible due to flying or falling objects, impact, or electrical shock or burns.

Eye and face protection are required whenever there is a danger of injury. Employees working with torches must wear appropriate filters and safety goggles. Goggles are a good safety measure when soldering, brazing, grinding, using hammer and chisel, and working with refrigerants. Always wear goggles when working with ammonia systems. Eye and face protection are covered at www.osha.gov/SLTC/eyefaceprotection/index.html.

Ear Protection

OSHA sets standards for maximum noise at job sites. If exposure levels surpass these levels, engineering and administrative efforts must be made to reduce the noise. If these efforts fail, workers must wear hearing protection. Plain ear cotton is not acceptable.

Table 1-C: OSHA Noise-Level Standards

Duration per day (Hours)	Maximum sound level (dB) (A slow response)
8	90
6	92
4	95
3	97
2	100
1 1/2	102
1	105
1/2	110
1/4 or less	115

Note: Exposure to impact noise must not exceed 140 dB peak sound pressure level. See further details at www.osha.gov/SLTC/noisehearingconservation/standards.html.

Gloves

Gloves are a smart precaution, especially when soldering, brazing, grinding, or handling other hot metal. Gloves are also useful when using a hammer and chisel, or working around leaking refrigerants or in cold areas.

Asbestos

The mineral fiber called asbestos was used as insulation for decades, and is found in numerous public and private buildings. Asbestos is known to cause cancer and lung disease when its fibers are inhaled or swallowed, so you must use great care when working around it. State hygiene laboratories and asbestos removal companies can test a sample for asbestos.

The hazard is greatest when the asbestos is damaged, flaking, or powdered. Undamaged asbestos is often coated and left alone since the hazard of removal is greater. Federal asbestos standards are summarized at www.osha.gov/SLTC/asbestos/index.html.

Electricity

OSHA requires compliance with the 1971 National Electric Code in most cases. Circuits of 15- and 20-amp, single-phase, 120-volt current at construction sites must use ground-fault interrupters or an assured equipment-grounding program if they are not part of permanent structural wiring. One or more employees at the job site should make daily inspections of temporary wiring and electrical equipment. Complete OSHA requirements for electrical safety are available at www.osha.gov/SLTC/electrical.

Below are some commonsense guidelines for electrical safety that are applicable to the ACR industry:

1. Check electrical equipment before using. Equipment must be grounded. Don't use equipment with frayed cords or damaged insulation.

2. Never operate electrical equipment when standing in wet or damp areas.

3. Electric cords must be the three-wire type. Do not hang cords from nails or wires. Splices must be soldered and adequately insulated.

4. Keep electrical wires off the ground. Never run over wires with equipment.

5. Plug receptacles must be the approved, concealed-contact type.

6. Exposed metal parts of electrical tools that do not carry current must be grounded.

7. Shut off power in case of a problem or accident.

8. Do not touch anyone who is in contact with live electrical current. Instead, first shut off the power. Then move the person by pushing him or her with a dry piece of lumber. Give mouth to mouth resuscitation if the victim is not breathing. Call 911.

Fire

On larger jobs, a firefighting program must be followed throughout the construction work. The job site must have an alarm system to alert employees and the fire department of a fire. Each floor of a building must have two separate fire exits to allow quick exit if one is blocked.

Work sites must follow these fire-prevention measures:

- Store oily or greasy rags in a tight-closing metal container.
- Remove all flammable waste daily.
- Maintain adequate clearance between heat sources and flammable materials.

For more complete OSHA standards on fire safety, see www.osha.gov/SLTC/firesafety.

Table 1-D: Extinguishing Agents

Material	How to Extinguish
Wood, paper, and rags	Use water or any fire extinguisher.
Flammable liquid	Smother with dry chemical, foam, carbon dioxide, sand, vaporizing liquid, or other approved fire extinguisher.
Electrical fires	Use dry chemicals, carbon dioxide, vaporizing liquid, or compressed gas.

Flammable Liquids

Flammable liquids pose a fire and explosion danger. Store gasoline in approved cans away from any possible fire, sparks, or mechanical hazard. Pour gasoline with an approved gooseneck filler. Keep the spout in contact with the metal opening to the tank to prevent sparks caused by static electricity. Do not smoke while filling. Never fill a machine while it is running.

2

Energy, Electricity, and Cooling Cycles

The key job of a refrigeration system is to transfer heat from the cooled space to the surroundings. Cooling systems must obey the laws of physics, especially laws on the interaction of various forms of energy, the transfer of heat, and the effects of temperature and pressure on fluids. Technicians need to know about the American and Standard International (SI) measuring systems, electricity and magnetism, the vapor-compression and absorption cooling cycles, corrosion, and psychrometrics—the study of temperature, humidity, and comfort. Understanding these principles will speed the diagnosis and repair of faulty systems. Since most cooling systems use the vapor-compression cycle, that is where we will focus.

Four States of Matter

Matter can take four states (also called phases): solid, liquid, gas, and plasma. The state of matter is determined by a substance's inherent properties, and by its temperature and pressure.

1. A *solid* retains its shape without needing a container because its temperature is low and the molecules are fixed in position. Ice is the solid form of water.

2. A *liquid* is a fluid—a substance that takes the shape of its container and has molecules that are tightly bonded together. The molecules move within the container by the force called convection; the warmer molecules rise and the cooler (denser) ones fall. Water is the liquid form of water.

3. A *gas* is the second type of fluid. A gas takes the shape of its container and has convection, but expands to fill the container because the molecules have too much energy to stick together. The trade often calls a gas "vapor." Steam is the gas form of water.

4. A *plasma* is an electrically charged state of matter found in the sun, electric arcs, and fluorescent lamps. Most plasmas exist only at high temperatures, and they play no part in cooling systems.

Measuring Systems

Two types of measuring units may be used to engineer and repair air conditioning and refrigeration equipment. The American system uses the familiar inches, pounds, and degrees Fahrenheit. The SI system uses centimeters, grams, and degrees Celsius. For many reasons, especially the ease of converting between units, the SI system is accepted by scientists and practically every nation except the United States.

In the American system, energy is measured in foot/pounds (ft. lbs.). One ft. lb. is a force of 1 pound operating through a distance of 1 foot. In the SI system, work is measured in joules, a force of 1 newton operating through a distance of 1 meter. One joule = 1 newton/meter (1 Nm). Electrical quantities (amperes, volts, and ohms) always use the SI system.

Quantities are listed here in both SI and American systems unless the conversion is unnecessary or irrelevant (See Appendix B for energy conversions and equivalents).

Energy

Energy is the ability to do work, so energy and work are measured by the same units: the foot-pound in the American system and the joule in SI. These principles of energy will help you understand a refrigeration system.

1. Energy is always "conserved." Energy always goes somewhere; it is not created or destroyed (except in a nuclear reaction). A refrigerator moves heat around; it does not destroy heat.

2. Energy may take several forms.

   a. *Potential energy* is energy that is available but not doing work. Potential energy is present in batteries that are not making electricity, water that is stored behind a dam, an object that is raised above a surface, and magnetic and electric fields.

   b. *Kinetic energy* is energy that is doing work. Kinetic energy is present in batteries that are converting chemical energy into electrical energy, water flowing through turbines, and falling objects.

   c. *Heat* is a form of energy held in the vibration of molecules. Faster vibration is the same thing as greater heat intensity, or a higher temperature. Heat energy is present in a flame, the element of an electric stove, and some forms of radiation. Temperature measures the intensity of heat energy, but *temperature and heat are different*. The amount of heat energy in a material is related to its temperature, mass, and specific heat capacity. Pressure is also a factor in *enthalpy*—the amount of heat stored in a fluid.

3. Substances expand as they warm because the molecules move faster and bounce off each other with more force. This expansion causes a reduction in density.

4. Heat flows *only* from warmer bodies to cooler ones. Cold is the absence of heat, and it cannot flow.

5. The various forms of energy can be converted. Batteries convert chemical energy to electrical energy, which can then be converted to heat, kinetic, or electromagnetic energy. Gasoline engines convert chemical energy to heat energy and then kinetic energy; automobile brakes then convert the kinetic energy back to heat energy. Electric motors convert electromagnetic energy to kinetic energy, which can be used to move refrigerant, air, water, or other fluids.

6. Liquids absorb heat (the latent heat of vaporization) as they change into a gas. Gases give off heat (the latent heat of condensation) when they change into a liquid. For a fluid, these quantities are usually equal.

7. Temperature remains constant during a change of state between gas and liquid if pressure also remains constant. In other words, water at atmospheric pressure will remain at 212°F (100°C) until all of it has boiled. Only then can the steam begin to warm above 212°F. However, the situation is a bit more complicated for zeotropic refrigerants, described in Chapter 9, "Refrigerants."

Heat Energy and Specific Heat Capacity

Heat is the most important form of energy for air conditioning and refrigeration. When a substance is warmed, it absorbs heat. In the American system, heat is measured in British Thermal Units, or BTUs. One BTU will raise the temperature of 1 pound of water by 1°F. In SI, heat is measured in joules, or the more practical kilojoule (1 kJ = 1,000 joules); 4.187 kJ will warm 1 kilogram of water 1°C. Calories are another SI heat unit. One calorie (cal) will warm 1 gram of water 1°C; 1 cal = 4.187 J. The larger kcal (1,000 calories) is often used instead; 1 kcal = 4.187 kJ.

The rate of temperature rise depends on the mass of the substance, its specific heat, the amount of heat added, and any change of state. Specific heat measures the ability of a material to absorb heat. In American units, specific heat capacity equals the BTUs that must be added or removed to change the temperature of 1 pound of a substance by 1°F. Temperature change is often expressed as ΔT.

BTU = mass in lb × specific heat capacity (in BTUs per pound) × ΔT (°F).

In SI, specific heat is the kJs added or removed to change the temperature of 1 kilogram of water by 1°C.

kJ = mass in kg × specific heat (in kJ/kg) × ΔT (C°).

To find the heat needed to raise the temperature (without changing state):

heat added = mass × ΔT × specific heat.

For water, the calculation is easer, because the specific heat is 1.

heat added = mass × ΔT × 1.

In the American system, the result is in BTUs. To heat 250 lb. of water 42°F: 250 × 42 × 1 = 10,500 BTU.

In SI, the result is in kcal. To heat 20 kg of water 12°C: 20 × 12 × 1 = 240 kcal.

To find kilojoules, multiply kcal by 4.187:
240 × 4.187 = 1004.88 kJ.

For cooling, the calculation is the same, except the heat is removed, not added.

Equivalents:
1 BTU/lb = 4.187 kJ/kg
1 kJ/kg = 0.2388 BTU/lb

Temperature Scales

In U.S. units, Fahrenheit is the common temperature scale. A variation called the Rankine scale starts at absolute 0 (–460°F). Units in each scale are the same size.

In SI, the Celsius Scale starts at 0°, the freezing point of water. The Kelvin Scale uses the same units, starting at absolute 0 (–273°C). See Table 2-A for comparisons of the four temperature scales.

Table 2-A: Temperature Equivalents and Scales

Rankine (R) to Fahrenheit (F):	R – 460	= F
Fahrenheit to Rankine:	F + 460	= R
Celsius (C) to Kelvin (K):	C + 273	= K
Kelvin to Celsius:	K – 273	= C
Celsius to Fahrenheit:	(9/5C) + 32	= F
Fahrenheit to Celsius:	5/9(F – 32)	= C

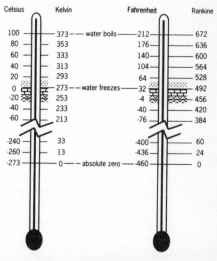

Celsius	Kelvin		Fahrenheit	Rankine
100	373	water boils	212	672
80	353		176	636
60	333		140	600
40	313		104	564
20	293		64	528
0	273	water freezes	32	492
-20	253		-4	456
-40	233		-40	420
-60	213		-76	384
-240	33		-400	60
-260	13		-436	24
-273	0	absolute zero	-460	0

fresh food storage temp.
fresh food evaporator temp.
frozen food storage

Temperature vs. Heat

Temperature measures how warm something is—how fast the molecules are moving. *Temperature does not measure the amount of heat.* The amount of heat energy present in a substance depends on temperature, mass, and specific heat. One ton of water at 100°F contains 2,000 times as much heat energy as 1 pound of water at 100°F, even though the temperatures are the same.

As temperature falls, molecular motion decreases. At absolute zero, all motion would cease. Because the properties of fluids are related to their absolute temperature (temperature above absolute zero), some refrigeration calculations use the Rankine or Kelvin Scales, which start at absolute zero, and are called "absolute temperatures." Absolute temperature is handy. For example, when you double the absolute temperature of a confined gas, its pressure doubles.

Sensible vs. Latent Heat

Heat can be "sensible" or "latent." One can feel the more familiar sensible heat with their hand and measure it with a thermometer. Latent heat is the amount of heat required to change the state of a substance, say from a solid to a liquid, without changing temperature. Latent heat cannot be measured by a thermometer.

A good refrigerant has a high latent heat of vaporization, which means more cooling can occur for each pound of refrigerant flowing through the system (all other things being equal).

Each substance has three latent heats and they may have different names, depending on whether heat is being added or removed:

Change of state	Temperature rising	Temperature falling
Solid—liquid	Heat of melting	Heat of fusion
Liquid—gas	Heat of vaporization	Heat of condensation
Solid—gas	Heat of sublimation	Heat of sublimation

The latent heat of vaporization equals the latent heat of condensation. If you were to add 970 BTU to boil (evaporate) a pound of water, you would remove 970 BTU to condense a pound of steam.

Some materials can sublimate—go directly from solid to gas—without passing through the liquid state. Solid carbon dioxide (dry ice) sublimates when it gains the latent heat of sublimation and becomes a gas.

Refrigeration technicians seldom worry about the latent heats of fusion or melting, because systems should not be operated at conditions that will cause refrigerant to freeze. However, the latent heat of fusion (freezing) for water is important when calculating refrigeration loads or using ice to cool something.

Calculating Heat Inputs and Outputs

When a substance changes state without changing temperature, it gains or loses latent heat. The heat gain or loss depends on the substance change (gas to liquid, or liquid to solid). Solid water requires 144 BTU per pound (335 kJ/kg) to melt (the latent heat of fusion). Water absorbs 970 BTU per pound (2,257 kJ/kg) when changing from liquid to vapor (the latent heat of vaporization).

To use these concepts, suppose 1 pound of water is heated from 0°F to 300°F. As the ice is thawed to 32°F, each BTU raises the temperature 1°. Because temperature is rising, this is sensible heat. When the ice reaches 32°F, the temperature stabilizes while 144 BTU of latent heat are added. Then the ice melts, and the water warms at 1° per BTU until it reaches 212°F. To vaporize the water, add the latent heat of vaporization—970 BTU. Finally, add another 88 BTU to heat the steam to 300°F.

Table 2-B: Heat Calculation for Changing State and Temperature

Temperature change	State change	BTUs added	Type of heat
0°F to 32°F	None	32	Sensible
None	Melting	144	Latent head of melting
32°F to 212°F	None	180	Sensible
None	Evaporation	970	Latent heat of vaporization
212°F to 300°F	None	88	Sensible

Notice that more heat goes to vaporizing the water than in the rest of the process: Boiling uses 69% of the total energy here. To cool the same amount, 69% of the energy loss would occur during condensation. This explains why the vapor-compression system, which depends on the latent heat of condensation, is so effective at moving heat.

Although temperature change cannot be detected during the latent heating stages, the water is still gaining heat energy. The molecular vibration is speeding up, so the molecules become more likely to break the bonds restraining them. Once enough heat is added, this vibration becomes so violent that a solid turns to liquid, or a liquid turns to gas.

Another way of understanding latent heat is to consider *vapor pressure* at the boundary between a liquid and a gas. Each liquid has a characteristic vapor pressure that results from the motion of the molecules. The warmer the liquid, the faster the molecules move and the higher the vapor pressure. While adding latent heat does not change the temperature, it does raise vapor pressure. When vapor pressure equals gas pressure in the container, the liquid molecules become energetic enough to break the bonds holding them as a liquid and overcome pressure from the gas above. At this point, the liquid molecules become gas molecules, and the liquid evaporates, or boils.

Latent heat explains what happens in the condenser (where hot, high-pressure refrigerant transfers its heat of condensation to the surroundings and becomes a liquid) and the evaporator (where liquid refrigerant boils as it absorbs the latent heat of vaporization from the cooled space). As the cooled space transfers this heat to the refrigerant, temperature in the cooled space drops. Note that the refrigerant remains at a steady temperature while changing state. Only when the change of state is complete does the refrigerant gain sensible heat and start to warm up. So every part of the evaporator where liquid refrigerant is boiling should be at the same temperature.

Heat Transfer

Heat transfer occurs because heat energy tends to flow from warmer to cooler objects. Heat can move in three ways:

1. *Radiation* is movement of electromagnetic energy through space. All warm bodies radiate, with the amount of radiation depending on their temperature, surface, and composition. The sun's heat reaches Earth by radiation. Fireplaces do most of their warming by radiation.

2. *Convection* is movement that occurs in fluids due to different density. Cool fluids are denser than warm ones, so convection causes cool fluids to move down and displace warm ones. Convection and a fan combine to move air around buildings with forced-air distribution.

3. *Conduction* is transfer of heat between materials that are touching. Heat is conducted from the cooled space, through evaporator tubes, to the refrigerant. The rate of heat transfer depends on temperature difference (ΔT), the extent of contact between the bodies, and the properties of the materials. Often, several means of heat transfer operate in unison. A pot on an electric stove absorbs radiated, convected, and conducted heat from the burner. A welder working in a closed room is warmed by convection and radiation.

Some materials, such as copper and aluminum, have a high rate of heat conduction. Insulators have a very low rate. Rapid heat transfer is necessary in compressor heads and sensing bulbs, and in the condenser and evaporator. The following factors increase heat transfer across the metal tubing of an evaporator or condenser:

- Thin walls
- Tubing made of heat-conductive material, such as copper or aluminum
- Rough or dull walls
- High fluid velocity
- Large ΔT between the fluid and the surroundings
- Large surface area (narrow tubes have greater wall area per volume than larger tubes)

Gas Laws and Fluid Physics

Refrigerant exists in a system as either a gas or a liquid. Fluids are the two states that take the shape of their containers. To understand what happens inside a system, we need to know about the physics of fluids. Let's start with pressure.

Pressure

Pressure is force applied per unit of area. The American system measures pressure in pounds per square inch (psi). In SI, it is measured in pascals (Pa), a force of 1 newton per square meter. Kilopascals (kPa) are often used because 1 pascal is a small amount of pressure; 6.895 kPa = 1 psi.

Although scientists say there is no such thing as suction, areas with low pressure do seem to pull things toward it. Even though the actual force of suction comes from greater pressure elsewhere, the trade finds terms like "suction line" and "pull down" exceedingly convenient.

Atmospheric pressure at sea level is 14.7 psi, or 101.3 kPa. In a perfect vacuum, pressure is 0. In the American system, vacuum is usually measured in inches of mercury vacuum instead of psi. A perfect vacuum is 29.92 inches of mercury (in/hg), and atmospheric pressure measures 0 inches of mercury. (See Table 2-C.) In SI, pressure measurements start at 0, and vacuum is measured in microns of mercury. One micron equals one-millionth of a meter.

Pressure affects the boiling point of liquids, because a liquid will not boil until its vapor pressure equals ambient pressure. At atmospheric pressure, water boils at 212°F, but at 10,000 feet altitude, reduced ambient pressure lowers the boiling point to about 193°F. Increasing pressure raises the boiling point, so water compressed to 100 psi boils at about 338°F. This explains why pressure cookers cook faster and hotter than boiling water.

Gauge and Absolute Pressure

A service technician using the American system of measuring must distinguish *gauge pressure* (pounds per square inch gauge, or psig) from *absolute pressure* (pounds per square inch absolute, or psia).

$$\text{Absolute pressure} = \text{atmospheric pressure} + \text{gauge pressure}$$

Most gauges read 0 at atmospheric pressure, although the actual pressure is 14.7 lb/in^2. Many calculations require absolute pressure instead of gauge pressure. Thus, a gauge pressure of 5 lb/in^2 equals an absolute pressure of 19.7 lb/in^2. "Psi" usually indicates gauge pressure, but the use of "psia" and "psig" will prevent confusion. In the SI system, a pressure of 0 indicates a complete vacuum; there is no gauge pressure.

Table 2-C: Vacuum-Pressure Conversion

Vacuum Pressure Scales			
Inches of Hg	mm of Hg	psia	Ft. of Water
30 (29.92)	760	15 (14.7)	33.40
29		14.5	
28	711	14	32.2
27		13.5	
26	660	13	29.9
25		12.5	
24	610	12	27.6
23		11.5	
22	559	11	25.3
21		10.5	
20	508	10	23.0
19		9.5	
18	457	9	20.7
17		8.5	
16	408	8	18.4
15		7.5	
14	356	7	16.1
13		6.5	
12	305	6	13.8
11		5.5	
10	254	5	11.5
9		4.5	
8	203	4	9.2
7		3.5	
6	152	3	6.9
5		2.5	
4	102	2	4.6
3		1.5	
2	51	1	2.3
1		0.5	
0	0	0	0

TABLE CONVERTS INCHES OF MERCURY (IN. HG) INTO POUNDS PER SQUARE INCH ABSOLUTE (PSIA).

The Gas Laws

The refrigerant in a vapor-compression cycle is confined inside the compressor, tubing, and heat exchangers. The combined laws of Boyle and Charles describe the relationships of pressure, volume, and temperature in a confined gas:

$$PV/T = pv/t$$

The left side of the equation describes the gas before a change, and the right side describes it afterward:

P and p = *absolute* pressure in lb/in^3 or kPa
V and v = volume (in^3 or m^3)
T and t = *absolute* temperature (in Rankine or Kelvin)

In a chamber with a constant volume, $P/T = p/t$. Thus, doubling the absolute pressure will double the absolute temperature.

The combined gas laws tell what happens inside a refrigeration system. In a compressor cylinder, increasing pressure and decreasing volume both raise temperature. In an evaporator, pressure decreases but volume remains constant, so temperature must fall.

Another way to view the relationship between temperature and pressure is through the law of conservation of energy: Energy cannot be created or destroyed except in nuclear reactions. The compressor does work, increasing the vibration of the gas molecules and raising their temperature. This energized fluid is pumped to the condenser, where the warm gas loses heat to the cool condenser walls. The gas molecules slow, and the gas condenses. In the evaporator, refrigerant pressure drops to saturation pressure, and the liquid starts to boil. The heat energy that powers the evaporation comes from the surroundings, so the surroundings are cooled.

Perfect Gas Equation

A more complete picture of confined gases comes from the *perfect gas equation*. This equation also takes into account the mass of gas present and the gas constant, (R), a mathematical factor unique to each gas.

PV = MRT
P = *absolute* pressure (lb/in^3 or kPa)
V = volume (in^3 or m^3)
M = mass (lb or kg)

R = gas constant

T = *absolute* temperature (Rankine or Kelvin)

The perfect gas equation can calculate one attribute of a gas if the other four are known. Thus, given the mass, identity, temperature, and volume of a gas, its pressure can be calculated.

Dalton's Law

Dalton's law of partial pressures explains the behavior of several gases in a mixture. The law states that the total pressure of gases confined together equals the sum of the individual gas pressures. Further, each gas behaves as if it occupies the space alone. These principles are crucial to the absorption cycle.

Enthalpy

Enthalpy is the amount of heat energy in a particular substance. Enthalpy is a function of the mass, temperature, pressure, and nature of a substance. Enthalpy is calculated by figuring out how much heat must be added or removed to bring the substance to reference conditions (for water: 32°F or 0°C; for refrigerant: −40°F or −40°C).

For changes in temperature without a change of state:

$H = M \times \Delta T \times$ specific heat

H = enthalpy

M = mass

ΔT = temperature difference

Because cooling systems use the latent heat of vaporization, the calculation usually must consider latent heat. (See Chapter 8, "Whole Systems.") The latent heat of crystallization only matters if ice is involved.

As shown later in Figures 2-D and 2-E, the refrigerant's enthalpy rises in the compressor (where both pressure and temperature increase) and the evaporator (as refrigerant absorbs heat from the cooled area). Enthalpy falls in the condenser (as refrigerant loses heat to the condensing medium).

Saturation Temperature-Pressure

At certain ranges of pressure and temperature (called saturation temperature-pressure), a fluid can exist as a liquid and a gas inside the same container. Saturation temperature-pressure exists in most parts of evaporators and condensers while cooling systems operate.

As pressure increases, the saturation temperature rises; as pressure falls, saturation temperature also falls. Saturation temperature for water at sea level pressure is 212°F (100°C). At higher altitudes, atmospheric pressure and saturation temperature are both lower.

Refrigeration engineers sometimes speak of a refrigerant's "pressure-temperature" to refer to saturation conditions. In other words, if you know the pressure of a saturated fluid, you can find its temperature by looking at a pressure-temperature chart.

Subcooling and Superheating

Subcooling and superheating are two basic concepts in refrigeration. Both conditions represent a change in temperature (but not pressure) from saturation pressure-temperature. While a fluid at saturation temperature-pressure will boil if it gains heat or condense if it loses heat, a subcooled liquid cannot *immediately boil* and a superheated gas cannot *immediately condense*.

Subcooled liquid: When a fluid that has just totally condensed starts to lose sensible heat, it becomes a subcooled liquid. A subcooled liquid is below the saturation temperature for its pressure, and it must gain sensible heat (its temperature must rise) and/or have its pressure reduced before it can begin to absorb latent heat and evaporate. This sounds fancy, but it's pretty simple. Liquid water at sea level pressure is subcooled when below 212°F (100°C). Sensible heat and then latent heat need to be added before water can be boiled.

Superheated gas: When enough heat has been added to entirely boil a liquid, it forms a gas at saturation conditions. As the gas gains sensible heat, its temperature will rise and it will become a superheated gas. A superheated vapor is entirely vapor because it is above saturation temperature for its pressure. This vapor must be cooled and/or subjected to greater pressure before it can condense. Vapor water (steam) at sea level is superheated when above 212°F.

Subcooling and superheating help insure safe conditions inside a refrigeration system. In the liquid line, subcooled liquid refrigerant should remain liquid until it passes through the metering device. (If liquid refrigerant is near saturation temperature, it can flash to a gas after a slight pressure drop, as in a filter-drier.)

Superheating in an evaporator ensures (1) against floodbacks (the liquid state cannot exist in superheated conditions), and (2) that all of the refrigerant's cooling power is used (because superheating can only occur after complete evaporation).

However, excessive superheat (1) wastes evaporator room and slows heat transfer, because the superheated area is warmer than the area of evaporation, and (2) reduces cooling of a hermetic compressor (because the suction gas will be too hot and not dense enough).

The superheat adjustment of an expansion valve is usually set at the factory to about 8° to 10°F. The most common reason to adjust this setting is a previous maladjustment. (For more on measuring and adjusting superheat, see Chapter 4, "Controls.")

Tons of Refrigeration

Cooling-system capacity can be rated by comparison to the cooling effect of ice. A 1-ton refrigeration machine cools as much in 24 hours as 1 ton of ice melting in 24 hours. One ton of 32°F ice melting to water at 32°F (with no gain of sensible heat) absorbs 288,000 BTU of the latent heat of fusion:

2,000 lb × 144 BTU/lb = 288,000 BTU

Thus, a 1-ton refrigerator can remove 288,000 BTU per day from a cabinet, or 12,000 BTU/hour (288,000/24).

The SI system has no equivalent to the ton rating. However, 1 ton of refrigeration equals about 303,845 kJ, or 12,660 kJ/hour (303,845/24). This equals 3.52 kW.

Fluid Flow

A fluid flows due to a difference in pressure caused by (1) different density, often due to convection, (2) a pump, or (3) the different heights of the containers. In cooling systems, a compressor pumps refrigerant through the piping. This flow may be resisted by (1) gravity (if the fluid must flow upward), (2) viscosity (the fluid's resistance to flow), and (3) friction caused by pipes and fittings. In a closed loop, you can ignore gravity because the falling fluid counterbalances the rising fluid.

Pressure drop is an important design consideration. The tubes must be large enough to conduct the fluid with little pressure drop, because a large drop reduces system efficiency. However, oversized tubes have relatively little surface area, reducing heat transfer, and the refrigerant may move too slowly to return oil to the compressor. Good pipe size is a compromise between minimum pressure drop and maximum heat transfer and oil return.

The type of fluid flow affects evaporator efficiency. Smooth-flowing fluids develop an insulating film that slows heat transfer from the evaporator wall to the refrigerant. Turbulent, quick-flowing, or rapid-boiling fluids all promote fast heat transfer into the refrigerant.

Magnetism and Electricity

A cooling-system technician may spend as much time dealing with electricity as with refrigerant. Electricity powers compressors and fans, and operates control circuits. Magnetic attraction and repulsion occur in motors, solenoids, and relays. To do this job right, an understanding of some basic principles and terminology of electricity is needed.

The first thing to notice about electricity and magnetism is their close relationship.

Electromagnetism: An electric current passing through a conductor creates a magnetic field.

Induction: When a conductor moves through a magnetic field, it induces an electric current.

These principles are fundamental to many electrical devices. Electromagnetism is basic to electric motors, and induction is used in generators, motors, and clamp-on ammeters, to name a few devices.

Magnetism

Magnetism is a field of force around a magnet that attracts certain substances toward the magnet. Each magnet has two poles—north and south—that are connected by the magnetic field. When the fields of two magnets overlap, unlike poles attract each other and like poles repel. Attraction and repulsion are used in motors, among many applications.

Some materials, including hardened steel, certain ceramics, and alnico (an aluminum-nickel-cobalt alloy) become magnetized through exposure to a magnetic field. A permanent magnet is made of materials that stay magnetized after such exposure. Permanent magnets are used in servo motors and some electrical contacts.

Electromagnetism occurs when a current passes through a conductor. To intensify the field, the wire is usually wrapped around a core of magnetic material, usually iron. Electromagnets are used in motors and solenoids.

Electricity

Electricity is the most versatile form of energy, as it can travel through wires and be converted into kinetic energy and heat energy. Electricity can flow only through a complete circuit: from a power source, through a resistance, and back to the power source.

DC and AC

Electricity may flow as direct current (DC) or alternating current (AC). AC is a rapid series of waves in a conductor, and these waves give AC some strange properties that we need to understand.

Direct current (DC) is the form of electricity produced by batteries. The current flows in one direction and does not have a wave form. Direct current is difficult to transmit and has other limitations, but it is widely used in semiconductors.

Alternating current (AC) is the form of electricity that is generated and distributed through power lines. For each complete cycle of single-phase current, the current and voltage start at 0, rise to a peak, fall to 0, rise to another peak, and then fall to 0 again. Thus, 60hz (hertz, or cycles per second) AC rises and falls 120 times per second.

Induction is the creation of a current in a conductor that is moving in relation to a magnetic field. Because the magnetic field around an AC electromagnet is constantly rising and falling, a nearby wire that is stationary still seems to be moving in relation to the rising-and-falling magnetic field, so a current is induced in the wire.

Cycle per second (hertz, or hz) is the number of complete oscillations of AC per second. In the United States, AC is delivered at 60 cycles per second, or 60 hertz (hz).

Phase is the number of waves of AC that coexist in a circuit. Single-phase AC (see Figure 2-A) is found in houses. In commercial and industrial installations, you may also find multiple-phase AC.

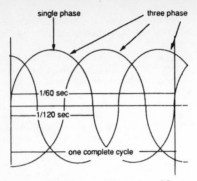

Figure 2-A: Single- and three-phase AC

Many power supplies deliver three-phase (3Φ) current, which superimpose three AC waves. When voltage and current for one wave reach 0, the other two waves are still carrying power, so the current can always power a motor. Three-phase motors are usually more efficient and smaller than single-phase motors. Single-phase motors are most common in smaller sizes and must be used when three-phase AC is unavailable. Motor plates indicate the required type of AC.

Electrical Units

Many units are used to measure and describe electricity:

Coulomb is the unit of electron flow. One coulomb is a flow of 6.24×10^{18} (6,240,000,000,000,000,000) electrons through a conductor.

Ampere (amp, or A) is the unit of current. One amp is 1 coulomb flowing past a point in a circuit each second. One milliamp equals 0.001 amp. Conductors are rated by how many amperes they can carry.

Volt (V) is the unit of electrical "pressure." One volt will push 1 ampere of current through a resistance of 1 ohm. "Line voltage" is the voltage supplied to a motor or device. Motors require a specific line voltage, and actual line voltage should not stray more than 5% below, or 10% above, the rating.

Volt-ampere (VA), the unit of AC power, equals volts times amperes (VA = V × A). Volt-amperes may be different from watts, which also takes power factor (see above) into account. However, VA = W when power factor = 1.

Ohm (Ω) is the unit of resistance. With 1Ω of resistance, 1 volt will push 1 ampere through a circuit.

Farad (f) is the measure of capacitance, or electrical storage. A device with 1f of capacitance can store 1 coulomb on capacitor plates separated by a potential of 1V. This is a lot of current, so the unit microfarad (.000,001f, or μF) is commonly used. The total capacitance of capacitors connected *in parallel* equals the sum of each capacitor's capacitance. To find the capacitance of capacitors *in series*: $1/f\text{(total)} = 1/C_1 + 1/C_2 + 1/C_3$, etc.

Power factor (PF) measures the percentage of actual power available in an AC circuit. Maximum power factor, 1, occurs when voltage and current are perfectly in phase:

$$W = V \times A.$$

When the peaks of voltage and current in AC do not coincide, we say the circuit is "out-of-phase," and less power is available, so power factor is below 1. An out-of-phase condition is generally caused by inductive loads, such as transformers and electric motors, and by capacitive loads such as capacitors. Heating and other resistive loads have less effect on power factor.

Although many motors use an out-of-phase condition to create starting torque, a low power factor cuts the efficiency and power of electric motors. Many utilities require their customers to maintain a power factor of 0.85 or above.

You can read power factor directly with a power factor meter, or calculate it with a voltmeter, ammeter, and wattmeter:

$$\text{Power factor (PF)} = W/(A \times V)$$

Another concept emerging from AC's wave nature is **RMS,** or **root mean squared voltage.** RMS voltage describes the effective voltage of an AC circuit. The peak voltage of 120V AC is actually 170V, but the circuit is called 120V because the wave only reaches peak voltage for two moments during each cycle.

Watt (W) is the unit of power—the rate at which electricity can do work. One kilowatt (kW) = 1,000 watts. One kilowatt hour (kWh) is the equivalent of 1 kW working for 1 hour. AC watts can be measured with a wattmeter or calculated if you know voltage, amperage, and power factor:

$$W = V \times A \times \text{power factor}$$
$$\text{DC has no power factor: } W = V \times A$$

Horsepower (hp) is another unit of power; 1 hp equals 746 watts.

Electric Circuits and Ohm's Law

The fundamentals of electric circuits are described by the relation of three units: current (measured in amperes), electromotive force (emf, or potential, measured in volts), and resistance (measured in ohms). Think of water flowing through a pipe: Amperage is like the amount of water moving, voltage is like water pressure, and resistance is like the drag from the piping and gravity.

Emf and resistance are related in Ohm's law: $I = E/R$
current (I)—measured in amps (A)
electromotive force (E)—measured in volts (V)
resistance (R)—measured in ohms (Ω)

Ohm's law says that current is equal to electromotive force divided by resistance: $I = E/R$. Knowing any two of these values, one can find the third: $E = IR$; $R = E/I$. In the more familiar amps, volts, and ohms, Ohm's law says:

amps = volts/ohms
volts = amps $\times$ ohms
ohms = volts/amps

Basic Electrical Components

Now that we know something about the terminology and measurement of electricity, let's look at some basic terminology and components.

Grounding is the connection to a "ground" for safety. Electricity always "wants" to return to its starting point. In 120V circuits, the ground wire allows safe return of the current if the neutral wire fails. In a second form of grounding, called "frame grounding," each component with a conducting frame or exterior is grounded to prevent metal parts from becoming "hot" when insulation fails. The standard ground wire color is green or green with yellow stripe. Never use wire with these colors for any other purpose.

Never cut off the grounding lug of a three-wire plug. Have a qualified electrician adapt the outlet to accept such a plug instead. If it is necessary to remove the ground wire on any fixture, control, or device during servicing, be sure to replace it before restoring the current.

For portable tools, the best protection against shock, especially when working outdoors or in damp locations, is to use an extension cord protected by a ground-fault circuit interrupter (GFCI), also called a ground-fault interrupter (GFI). This device will detect if a current as low as 5 milliamperes leaks from a circuit (indicating a fault in the insulation) and immediately shut off the current. (See Chapter 1, "Tools, Equipment, and Materials.")

Capacitors are devices that store electricity as free electrons and release them on demand; they are used to start electric motors and to increase the power factor. Capacitors are measured in Farads or microfarads.

> **CAUTION:** Capacitors can store large amounts of electricity even after the current is turned off. Capacitors must be discharged before they are touched or carried. Contact the terminals with a steel tool that has an insulated handle, or better, with a 100,000-ohm resistor.

A **solenoid** is a magnetic actuator that can be used to move a valve or a switch. The device works because an electromagnet tends to pull a magnetic core to the center of the coil when current flows. By attaching a switch, valve, or lever to the iron core, a solenoid can use electrical energy to control a system. (See Figure 2-B.)

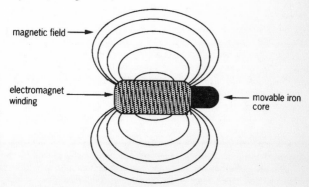

magnetic field →

electromagnet winding

movable iron core ←

Figure 2-B: Principles of a solenoid

A **thermocouple** is an electric device that measures temperature. The thermocouple works because an emf develops if the connection between two metals is heated. This voltage can be measured and converted into temperature on a scale. A thermocouple may read extremely high temperatures.

A **thermistor** is a semiconductor that can sense temperature because its resistance changes as temperature changes. The signal can be directed to an electronic control unit. A thermistor may be positive temperature coefficient (PTC): ohms and temperature go up together, or negative temperature coefficient (NTC): ohms go down as temperature goes up.

A **transformer** changes the voltage of current passing through it. The "primary" coil in a transformer is connected to the input, and the "secondary" coil is connected to the load. The primary coil induces a current in the secondary coil. The ratio of the number of windings in each coil determines the voltage of the secondary current. A "step-up" transformer increases the output voltage, while a "step-down" transformer decreases it.

A **correction line-voltage transformer** may be installed in a line to get the correct value—from 208 to 240 volts, or from 120 to 240 volts.

Rectifiers change AC to DC. Rectifiers are called diodes in electronics, where they create the DC needed by most electronic devices.

Circuits

A circuit is a complete path allowing electrons to travel from a source of electricity, through a load (also called a resistance), and back to the source. A circuit must have some resistance. Looking at Ohm's Law, current equals voltage divided by resistance. In a circuit with 0 resistance, the current is theoretically infinite—a rather dangerous amount. A large current due to such a *short circuit* should heat the conductor until the fuse or circuit breaker blows; otherwise, a fire or other damage is likely.

In a *closed* circuit, current can flow all the way around. In an *open* circuit, no current flows because something is disconnected or a switch is open. In a *grounded* circuit, a conductor is touching ground and the circuit will not work. Insulation failure generally causes a grounded circuit, which can look like a short circuit as it overheats and trips the circuit protector.

The two basic types of circuit designs are *series* and *parallel*. Current in a series circuit passes through each component in turn. The resistance is the sum of the resistance of each component. Voltage is the sum of the voltage drop across each load. The current is equal everywhere, but the voltage drops as the current proceeds.

In a parallel circuit, the current can flow through multiple conductors ("branch circuits") on its round trip from supply through load and back to supply. Voltage is equal in the branch circuits. Total current equals the sum of the current in each branch circuit.

Many "series-parallel circuits" circuits combine series and parallel wiring. (See Figure 2-C.)

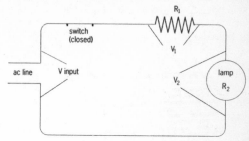

(a) Series circuit current is constant at all points.

$$V_{input} = V_1 + V_2$$

$$R_{total} = R_1 + R_2$$

$$I = \frac{V_{input}}{R_{total}}$$

Figure 2-C: Circuit types

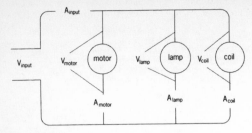

(b) Parallel circuit voltage is constant at all points.

$$\frac{1}{\text{Total Resistance}} = \frac{1}{R_1} + \frac{1}{R_2} + \frac{1}{R_3}$$

$$A_{input} = A_{motor} + A_{lamp} + A_{coil}$$

$$V_{input} = V_{motor} = V_{lamp} = V_{coil}$$

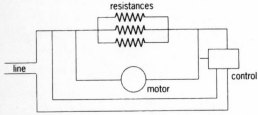

(c) Series-parallel circuit

Figure 2-C: Circuit types (continued)

Reading Drawings

Electrical diagrams, or drawings, are the road maps to electrical circuits. Drawings describe what controls and switches are in a system, how they are linked together, and (sometimes) where the components are located. Technicians must read electrical diagrams to troubleshoot or help an electrician install a system. (Electricians may not know enough about cooling equipment to wire them correctly.)

Diagrams rely on symbols shown in Table 2-D. Symbols unique to a particular manufacturer are usually defined in a block on the diagram.

Refer to electrical diagrams when diagnosing electrical problems. To read a diagram, start at the supply and work toward the suspect component. Note which terminals the current should pass through and which switches and contacts control the current. Test the current at these locations to see whether it is being switched properly.

The following different types of drawings may be used to describe electrical circuits in a cooling system:

1. A *connection diagram* shows the components in their relative positions, with the terminals numbered. Although wires are not shown, terminals with the same number are connected by a wire. This method is often used for control panels in large systems. It is easy to read because you don't need to trace through a maze of wires.

2. A *schematic diagram* shows symbols for the various components, and links them with lines for the wires. The diagram can be laid out vertically or horizontally. Power wiring usually appears heavier; power supply is usually located at the top or left side. Wire colors and terminal colors may be noted to help trace the connections. Schematics are mostly used to diagram control systems. A schematic diagram follows these conventions.

   • Switches and relays are shown in the deenergized position.

   • A switch is always located between motor windings and L1 (the hot wire) in single-phase motors.

   • Lower-voltage circuits are shown toward the bottom.

   • The ladder (or vertical) schematic use the same conventions as the standard schematic. The supply wiring is located at the left and right sides and the "rungs" are individual circuit branches between them. Power wires to the motors are not usually shown. Lines are numbered because switches in one line may affect actions in another line. The contacts controlled by an electromagnetic relay are usually listed alongside it.

3. A *line diagram* shows each component as a unit. All switches that are physically located on the component are placed together. Connecting wires run from hot to ground through each component, so you can find problems with components by locating and testing switches and controls that affect their operation. The diagram shows both control circuits and line voltage circuits. Power wiring appears heavier. This can get pretty confusing and cluttered but it does show the action of the contacts.

Diagrams may combine different diagram types, or show only part of the system for ease in reading. Some manufacturers supply multiple types of diagrams to simplify matters.

Table 2-D: Electrical Symbols Recommended by the R.S.E.S. Educational Assistance Committee

Capacitor

• = terminal nearest ground

Circuit Breakers

Thermal

Magnetic Coils (relay, timer, solenoid)

• = device

Contacts

Open

Closed Fuse

Fusible Link

Ground Connection

Rectifier

Resistor

Shielded Cable

Multiple Conductor Cable

Thermocouple

Transformer

**Table 2-D: Electrical Symbols Recommended by the R.S.E.S.
Educational Assistance Committee (continued)**

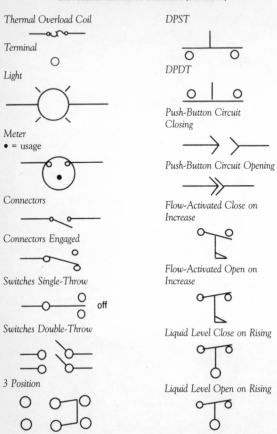

Thermal Overload Coil

Terminal

Light

Meter
• = usage

Connectors

Connectors Engaged

Switches Single-Throw   off

Switches Double-Throw

3 Position

DPST

DPDT

Push-Button Circuit
Closing

Push-Button Circuit Opening

Flow-Activated Close on
Increase

Flow-Activated Open on
Increase

Liquid Level Close on Rising

Liquid Level Open on Rising

Disconnect

General Selector Switch (any number of paths may be shown)

Segment Switch

Push Button—Two Circuits

Make Before Break

Pressure N.C.

Pressure N.O.

Temperature-Close on Rising

Temperature-Open on Rising

Conductors Power (factory-wired)

───────────

Control (factory-wired)

───────────

Power (field-installed)

▬ ▬ ▬ ▬ ▬

Control (field-installed)

- - - - - -

Alternate Segment Switch

Thermal Relay

Alarm

Bell

Horn Motors (symbol to be 1.5 times larger than relay coil)

**Table 2-D: Electrical Symbols Recommended by the R.S.E.S.
Educational Assistance Committee (continued)**

Squirrel Cage Induction

Transistor—PNP type

Single Phase

main

aux

Transistor—NPN type

Electrical Codes

The National Electric Code has been developed to standardize safe practices in electrical construction and installation. Many localities add regulations on top of the National Code. The National Code permits cooling-system technicians to make Class 2 connections. Class 2 circuits are used in relays, control, signals, and communications, and are defined as up to approximately 100 volt-amperes:

Less than 15V	up to 5 A
15 to 30V	up to 3 A
30 to 60V	up to 1.5 A
Above 60V	less than 1 A

Cooling Cycles

A refrigeration system is basically a device that transfers heat from one place to another. A modern comfort-cooling or refrigeration system uses either the vapor-compression or the absorption cycle to move heat. Within each of these cycles, a great variety of systems can be developed to achieve specific operational and economic objectives. The compressor, controls, and components can be altered for cold-weather operation, defrosting, capacity control, or the use of multiple evaporators.

The elements of the system are described in Chapter 3, "Compressors"; Chapter 4, "Controls"; Chapter 5, "Components"; and Chapter 6, "Motors." The objective here is to describe the two basic systems in terms of energy and basic design.

Absorption Cycle

In the absorption cycle, heat energy moves the refrigerating fluid and energizes the heat transfer. (In contrast, the vapor-compression cycle uses mechanical energy for this purpose.) The basic absorption cycle involves the repeated absorption, separation, condensation, evaporation, and reabsorption of the refrigerant. Instead of using a compressor to compress gaseous refrigerant, the system absorbs it in an absorbing fluid (the absorbent). Heat added in the generator raises the solution temperature and drives the refrigerant gas from the absorbent (because warm liquids can dissolve less gas than cool liquids). The gas then condenses and is evaporated in an evaporator, much like in the vapor-compression cycle.

Absorption machines have several advantages. They are simple, requiring neither metering devices nor moving parts (although they often use thermostats, fans, pumps, and other components). They require relatively little maintenance. Because some absorption systems require no electricity, they can be used in remote locations and in campers. Because steam may be an inexpensive source of heat for the generator, absorption systems are also used in industrial refrigeration and in chilling applications in buildings, like hospitals or laboratories, with a year-round supply of waste steam. (See Chapter 8, "Whole Systems".)

Vapor-Compression Cycle

Most refrigeration units move heat using the vapor-compression (mechanical refrigeration) cycle: vapor refrigerant is compressed to a hot, high-pressure gas, cooled and condensed to a liquid, evaporated to a cold gas, and compressed again.

Vapor-compression cycle systems have a high-pressure side and a low-pressure side. The high side starts at the compressor outlet and ends at the metering device. In this side, the refrigerant exists as first a hot, high-pressure vapor and then as a warm, high-pressure liquid. The low side starts at the metering device and ends at the compressor outlet. Pressure on each side of the system remains relatively constant, but pressure drops at the metering device and rises at the compressor.

Energy in the Vapor-Compression Cycle

In the vapor-compression cycle, the motor converts electrical energy to magnetic and then kinetic energy. This kinetic energy moves the compressor, which compresses the gas, adding heat energy to the refrigerant.

Because the cycle is continuous, it can be said to begin at any point. (See Figure 2-D.) High-pressure liquid refrigerant is held in the receiver (A) at roughly ambient temperature. Refrigerant goes through the liquid line (B) to the metering device (C), which allows refrigerant to enter the evaporator (D) at reduced pressure. This reduction in pressure causes the refrigerant to boil into a cold vapor. The latent heat that drives the boiling comes from the cooled space outside the evaporator. The evaporator is linked by the suction line (E) to the compressor (F), which pulls refrigerant from the evaporator. The compressor squeezes the gas, adding energy and warming it. Hot gas leaves the compressor through the discharge line (G) and enters the condenser (H), where the latent heat of vaporization is lost to the surrounding air or water. The refrigerant condenses and the liquid returns to the receiver (A). The system is commonly controlled by a thermostat (I) which measures temperature in the evaporator or cooled space and signals the motor through the control wire (J) to operate when needed.

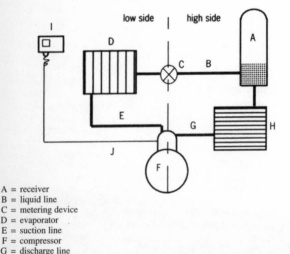

A = receiver
B = liquid line
C = metering device
D = evaporator
E = suction line
F = compressor
G = discharge line
H = condenser
I = thermostat
J = control wire

Figure 2-D: Basic components of the vapor-compression cycle

The refrigerant remains in a saturated condition at every point in the evaporator, because liquid and vapor should both be present. Thus, the evaporator has a characteristic pressure-temperature of saturation, so the temperature does not rise even though the refrigerant is absorbing the heat of vaporization. This allows the evaporator to cool the load evenly, with the rate of heat transfer determined largely by surface area, temperature difference, and refrigerant flow.

The Pressure-Heat Diagram

Engineers use a diagram called a pressure-heat (or pressure-enthalpy) diagram to describe the interactions of heat, pressure, temperature, heat content, and cooling capacity of a vapor-compression system. This diagram charts pressure along the vertical axis and enthalpy (the heat content of the refrigerant) along the horizontal axis.

Figure 2-E is a pressure-heat diagram showing energy flow and changes of state in the vapor-compression cycle.

The curve for the refrigerant crosses several important lines and areas in the pressure-heat diagram:

- In the *all-liquid area,* all refrigerant is a subcooled liquid.

- In the *all-vapor area,* all refrigerant is a superheated gas.

- In the *saturated-vapor area* (also called the liquid-vapor area), refrigerant is a saturated mix of liquid and vapor. This condition is found in the condenser and the evaporator.

- The *saturated-liquid line* separates the saturated-vapor area from the all-liquid area. Refrigerant along this line is not subcooled, but it becomes subcooled as it enters the all-liquid area.

- The *saturated-vapor line* separates the saturated-vapor area from the all-vapor area. Superheating begins when the gas moves from this line into the all-vapor area.

- Along the *line of constant quality,* the refrigerant has a constant proportion of gas and liquid.

- Along a *line of constant heat* (enthalpy), refrigerant has the same heat content.

- Along the *line of constant temperature,* the refrigerant has constant temperature. The line is vertical in the all-liquid area, horizontal in the saturated vapor area, and nearly vertical in the all-vapor area.

- Along a *line of constant pressure,* every location has the same pressure.

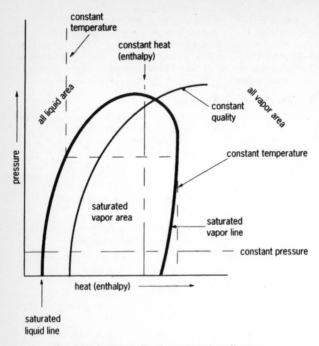

Figure 2-E: Understanding the pressure-heat diagram

The pressure-heat diagram can be used to show the *action of the vapor-compression cycle*. During this cycle, refrigerant follows the letters **A-B-C-D-E-F-G.** (See Figure 2-F.) Notice that the refrigerant spends most of its time in the saturated vapor area, in both the evaporator and the compressor, and only briefly becomes a subcooled liquid or a superheated vapor.

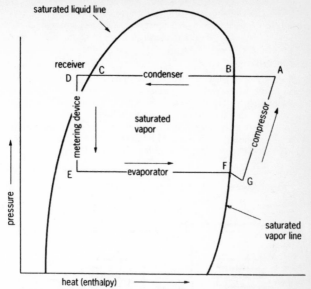

Figure 2-F: Pressure-heat diagram showing the vapor-compression cycle

At **A,** the hot vapor has been compressed in the compressor and reaches maximum pressure, temperature, and enthalpy. Without losing pressure, the vapor enters the condenser (**B**) and begins to lose the latent heat of condensation, as shown by its leftward movement (loss of enthalpy). The condenser pressure remains constant while the refrigerant loses heat. At **C** the refrigerant is totally condensed (it has reached the saturated-liquid line). The condenser continues drawing heat from the refrigerant, which is now a subcooled liquid, so it is losing sensible heat. Now the liquid refrigerant enters the receiver. Temperature and pressure remain constant in the receiver until at the metering device (**D**). Pressure falls suddenly, and the refrigerant recrosses the saturated-liquid line to enter the evaporator at **E.** Pressure is low and the liquid refrigerant vaporizes. On the horizontal section, evaporator pressure is stable; the refrigerant gains heat from the surroundings until **F,** where it is fully vaporized. Refrigerant vapor begins to superheat in the suction line (F–G) until it reaches the compressor at G. The compressor squeezes the refrigerant, raising pressure, temperature, and enthalpy, and the cycle repeats as the refrigerant reaches A, the point of maximum enthalpy.

Heat Pump

A heat pump is a combined refrigerating and heating system that uses vapor-compression techniques to produce cooling or heating. A heat pump (see Figure 2-G) has two reversible heat exchangers, one inside the cooled space and the other outside it. These heat exchangers accept the role of condenser or evaporator according to whether the system must heat or cool. This allows the heat pump to transfer heat to or from the conditioned space, depending on the control and valve settings.

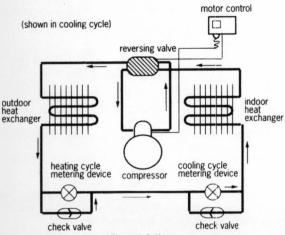

Figure 2-G: Heat pump

The key feature of a heat pump is a four-way valve that directs the discharge gas from the compressor to the proper heat exchanger. (See Chapter 7, "Pipe, Tube, Fittings, and Valves.") (Because the roles of the evaporator and the condenser are reversed in winter and summer, it is best to call them heat exchangers when discussing heat pumps.) The outdoor heat exchanger serves as a condenser during the cooling cycle (normal for an air conditioning unit) and as an evaporator during the heating cycle.

Two metering devices are required for a heat pump: one thermostatic expansion valve (TXV) in each heat exchanger. A check valve allows refrigerant to bypass the TXV when it is exiting the heat exchanger that is serving as a condenser. Although refrigerant always flows in the usual direction through the compressor, it can change direction elsewhere.

During the *heating cycle*, the compressor pumps hot, high-pressure gas to the condenser, which is in the conditioned space. While condensing, the refrigerant releases the latent heat of condensation to the building. The high-pressure liquid flows to the outdoor heat exchanger, which is now an evaporator. As long as the saturation temperature in the evaporator is below ambient temperature, the refrigerant picks up the latent heat of vaporization from the outside. This gas returns to the compressor, where the cycle repeats. During the *cooling cycle*, the four-way valve directs hot, high-pressure gas to the outdoor heat exchanger, and the system functions as a normal air conditioning system. The system may dispose of condenser heat to air, water, or underground piping.

A heat pump can only heat effectively if the minimum outdoor temperature does not run much below freezing, and it is most efficient if the heating and cooling loads are approximately equal. Some systems use supplemental electric heaters in the inside heat exchanger when the outside temperature is too low for the heat pump to handle the full heating load.

Acidity

Solutions have a quality called acidity or alkalinity. Acids are liquids with excess hydrogen ions, while bases are liquids with the ability to take up extra hydrogen ions. Thus, acids and bases neutralize each other. Refrigerants and oils can both get acidic when they absorb moisture, which helps explain the emphasis on keeping refrigerant dry.

Acidity and alkalinity are measured on the pH scale. pH 7 is neutral; numbers higher are basic and lower are acidic. Because each unit below 7 indicates a tenfold increase in acidity, pH 5 is 100 times as acidic as pH 7 and pH 3 is 100 times as acidic as pH 5.

Corrosion

Corrosion is the degradation of metal by oxidation. Corrosion not only weakens metal but also decreases its ability to conduct electricity and heat, and damages appearance. Unchecked corrosion can cause total failure, but even moderate amounts can cause great damage. The National Bureau of Standards has estimated annual U.S. corrosion losses at about $70 billion annually.

Corrosion affects the air conditioning and refrigeration trade in two important ways. First, it can damage connections between wires, terminals, and contacts on motor starters and other relays. Second, in tubing and evaporators, corrosion can reduce transmission of heat, reduce strength, and eventually, cause leaks and failure.

The rate of corrosion depends on the metal, the electrical and chemical environments, and the effectiveness of any coatings used. Corrosion is greatly accelerated by the presence of acids, bases, water, and salts. Certain metals, notably iron and steel, are extremely prone to corrosion and suffer the familiar form called rust. Some metals, such as copper and aluminum, corrode on the surface but are then protected when the oxide sticks to the metal, hindering further corrosion. In acidic conditions, or with rapid fluid flow, this "self-protection" fails, and the metal may corrode all the way through. Three general types of corrosion can cause problems:

1. *General attack* is a uniform attack to an entire surface.

2. *Pitting* (localized attack) can perforate metal very quickly and is considered the most dangerous form of corrosion.

3. *Galvanic corrosion* occurs between certain metals when they touch and an electric current is produced. Galvanic corrosion can degrade metal very quickly, and is common when ferrous metals contact nonferrous metals, such as galvanic pipe connected to copper fittings. Galvanic corrosion can also affect steel touching brass, and aluminum touching zinc and brass.

Many measures can be taken to reduce corrosion:

- Prevent contact between galvanic metals.
- Minimize system acidity.
- Add anticorrosion solutions to closed-circuit cooling-water systems. These solutions are classified as anodic and cathodic, depending on what part of the galvanic cell they coat. General corrosion inhibitors reduce corrosion in both parts of the corrosive cell.
- Use effective coatings and keep them intact.
- Install dielectric unions when joining dissimilar metals.
- Do not allow condensation to drip onto surfaces that may corrode.

- Establish electrical currents that counteract the electrochemical processes that speed corrosion.

Humidity and Psychometrics

Psychrometrics, the study of the relationship between humidity and air, is important to cooling-system technicians because of the intimate relationship between humidity and comfort. Because skin evaporation is a major source of cooling, temperatures that are comfortable in low humidity can be unbearable when the humidity cranks up. Thus, humidity is almost as important as temperature when analyzing complaints about comfort.

Although psychrometrics properly is limited to humidity and air, the study of comfort requires a consideration of the third important factor in our ability to dispose of heat: air flow. Air flow can increase evaporation as well as provide fresh air and remove odors.

Relative humidity is a percentage, showing how much water vapor is in the air, compared to the maximum the air could hold at the particular temperature.

$$\text{Relative humidity} = \frac{\text{absolute humidity}}{\text{maximum possible humidity}}$$

Absolute humidity is the number of grains or pounds of moisture per pound of air. (One pound equals 7,000 grains.) This value does not change as a given volume of air warms or cools, unless condensation takes place. Relative humidity, however, does change with temperature. As air warms, it can hold more moisture, so relative humidity falls if absolute humidity remains the same. (This is why houses can be so dry in winter—cold air holds little moisture, and when it is heated, relative humidity plummets.)

As air cools, it loses the ability to hold moisture. The falling temperature can reach the dew point if relative humidity reaches 100%. Further cooling will produce condensation on the walls of the container, or rain. This reduction in air's ability to hold moisture accounts for condensation buildup on evaporators. While this condensation can cause frost problems, it may be beneficial. For example, condensation lowers the absolute (and relative) humidity in a comfort-cooling system, boosting comfort in humid weather.

Psychrometrics also matters in commercial cooling. Each stored food product has an ideal temperature and humidity that the cooling system should attain. (See Table C in Appendix C.)

Measuring Humidity

Humidity can be measured in a number of ways. Direct-reading instruments are available, but for much less money, you can buy a sling psychrometer or aspiring thermometer to measure wet-bulb and dry-bulb temperatures. These readings can be converted into relative humidity with a relative humidity table as follows:

1. Swing the sling psychrometer around (or run the aspiring thermometer) until both thermometers reach stable readings.

2. Note both wet- and dry-bulb readings.

3. Subtract the dry-bulb reading from the wet-bulb reading to find the wet-bulb depression.

4. Find the dry-bulb reading on the left column and the wet-bulb depression on the top row.

5. Read down from the top and across from the left, and read relative humidity at the intersection. (See Table 2-E.)

Table 2-E: Finding Relative Humidity

Dry Bulb Degrees F	1	2	3	4	5	6	7	8	9	10	12	14	16	Wet Bulb 18	20
30	89	78	67	56	46	36	26	16	6						
32	89	79	69	59	49	39	30	20	11	2					
34	90	81	71	62	52	43	34	25	16	8					
36	91	82	73	64	55	46	38	29	21	13					
38	91	83	75	66	58	50	42	33	25	17	2				
40	92	83	75	68	60	52	45	37	29	22	7				
42	92	85	77	69	62	55	47	40	33	26	12	2			
44	93	85	78	71	63	56	49	43	36	30	16	7			
46	93	86	79	72	65	58	52	45	39	32	20	11			
48	93	86	79	73	66	60	54	47	41	35	23	15			
50	93	87	80	74	67	61	55	49	43	38	27	20	5		
55	94	88	82	76	70	65	59	54	49	43	34	26	14	5	
60	94	89	83	78	73	68	63	58	53	48	40	32	21	13	5
65	95	90	85	80	75	70	66	61	56	52	44	37	27	20	12
70	95	90	86	81	77	72	68	64	59	55	48	42	33	25	19
72	95	91	86	82	77	73	69	65	61	57	49	43	34	28	21
74	95	91	86	82	78	74	69	65	61	58	50	45	36	29	23
76	96	91	87	82	78	74	70	66	63	59	51	46	38	31	25
78	96	91	87	83	79	75	71	67	63	60	53	47	39	33	27
80	96	91	87	83	79	75	72	68	64	61	54	49	41	35	29
85	96	92	88	84	81	76	73	70	66	62	56	49	44	38	33
90	96	92	89	85	81	78	74	71	68	65	58	52	47	41	36
95	96	93	89	85	82	79	75	72	69	66	61	55	50	43	38
100	96	93	89	86	83	80	77	73	70	68	62	56	51	46	41

For example, if the wet-bulb reading is 74°F and the dry-bulb reading is 70°F, the wet-bulb depression is 4°F, and relative humidity is 81%.

A *psychrometric chart* is a graph showing the relationship of many physical variables in a volume of air. A complete psychrometric chart will cover absolute humidity, temperature (dry-bulb and wet-bulb), dew point, vapor pressure, total heat (enthalpy), and relative humidity. If you know any two of these quantities about a volume of air, you can find any other factor from the chart. The chart is often used to find relative humidity with a sling psychrometer, and should be available from psychrometer manufacturers.

On a psychrometric chart, dotted lines indicate relative humidity in percent. Dry-bulb (db) temperature is shown at the bottom. Wet-bulb (wb) temperature is along the top curve. The right side gives absolute moisture in grains/lb. On the "SHR" (Sensible Heat Ratio) scale, each line angles away from the central comfort zone (point B).

To find relative humidity with a psychrometric chart:

1. Swing the sling psychrometer around (or run the aspiring thermometer) until both thermometers reach stable readings.

2. Find the dry-bulb temperature on the bottom "db °F" scale. Put your finger on the vertical line up from this temperature.

3. Find the wet-bulb temperature on the curving "wb °F" scale on top and follow the line down and to the right.

4. Pinpoint the intersection of the lines identified in steps 2 and 3. Read relative humidity where this line meets a third line, curving toward the upper right. This line is marked %.

3

Compressors

The compressor is the heart of the modern vapor-compression system. Technicians are likely to encounter five types: centrifugal, helical (screw-type), rotary, scroll, and reciprocating. But before we meet the compressors, we need to look at open and closed systems and compressor cooling.

OPEN AND CLOSED SYSTEMS

In *open-drive* or *open* systems, the compressor is driven by an external motor, as shown in Figure 3-A. In return for being easier to service, these systems need tight seals at the crankshaft bearing. The motor usually drives the compressor through V-belts or flexible couplings. (See Chapter 6, "Motors.")

DIRECT DRIVE COMPRESSOR FEATURES

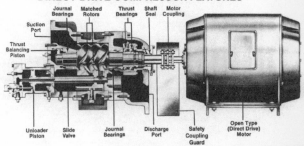

Figure 3-A: Open system
Courtesy of Dunham-Bush, Inc.

In a *hermetic* (closed) system, the motor and compressor are inside a housing, eliminating the seal and chance of leaks at the crankshaft bearing. The motor is cooled by refrigerant vapor, the crankcase serves as the intake manifold, and the intake valves need no direct connection to the suction line. Motors in hermetic systems cannot use brushes—the arcs would pollute the refrigerant and oil, and cause a burnout.

Full hermetic systems, used in domestic refrigerators, have welded housings and are not serviceable. If the motor or compressor fails, the entire unit must be replaced. Sometimes, failure-prone components are located outside the housing and connected through leak-proof devices to the compressor or motor.

Serviceable hermetic, or *semihermetic*, systems are common in large reciprocating and centrifugal compressors. The housing is bolted and gasketed together and may be dismantled for major service.

COMPRESSOR COOLING

Compressors build up considerable heat while compressing refrigerant vapor. Most of this heat travels with the high-pressure vapor to the condenser, but to remain at safe operating temperature, the compressor head must also dispose of heat. This is normally done through fins or water passages.

In hermetic and semihermetic systems, the suction line feeds a stream of cool refrigerant to the cylinder heads, so suction-gas temperature and pressure are critical to compressor cooling. Suction gas should enter the compressor below 65°F (18°C) on a low-temperature installation, or 90°F (32°C) on a high-temperature system. A hotter gas picks up less compressor heat because it is less dense, and the ΔT is lower between the motor and the suction gas. Hermetics have a low-pressure cut-out to protect the motor from low suction-line pressure.

Air-cooled open compressors may be cooled directly by the blast of the condenser fan, or the compressor may have its own cooling fan. Water-cooled compressors have a jacket allowing water to circulate through the head. Heat picked up in this water is dumped to water or air in the condenser.

CENTRIFUGAL COMPRESSOR

Centrifugal compressors have impellers that spin and fling the refrigerant away from the axis of rotation. Centrifugal compressors create centrifugal force. Because each impeller adds relatively little pressure, several impellers are often ganged together to create the necessary high-side pressure.

Centrifugal compressors are used in large systems, often in semihermetic or open configurations. The system may operate at positive pressure or under a vacuum, depending on the refrigerant and evaporator temperature. A large centrifugal system may be shipped ready-charged with refrigerant and oil.

The centrifugal compressor has no connecting rods, pistons, or valves, so the shaft bearings are the only wear points. The compressor "head" (pressure gain) is a function of gas density and impeller diameter, design, and speed. Centrifugal compressors rotate fast, as shown here:

Low speed	3,600 rpm
Medium speed	9,000 rpm
High speed	9,000+ rpm

Power is supplied by an electric motor or steam turbine. Vapor enters the intake near the impeller shaft, and is caught by the impeller blades. As the impeller accelerates the gas, the kinetic energy of the impeller is converted to the kinetic energy of fast-moving gas. As the gas meets the housing, or volute, it is compressed, and the kinetic energy is converted to the potential energy of compressed gas. The gas leaves the impeller at high velocity.

Capacity may be controlled by vanes in the inlet that regulate the supply and direction of vapor. Large compressors, with more than three stages, may omit the inlet vanes.

Floodback on a centrifugal compressor is dangerous due to the high speed of the impellers. To prevent floodback, avoid overcharging with refrigerant, and maintain adequate superheat.

Many centrifugal compressors have a built-in purge device to rid the system of unwanted air. The purge unit is a compressor and condenser that draws vapor from the top of the system condenser, then compresses and condenses it. Because only refrigerant can condense at the pressure created by the purge system, air collects on top, where it can be purged manually through a valve. Liquid refrigerant flows through a float-operated valve in the purge unit's condenser, back to the main system.

A filter-drier can be placed in a bypass around the float valve. Placing the filter-drier in the main output would impair the compressor's operation too much. Even though the bypass only takes a portion of the flow, the filter-drier will eventually pull out enough moisture to control system acidity.

HELICAL (SCREW) COMPRESSOR

Screw-type compressors are generally used in systems with capacity of at least 20 tons. These compressors (see Figure 3-B) rotate a pair of helical screws, or rotors, inside a chamber, forcing refrigerant toward one end of the chamber. As the gas is forced forward, it is compressed into the shrinking gaps between the screws, creating the compression. No valves are needed at the intake and exhaust ports. Because the rotors spin continuously, vibration is less than with a reciprocating compressor. Helical compressors are used in open or hermetic systems.

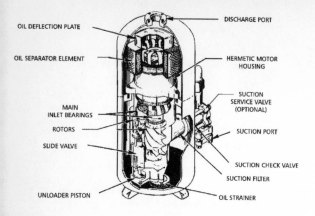

Figure 3-B: Vertical screw compressor
Courtesy of Dunham-Bush, Inc.

The rotors are termed "male" for the drive rotor and "female" for the driven rotor. The male has more lobes and spins faster than the female. Capacity control is accomplished by a slide valve that opens in the compression chamber and allows vapor to exit uncompressed. Some units can operate efficiently at only 10% of rated capacity.

ROTARY COMPRESSOR

Rotary compressors use one or more blades to create compression inside a cylinder. Unlike the reciprocating compressor, no piston is used. There are two basic types—the rotating vane and stationary blade.

In both types, the blade must slip within a housing in the impeller, which rotates off-center in the cylinder. Inlet ports are much larger than discharge ports because the suction gas is less dense than the inlet gas. Intake and discharge valves are not needed, eliminating a major source of trouble. However, check valves are helpful in the suction line to prevent oil and high-pressure vapor from entering the evaporator when the compressor is not operating. (See Figure 3-C.) Tolerances are so tight in rotary compressors that gaskets are not needed.

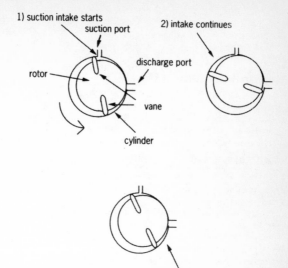

Figure 3-C: Rotating-blade rotary compressor

Rotating Blade (Vane)

In a rotating-vane compressor, a shaft rotates inside a cylinder, but the center axes of the cylinder and the shaft are different. The rotating shaft has grooves for sliding vanes. As the shaft spins, centrifugal force pushes these vanes against the cylinder. As gas enters from the suction line, it is swept around by the vanes. Because the rotor is not centered, the space holding the gas shrinks as the vanes rotate, causing compression. When the gas reaches minimum volume and maximum compression, it is forced out the discharge port. The clearance volume is quite low and the compression efficiency is high.

Rotating-vane compressors are common as the first stage of a cascade system. These units may have two to eight blades in a larger system. The edge of the blade that meets the cylinder must be smooth and accurately ground to avoid leakage and excess wear. The blade must fit precisely into the rotor slots.

Stationary Blade (Divider Block)

In the stationary-blade rotary compressor, a sliding blade in the cylinder housing separates the low-pressure vapor from the high-pressure vapor. The impeller rotates on an eccentric on the compressor shaft and draws vapor from the suction line and squeezes it toward the discharge port. Pushed by a spring, the blade retracts and protrudes to seal between the impeller and the cylinder.

SCROLL COMPRESSOR

The heart of a scroll compressor looks like the inside of a nautilus, that familiar, spiral-shaped seashell. In the compressor, one scroll, or "involute," is meshed inside the other. The moving scroll orbits inside the fixed scroll with an eccentric motion. Each involute is bonded to a plate at one end. (See Figure 3-D.)

The compressor draws in vapor at the outside of the scrolls, and traps it in pockets that immediately start to shrink. The orbital motion of the moving scroll forces the vapor toward the center of the chamber, where vapor reaches maximum pressure and temperature. The discharge port at the center allows hot vapor to move toward the condenser. Because many pockets of gas are getting compressed at once, the scroll compressor operates continuously, without intake or discharge valves.

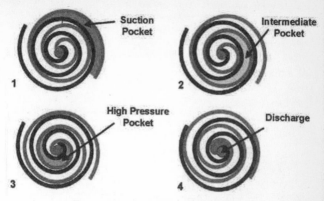

Figure 3-D: How a scroll compressor works
Courtesy of Dunham-Bush, Inc.

Several advantages of scroll compressors account for their quick acceptance in the ACR industry. The scroll compressor:

- can be completely oil-free (true of some models only);
- is quiet and produces little vibration, due to the rotary motion;
- has no valves and few wearing parts, increasing reliability (see Figure 3-D); and
- has positive displacement, so it can efficiently create high pressure (see Figure 3-E).

Scroll compressors should only operate in one direction. If some electrical snafu causes one to run backwards, it will not compress, and may be damaged. During backward operation, suction pressure will not drop, discharge pressures will not rise, and the motor will draw less than normal current. Large scroll compressors on three-phase motors may have built-in phase monitors to prevent backward operation.

RECIPROCATING COMPRESSOR

Reciprocating compressors compress refrigerant by sliding a piston up and down inside a cylinder; the whole system is similar to what you would see inside an internal combustion engine. During the intake stroke, the piston draws in refrigerant through the open intake valve. When the piston reaches the bottom of the stroke ("bottom dead center"), the intake valve closes and the piston begins rising and compressing vapor. The vapor exits through the discharge valve, which opens when the piston approaches the top of the stroke ("top dead center"). The hot, compressed vapor passes toward the condenser.

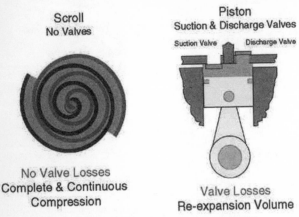

Scroll
No Valves

Piston
Suction & Discharge Valves

Suction Valve   Discharge Valve

No Valve Losses
Complete & Continuous
Compression

Valve Losses
Re-expansion Volume

Figure 3-E: Scroll compressor vs. reciprocating compressor
Courtesy of Dunham-Bush, Inc.

At the top of the stroke, the piston must come close to the cylinder head. The smaller the clearance, the higher the pressure from the compressor. This clearance may range from .010" to .020" (.254 mm to .508 mm).

Small systems use a single piston, while larger systems use several. The crankcase must be designed to dispose of the heat of compression. Compressor crankcases are made of cast iron and have fins for air cooling or a water jacket, which operates much like an auto engine's cooling system.

Pistons in large reciprocating compressors have separate oil and compression rings. Oil rings, lower on the piston, reduce the amount of oil entering the cylinder from the crankcase. Small systems may have oil grooves instead of oil rings. Compression rings make a tight seal against the cylinder walls, ensuring the maximum output from each stroke.

Crankshaft and Connecting Rods

The crankshaft converts the motor's rotary motion into reciprocating motion to drive the pistons. Crankshafts rotate within main bearings that must firmly support the crankshaft against loads from the motor and connecting rods. The exact end play should be specified in manufacturer's literature.

Several types of linkages may connect the connecting rod to the crankshaft, including:

1. A conventional connecting rod, the most common linkage on commercial systems, is clamped to the throw.

2. The eccentric crankshaft has an off-center, circular boss on the crankshaft to create the up-and-down motion. This system eliminates the need for caps or bolts on the connecting rod. Instead, the one-piece rod end is fitted to the crankshaft before final assembly.

3. The Scotch yoke uses no connecting rod. Instead, the lower portion of the piston contains a groove that holds the throw on the crankshaft. The groove permits the crank throw to travel laterally and to drive the piston only up and down. Both the Scotch yoke and the eccentric are found mainly on domestic and automotive systems.

Crankshaft Seal

In open-drive systems, the seal between the crankshaft and the crankcase is a common source of problems. The seal is subjected to a great deal of pressure variation and must operate whether the crankshaft is rotating or stationary. Clearances between the rotating and stationary surfaces must be accurate to .000001" (.0000254 mm), and lubrication must fill that tiny gap. The seal is commonly made of hardened steel and bronze, ceramic, or carbon. The absence of the crankshaft seal is the major advantage of the hermetic design.

The rotary-type seal is a simple, common seal that rotates on the shaft. (See Figure 3-F.) A spring, plus internal pressure, forces the seal face against a stationary seal face.

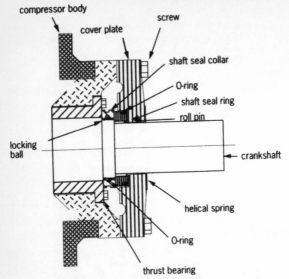

Figure 3-F: Crankshaft seal

The major cause of crankshaft-seal leaks is misalignment. Take care when aligning the motor to the compressor so the seal will not be stressed during operation.

The seal is usually lubricated by the oil pump. Make sure the compressor operates occasionally during long shutdowns, so the seal stays lubricated. A slight leak after startup, while a dry seal gets lubricated, may be normal. A leaking seal can be detected with a leak detector.

To inspect a leaking seal:

1. Pump down the system into the high side (receiver or condenser).
2. Remove the coupling at the shaft end.
3. Remove the seal cover and any rings holding the rotating seal in place.
4. Clean the ring surfaces with a very soft cloth.
5. Inspect the sealing surfaces and replace the entire seal if any scoring, scratching, or grooving is apparent.

6. Reassemble the system.
7. Check the alignment of the seal.
8. Evacuate the system and open necessary valves to restore operating conditions. (See Chapter 11, "Standard ACR Procedures.")

Heads and Valve Plates

Cylinder heads, generally made of cast iron, hold the gaskets and valve plate against the block. The valve plate is the assembly holding both valves tightly in place. Cylinder heads have passages that admit suction gas into the cylinder. The head is generally affixed to the block with cap screws.

Intake valves admit refrigerant during the intake stroke and close during the compression stroke. Discharge valves are closed during the intake stroke and opened at the end of the compression stroke. Valves are usually made of spring steel and designed to make a tight seal until opened by the pumping action of the piston. The mating surfaces of valves must be perfectly flat, and defects as small as .001" (.0254 mm) can cause unacceptable leaks. In service, the valve must open about .010" (.254 mm). Larger openings cause valve noise, while smaller openings slow refrigerant flow.

Operating temperature greatly affects valve durability. Intake valves operate in a relatively cool environment and have constant lubrication from oil vapors. Discharge valves probably are the hottest part of a refrigeration system, operating up to 50° to 100°F above the discharge line, so they more commonly cause trouble. Fit discharge valves with special care. Heavy molecules of oil tend to accumulate on them, causing carbon buildup and interfering with performance. Discharge valves and oil are both damaged by temperatures above 325° to 350°F (163° to 177°C). In general, keep the discharge-line temperature below about 225° to 250°F (107° to 121°C).

Discharge valves may have a relief spring so they can open extra-wide if slugs of liquid refrigerant or oil enter through the suction line.

Measuring Reciprocating Compressor Output

Two important concepts about the action of a reciprocating compressor are *volumetric efficiency* and *pumping ratio*.

The following abbreviations appear in compressor formulas:

π = 3.14
D = diameter of cylinder
r = radius of cylinder = D/2
L = length of stroke
RPM = revolutions per minute

N = number of cylinders
cfm = cubic feet per minute
h = height from piston at top dead center to cylinder head

1. *Volumetric efficiency* is the actual amount of refrigerant gas pumped, compared to the compressor's theoretical maximum (which equals piston displacement).

$$\text{Volumetric efficiency} = \frac{\text{quantity of refrigerant gas pumped}}{\text{piston displacement}}$$

An efficient system requires high volumetric efficiency. The following factors can reduce volumetric efficiency:

- High head pressure
- Low low-side pressure (makes it tougher for the compressor to draw in vapor)
- Large clearance space
- Valves that stick, don't open fully, or are undersized
- Restrictions in intake or discharge lines

2. *Pumping ratio* (or *compression ratio*) equals absolute high-side pressure divided by absolute low-side pressure. Excess pumping ratio will reduce compressor efficiency and raise discharge temperature, possibly degrading oil, refrigerant, and equipment. Constant pressure on the piston can starve the piston pin of lubricant and cause abnormal wear.

$$\text{Pumping ratio} = \frac{\text{absolute high-side pressure}}{\text{absolute low-side pressure}}$$

To understand how a high pumping ratio can cut efficiency, think about the cylinder of a reciprocating compressor. When the piston reaches top dead center, all the gas has roughly equal compression. Most of the gas exits the discharge port, but pressure from gas remaining in the cylinder prevents suction gas from entering the cylinder. Only when the piston falls, and cylinder pressure drops below suction pressure, can suction gas enter the cylinder and be compressed.

For proper operation, keep the pumping ratio to a maximum of about 10:1. Higher pressures cause heat, carbonizing oil in the discharge gas. The pumping ratio may be lowered by raising the suction pressure, which also increases compressor cooling (in hermetics), raises efficiency, and reduces deterioration of oil, refrigerant, and equipment.

When calculating pumping ratio, make sure to convert gauge pressure to absolute pressure. For a system with a discharge pressure of 150 psig and a suction pressure of 5 psig, the calculation would be as follows:

$$\frac{150+15}{30+15} = \frac{165}{45} = 3.7$$

Because vacuum is measured by inches of mercury, calculating compression ratio is somewhat complicated when suction pressure is below atmospheric pressure. Convert a mercury vacuum reading to pounds absolute pressure with this formula:

$$\text{Absolute suction pressure} = \frac{30 - \text{vacuum in inches Hg}}{2}$$

The actual output of a reciprocating compressor depends on the:

- type of refrigerant;
- compression ratio;
- volumetric efficiency;
- cooling system's efficiency and suction-line pressure (Cooler suction gas is denser, so more gas is drawn into the cylinder.);
- cylinder cooling (Cooling increases volumetric efficiency.);
- compressor speed (At high speed, valve inertia can reduce gas flow.);
- valve type and size (Large valves with good seals will increase output.);
- friction (An elaborate evaporator impedes flow and reduces refrigerant supply to the compressor.);
- mechanical condition of equipment (Good seals, piston rings, bearings, and valves raise output.); and
- lubrication (Proper amounts, type, and distribution of oil decrease friction and promote a seal between piston and cylinder.)

Checking Head Valves

To check the operation of head valves in a reciprocating compressor (see Figure 3-G):

1. Install the gauge manifold with both valves closed.
2. Frontseat the suction-service valve.

3. Crack the discharge-service valve just off the backseat to get a gauge reading.

4. Allow the compressor to run down to 10 psig (172 kPa) on the suction side. (The low-pressure cut-out might need to be held in by sticking a screwdriver under the lever in the switch.)

5. Stop the compressor when it reaches about 10 psig. (If the compressor cannot do this, the suction valves are probably bad, or a head gasket is blown between the suction and discharge sides.)

6. If the compressor can pull down, watch for a rapid rise in suction pressure after shutdown. (If this occurs, the discharge valve is leaking back. Discharge any excess pressure to a recovery apparatus and pull off the heads and investigate.)

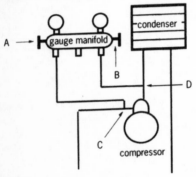

A. low-side manifold valve (closed)
B. high-side manifold valve (closed)
C. suction-service valve (frontseated)
D. discharge-service valve (backseated)

Figure 3-G: Checking compressor head valves

Reciprocating Compressor Troubles

If a compressor fails, use Table 3-A to analyze the failure. Many problems in reciprocating compressors emerge from problems elsewhere in the system, and replacing a compressor may only lead to further expense after that problem destroys the new compressor. For example, compressor overheating may be due to excess superheating in the suction line, failed motor safeties, or lubrication problems. (See Chapter 10, "Troubleshooting.")

Most compressors fail due to system malfunctions, not compressor problems. Examine the failed compressor for symptoms of system problems, then correct them to prevent future failures.

Table 3-A
Identifying Compressor Failures

Liquid Slugging

Symptom(s): Broken reeds, rods, or crankshaft; loose or broken discharge bolts; blown gaskets.

Explanation: Slugging is a result of trying to compress liquid in cylinders. Liquid may be either refrigerant or oil or, more likely, a combination of both. Slugging is primarily the result of off-cycle refrigerant migration on refrigerant-cooled compressors and floodback on air-cooled compressors.

Remedy:

1. Maintain proper compressor and evaporator superheat.

2. Prevent uncontrolled liquid return (particularly oil) with accumulators.

3. Locate the compressor in warm ambient or install a pump-down cycle.

4. Correct abnormal low-load conditions.

Liquid Washout

Symptom(s): Worn rods and bearings; worn pistons and cylinders on lower end; worn crankshaft and oil pump; scored cover bearing and crankshaft.

Explanation: This is a result of refrigerant washing oil off wearing surfaces. There is off-cycle migration of saturated refrigerant into the crankcase. Compressor starts up, resulting in a mass of foam that, when pumped, washes bearing surfaces clean of the oil film necessary for proper lubrication. Severe migration results in slugging.

Remedy:

1. Locate the compressor in warm ambient or install a pump-down cycle.

2. Check crankcase heater operation.

Liquid Dilution

Symptom(s): Rotor drag/shorted stator; worn bearings; scored and/or broken rods; scored crankshaft; worn oil pump.

Explanation: This is a result of liquid refrigerant returning to the compressor during the running cycle. Oil becomes diluted; lubrication for the oil pump and end bearing may be adequate, but as it progresses down the crankshaft, insufficient oil to lubricate the rods and main bearings will occur. This may allow the rotor to drag on the stator and short out the stator.

Remedy:

1. Maintain proper compressor and evaporator superheat.
2. Prevent uncontrolled liquid return with accumulator if necessary.
3. Correct abnormal low-load conditions.
4. Check defrost cycle.
5. Check for oversized TXV.

High Discharge Temperature

Symptom(s): Discolored valve plate (cannot rub off); overheated or burned valve reeds; worn rings and pistons; worn cylinders; scored rods, bearing, and crankshaft; spot burn in the stator.

Explanation: This is a result of temperatures in the compressor head and cylinders becoming so hot that the oil loses its ability to lubricate.

Remedy:

1. Check for low suction and high discharge pressures and low load and evaporator problems.
2. Check low pressure control setting.
3. Check the ambient temperature; check for dirty condenser, inoperative condenser fan.
4. Check air flow across compressor.

Lack of Oil

Symptom(s): Scored bearings; broken rods; scored crankshaft; low oil in crankcase.

Explanation: This is a result of not enough oil in the crankcase to properly lubricate the running gear.

Remedy:

1. Check oil failure switch operation.
2. Check pipe sizing and for oil traps.
3. Check for inadequate defrost.
4. Correct abnormal low-load conditions.
5. Eliminate short cycling.

Courtesy of Copeland Industries

4

Controls

Air conditioning and refrigeration systems rely on several types of controls. Some controls serve multiple functions, and several types of controls can be housed in a single component, especially with solid-state controls.

These controls are described here:

1. *Capacity controls* determine how much refrigerant the compressor pumps to the condenser.

2. *Operating controls* regulate electric current to the compressor motor.

3. *Refrigerant controls*, or *metering devices*, regulate the flow of refrigerant through the system.

4. *Safety controls* prevent the system from operating when it might harm people, equipment, or facilities.

Other components that help control system operation, such as two-temperature valves and pressure limiters, are described in Chapter 6.

Faulty controls can cause almost any sort of problem in a cooling system, but the complicated nature of modern controls can interfere with troubleshooting. If a control problem is suspected, try to bypass the control and watch the result. If the bypass corrects the problem, then the problem has probably been isolated. Another simple troubleshooting technique is to replace the questionable control with one that is good.

PRINCIPLES OF CONTROLS

The goals of a control system are to:

- establish design conditions (pressure and temperature);
- restore conditions quickly when they deviate;
- ensure safety for building occupants, products, and mechanical equipment; and
- ensure economical operation.

In a *closed-loop control system*, the controller senses a variable and changes it when necessary. Closed-loop systems are common in air conditioning and refrigeration systems. A closed-loop control system typically has these basic components:

- An *element* that senses a change in the controlled variable;
- A *controller* that receives a signal from the sensor and causes an action (such as sending a current) when the set point is exceeded; and
- A *final control element* that responds to the signal from the controller (such as the compressor-motor relay)

Detecting disturbance, the first step in establishing control, can be done by several techniques, including:

Table 4-A: Detecting Disturbance

Disturbance in	Mechanism
Liquid level	Float
	Static-pressure element
Pressure	Diaphragm
	Bellows
	Pressure bell
Temperature	Piezoelectric crystal
	Bimetallic strip or coil
	Rod-and-tube element
	Sealed bellows
	Remote bulb
	Thermistor
	Resistance bulb
	Thermocouple

In recent years, a spate of integrated electronic controls has entered the market. These controls have many advantages in reliability and flexibility, but they can be difficult and confusing to service. The technician should become familiar with the most common electronic controls first, and increase knowledge when opportunities arise. Manufacturer's troubleshooting guides are a good place to learn to service integrated controls. Manufacturers of integrated controls often have their own technicians who are expert in that particular brand.

TERMINOLOGY

To read product literature and discuss problems with specialists, technicians must understand the language of controls.

An **actuator** converts a signal into a movement that then changes the controlled variable. EXAMPLE: upon receiving a signal, a solenoid valve regulating liquid refrigerant flow into an evaporator

A **close-on-rise** control makes contact when temperature or pressure rises. Close-on-rise thermostats are common in refrigeration systems.

A **closed-loop** system is a group of components with feedback: The action of the final control element changes conditions, which the sensor detects. Practically all cooling systems have closed-loop control systems.

A **control agent** is whatever is manipulated to achieve the desired conditions. EXAMPLE: the cold air in a forced-air cooling system

A **control fixture** is the fixture containing the control device. EXAMPLE: the cabinet containing a thermostat

A **controlled device** responds to a signal from the controller. EXAMPLE: a compressor motor

The **controlled variable** is the condition regulated by the control system. EXAMPLE: temperature in most ACR systems

A **deviation** is the difference between the value of the controlled variable and the set point of the control for that variable.

A **differential** (in a two-stage control) is the gap between the cut-in and cut-out settings.

A **direct-acting control** has an output that changes in the same direction as the controlled variable. (See Reverse-acting control.)

Hunting (**surging** or **cycling**) is the tendency of a feedback mechanism to overcorrect, adjusting too far in one direction, then too far in the opposite direction. In cooling systems, hunting commonly refers to metering devices.

A **limit control** is a device that prevents unsafe conditions in the controlled variable. EXAMPLE: a high-pressure cut-out preventing overpressure in the discharge line

A **normally closed (NC)** device closes when the control signal is removed.

A **normally open (NO)** device opens when the control signal is removed.

An **open-on-rise** control breaks contact when temperature or pressure rises. EXAMPLE: a heating system thermostat

A **reverse-acting control** produces an output in the opposite direction from the controlled variable.

A **sequencing control** energizes several stages of a cooling system according to need. EXAMPLE: a control signaling several compressors to operate in response to load conditions

A **set point** is the point at which a controller acts to make a change in the controlled variable.

In a **slave fixture,** the condition (usually temperature) depends on measurements taken elsewhere; the fixture has no device for measuring pressure or temperature.

Supply pressure is the pressure of compressed air in a pneumatic control system, usually 15 or 20 psi.

System feedback is the return of information about the controlled variable to the controller; it's essential in a closed-loop system.

A **transducer** changes energy from one form to another. EXAMPLE: the bimetallic strip of a thermostat converting heat into kinetic energy.

ELEMENTARY CONTROL SYSTEMS

Control systems may use these modes of control:

- An *on-off* (two-position) is the simplest type of control device. The device can only be on or off; it has no intermediate positions. On-off control is suited to simple heating and some cooling systems.

- A *multiposition* (multistage or sequencing) control can actuate several on-off devices. EXAMPLE: A control that brings more compressors on line to meet increasing demand.

- In a *floating control,* the final control element may take any position between full on and full off. When the controller rests in "neutral," it sends no signal to the final control element.

- A *modulating* (or *proportioning* or *throttling*) control is like a floating control, but lacks the neutral zone, so a signal always goes to the final control element. EXAMPLE: A thermostatic expansion valve can vary the entry to the evaporator.

- A *step controller* can operate several circuits. The controller may have an electronic or mechanical timer; cams on a shaft trip switches to control the various functions.

The final control element generally uses one or more of these *sources of power* to make changes in the system:

- **Electricity:** A low-voltage or line-voltage circuit delivers power to a control device. EXAMPLE: a solenoid valve

- **Manual:** Certain devices depend on a human operator. EXAMPLE: manual-resetting valves and switches

- **Oil pressure:** Oil pressure developed by the compressor oil pump is directed to devices. EXAMPLE: a cylinder unloader

- **Pneumatic (air):** An air circuit delivers air pressure to the control element at 15 psi or 20 psi (207 kPa or 241 kPa). The air presses on a piston to move the final control element. EXAMPLE: a pneumatic valve

- **System pressure:** The device is actuated by refrigerant pressure in the system. EXAMPLE: The pilot valve on the four-way valve in a heat pump directs refrigerant pressure to the slide that controls refrigerant flow through the four-way valve.

Sensing Elements

A variety of electromechanical temperature sensors appear in controls.

A *bimetallic element* is a sandwich of two metals with different coefficients of expansion. The element bends as temperature changes. Usually the element has a spiral or curved shape, to save space and increase accuracy.

The *rod-and-tube* is a variation of the bimetallic element. A rod of low-expansion material is housed in a tube of high-expansion material. The components are bonded at one end, and the relative movement of the tube versus rod at the other end gives the signal.

A *sealed bellows* is filled with a gas or liquid charge. As the controlled device changes temperature, the bellows expands or contracts.

A *remote bulb* works like a sealed bellows: the fluid expands or contracts with changing temperature. The bulb is connected by a capillary tube to a bellows or diaphragm, which registers the change in temperature and affects the final control element.

A *fast-response element* is a variation on the remote bulb; a coil of capillary tube replaces the bulb. With its higher ratio of surface to volume, the device responds faster than a remote bulb.

An *averaging element* is a variation on the fast-response element; the capillary tube is wrapped around a duct to take an average temperature reading.

A *thermistor* is an electronic device whose resistance depends on temperature.

A *resistance bulb* is a coil of wire around a bobbin. Resistance increases with temperature.

A *thermocouple* registers the change in voltage that changing temperature creates at the junction of two metals.

Switches and Electrical Mechanisms

Several mechanisms are used to control the electrical signal from a controller to an actuator or controlled element. Relays (power-operated switches) are widely used because they eliminate the need to run heavy cables from the control device to the motor, saving space, money, and hazard.

Switches must rapidly connect and disconnect to reduce arcing, the flow of electricity across the narrow gap that forms when contacts open and close. Arcing causes heat and corrosion, which raises resistance across the contacts and can destroy the switch or associated equipment.

Switch Classification

Switches are classified by number of poles and throws. A *pole* is a single current path through the switch. A *throw* is a position in which the switch can complete a circuit. Thus, a single-pole, double-throw (spdt) switch has a single power input that can be connected to either of two outputs. A double-pole, double-throw (dpdt) has two paths, and two possible "made" positions. (A switch that's "made" is closed and "open" when not closed.) A "single-break" switch opens and closes the conductor(s) in one place; a "double-break" switches the conductors(s) in two places. (See Figure 4-A.)

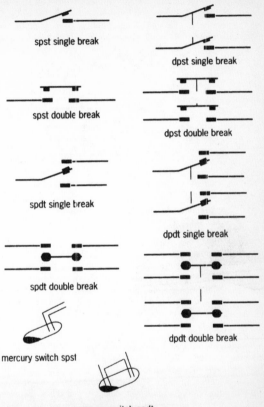

spst single break

dpst single break

spst double break

dpst double break

spdt single break

dpdt single break

spdt double break

dpdt double break

mercury switch spst

mercury switch spdt

Figure 4-A: Switch diagrams

Snap-Acting Switch

This type of switch (spst or spdt) uses a sprung piece of metal that a plunger moves in response to a signal from the sensing element. The metal contacts move quickly apart, minimizing arcing. The switch need not be installed level, vibration is not a problem, and the switch can be actuated by a slight movement of the plunger. However, you cannot see the degree of contact in the switch. Unlike a mercury switch, this switch cannot be fully sealed against dust. (See Figure 4-B.)

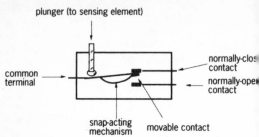

Figure 4-B: Snap-acting switch (spdt)

Mercury Switch

The simple, reliable mercury switch is used in many thermostats. A bulb holding mercury and contacts is attached to a rocking plate that is actuated by the sensing mechanism. When the tube tilts toward the contacts, the mercury quickly fills the gap, closing the circuit. Mercury switches are sealed, and the action is visible, but they need careful leveling. Do not use in vibrating locations or where temperature reach −38.87°C, mercury's freezing point. Spst or spdt mercury switches are made to switch currents from 0.1A to 10A.

Mercury Plunger Relay

Like the mercury switch, this device closes the contacts with mercury. But the mercury is displaced by a plunger, not a tilting bulb, and the relay can handle up to 60A. When the coil surrounding the relay is de-energized, the plunger, containing a small pool of mercury and one contact, floats in a large pool of mercury. When the coil is energized, the plunger is pulled into the large pool, displacing mercury and forcing the two pools into contact with each other. Since each pool is already touching one contact, the switch closes. It remains closed as long as the coil gets current.

Electromagnetic Relay

This is another form of electrically operated switch. Like the mercury plunger, it can be used to switch heavy currents, but it can also be used for more complex switching applications, such as energizing several loads from a single current source, or signaling several control circuits to operate in sequence.

A rocking armature holding the contacts is regulated by springs and controlled by an electromagnet. Unlike the solenoid switch, the armature is outside the magnet. Each circuit gets a pair of contacts, one fixed and the other on the armature. When the magnet is deenergized, the spring moves the contacts to the normal position. When the magnet is energized, it overpowers the spring and the contacts move to the opposite position. The switch can be normally open or normally closed, and the relay can contain many combinations of poles and throws. (See Figure 4-C.)

Potentiometer

A potentiometer is a proportioning control that sends a signal of varying voltage to another device. The remote device responds proportionately to the voltage, so this is used in a modulating control. The coil of a potentiometer has fine wire with a potential across it. A lever called a wiper slides across the coil and completes the circuit to any point on the coil. As the wiper moves, the resistance between its terminal and either coil terminal changes, so the output voltage reflects the wiper position.

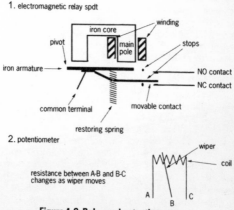

1. electromagnetic relay spdt

2. potentiometer

resistance between A-B and B-C changes as wiper moves

Figure 4-C: Relay and potentiometer

Electronic Controls

An electronic controller compares the signal from a sensor to a reference value (the set point) and gives an output called an error signal. The error signal is amplified and wired to the final control element. The degree of amplification is called "gain."

Electromechanical relays have better ability to handle large current, so they are often used to switch the output current, even in systems using electronic controls.

The most common type of electronic controller is a form of the resistance bridge called the Wheatstone bridge. A bridge compares the sensor signal to the set point and amplifies the resulting error signal into a useful output signal. The variable resistor of a Wheatstone bridge can be replaced by a thermistor or other electronic sensor. With modifications, this device can be adapted to all modes of control, including two-position and proportional. **Electronic controls vary widely, and the manufacturer is the best reference on them!**

Pneumatic Controls

Pneumatic controls generally use the same combination of sensing element and relay as electromechanical and electronic controls. The air supply—at 15 to 20 psi (207 to 241 kPa)—provides volume to fill the control and associated piping, and pressure to move the final control element.

A pneumatic control uses pilot and amplifier circuits. The pilot circuit takes the signal from the sensor and actuates a device that regulates the amplifier circuit. The amplifier circuit handles a larger volume of air to move the final control device. The output signal can be on-off or proportional. The engineer or system manufacturer will supply a pneumatic control diagram.

Capacity Controls

Capacity controls allow a system to meet varying cooling needs. The obvious example is an office-building system. During the day, the heat load comes from equipment, appliances, lighting, solar energy, and people. At night, most loads are reduced or eliminated, but operating at minimum cooling load can cause serious problems. Low suction pressure can cause frosting of dry evaporators and freezing of water chillers. Reduced suction-gas density can overheat a hermetic compressor or impair oil return, causing loss of compressor lubrication and oil logging in the evaporator. For these reasons, larger systems commonly have capacity controls in addition to on-off motor controls. These capacity controls include the multistage compressor, the variable-speed motor, the hot-gas bypass, and various unloader devices.

On-Off

On-off operation is fine for controlling capacity in small systems, but in large systems with light loads, it can cause short cycling. In some systems, technicians try to prevent short-cycling by lowering the cut-out pressure to extend the on cycle, but operating at extremely low suction pressure can cause problems.

Multistage Compressor

Several conventional compressors can be linked in parallel, so more compressors come on-line as the load increases, and then go off-line as the load is reduced. Each compressor feeds refrigerant into a header that supplies the condenser. The system offers a built-in backup: if one compressor fails, others can handle the load. Electricity consumption is proportional to the load.

Variable- or Multispeed Motor

Variable-speed motors are sometimes used for capacity control, mostly in larger installations with centrifugal or reciprocating compressors. These motors are expensive and usually require three-phase power. An alternative, the two-speed motor, may be controlled by a two-stage thermostat, which drives the motor at the appropriate speed.

Hot-Gas Bypass

A hot-gas bypass directs refrigerant gas from the high side to the low side, bypassing the condenser. This reduces cooling capacity because the gas cannot dispose of its heat. Instead of using compressor energy for cooling, this bypass uses it to increase the heat load, allowing a compressor to operate down to zero load.

When low-side pressure drops below the setting, a modulating-discharge bypass valve opens, allowing gas to exit the discharge line toward the low side. The valve closes when low-side pressure exceeds the setting. The valve may be directly operated or pilot operated.

Limit the length of the bypass to 35" (10.7 m), and insulate it so refrigerant does not condense and oil does not gather. An oil return, as shown in Figure 4-D, may be used to promote oil return in long or cold bypass lines.

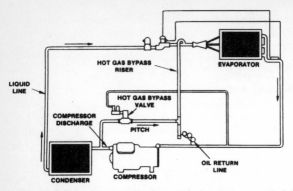

Figure 4-D: Hot-gas bypass capacity control—bypass to evaporator inlet
Courtesy of American Standard

1. A bypass to the *evaporator inlet* (see Figure 4-D) controls capacity and prevents oil logging in the evaporator. The system can modulate capacity down to zero on systems that have cylinder unloaders for initial capacity control. This bypass setup can, in some cases, impair motor cooling. Oil return is assisted by the increased volume of gas in the evaporator. This method is the simplest and least expensive bypass system. The line between the suction line and the bypass valve is a pilot line that detects low pressure (indicating low demand). When pressure drops below the set point, the bypass opens, routing hot vapor to the evaporator. The valve keeps suction pressure high enough so the low-pressure cut-out (LPCO) does not shut down the compressor.

2. A bypass to the *suction line* may be installed in a multiple-evaporator system, or in a system with a remote evaporator. This raises the danger of motor overheating, so a desuperheating valve may be placed at the inlet into the suction line, and a mixing chamber is helpful as well.

3. A bypass to the *chiller inlet* can create a hot-gas cooling load equal to the compressor's minimum capacity with all unloaders operating. Hot gas maintains suction pressure and temperature down to zero load.

Unloader

Several types of unloaders can improve efficiency at low demands by gradually reducing output to almost zero. These devices will allow, for example, a six-cylinder compressor to simulate the output of a smaller device. They also reduce high-side pressure to ease motor and compressor starting. The unloader may be powered by electricity or oil pressure.

Unloaders come in two basic types:

1. The unloader *holds the suction valves open*, causing some cylinders on a multicylinder compressor to pump vapor into the suction line, not the discharge line.

2. The unloader *routes refrigerant from the discharge side to the suction side* without letting it lose heat. These unloaders act like bypasses (see above), but since they are built into the compressor, we call them unloaders. Like a bypass, they return hot gas to the low side, avoiding the condensers. These unloaders, which are getting rarer because they tend to heat the compressor, come in two varieties:

   a. During low demand, a *three-way bypass valve* in the compressor head directs gas to the suction side instead of the discharge side.

   b. An *external bypass* routes refrigerant through a pipe back to the suction inlet. A solenoid valve controlled by a timer (for start-up unloading) or a pressure switch (for capacity control) determines whether vapor goes to the condenser or directly to the suction side.

Operating Controls

Operating controls direct an ACR system to deliver the right amount of cooling without wasting energy. Many control systems are integrated, such as a combined heating-cooling thermostat, or a "smart-building" control that also handles fire-detection and security services.

Thermostat

A thermostat is a control that stops and starts components depending on temperature at the sensor location. The sensor may be in the cooled area or on the evaporator tubing. A duct thermostat, or "duct stat," measures temperature in an air duct. Thermostats can sense heat with most of the techniques listed under "Sensing Elements," above. The bimetallic strip is a common sensing element for small air conditioning systems.

Heating and cooling systems use different types of thermostats. A heating thermostat starts the system when the temperature drops below the set point (called "close-on-drop"); a cooling system thermostat starts the system when the set temperature is exceeded (called "close-on-rise"). In practice, both functions often are housed in one device. In addition to turning on a compressor, a cooling system thermostat may operate louvers, pumps, power circuits, or a dehumidifier. A mercury switch is often used to make quiet contacts in a thermostat.

Thermostats operate on 24V, 120V, or 240V current. Low-voltage thermostats are desirable because high-voltage wires can warm the unit, causing an error called "thermostat droop." Low-voltage wires are also easier, cheaper, and safer to run through a building. Current from a low-voltage thermostat drives a relay, motor starter, or a contactor, which supplies line current to the compressor motor.

Thermostat-controlled systems may overshoot the set point after shutoff, because the heating or cooling system continues adding or removing heat for a time. A heating thermostat can control overshoot with an anticipator—a resistor that adds a little heat, causing the thermostat to shut off prematurely so residual heat will warm the room to the set point. In a cooling thermostat, the anticipator is a fixed resistor that is energized during the off cycle, warming the thermostat and starting the cooling sooner. By reducing "lag" time, the anticipator prevents the room from getting too hot.

In buildings with pneumatic controls, large refrigeration systems may use pneumatic-operated relays and valves. In this setup, a thermostat controls a variable air-pressure supply to the control device. When temperature and air pressure exceed the set point, the air closes or opens a pressure-electric ("PE") switch. The electric circuit then powers a solenoid valve in the system or a relay that powers a motor.

To test and calibrate a thermostat, measure ambient air temperature and adjust the thermostat to make or break at that temperature. If one cannot see when the mercury bulb flips over, use a VOM or continuity meter to detect the instant of contact. If the thermostat does not make or break at that point, the temperature setting may be able to be adjusted. The thermostat will also have some sort of delay arrangement to prevent short-cycling; this may need adjustment as well.

Programmable thermostats are electronic controls that can vary the temperature according to time of day and day of the week, with a possible manual override. Many thermostats have digital displays, and a battery backup to preserve memory during power loss. Solid-state thermostats have complicated functions; many can save energy by changing the set point according to time of day and/or day of week.

Checking Operation

First check continuity between the thermostat and the motor control. Then make sure all other system components are working properly by bypassing or testing with a VOM. Bypass a mechanical thermostat and see if the compressor will start. If a good thermostat is wired in the circuit and it solves the problem, leave it in place.

Integrated controls and electronic thermostats present a special challenge. This equipment is sensitive and must be tested carefully. Aside from swapping in a good control, troubleshooting charts from the equipment manufacturers are essential for dealing with these devices.

Locating the Thermostat Sensing Bulb

The thermostat sensing element can measure the temperature of the (1) product, (2) evaporator, (3) evaporator return air, or (4) conditioned space. Important: the sensing bulb must directly contact the component or area being controlled.

1. A *product-temperature sensor* is used for a system that cools a liquid, such as milk or ice cream. The sensor may be inserted into a well surrounded by product and insulated from ambient air. A capillary tube may be wrapped around the drum holding the product.

2. An *evaporator sensing element* may be clamped to evaporator tubing, placed in a well touching the tubing, wound around the tubing, or affixed to a plate evaporator.

3. Place a *space sensor* in a cooler away from doors, in a place with good air circulation. Locate return air sensors in the return air stream to the evaporator, but not touching the evaporator.

4. Place a *comfort-cooling thermostat* so it accurately measures the cooled rooms. The thermostat should be about 5' (1.5 m) above the floor on an inside wall. Keep it away from drafts, ducts, radiant heating devices, or concealed sources of heat or cold in the wall.

Pressure Motor Control (Low-Pressure Cut-Out)

A pressure motor control, or low-pressure cut-out (LPCO), operates the compressor motor by measuring pressure in the evaporator or suction line. Low-side pressure gives a good picture of evaporator temperature. When evaporator pressure exceeds the control's set point (indicating that the evaporator is too warm), the bellows expands, tripping a switch and starting the motor. The LPCO can also serve as a safety control to shut off motor current when suction-line pressure falls dangerously low.

Some pressure motor controls have separate adjustment screws for cut-in and cut-out, while others have adjustments for range and cut-out. Adjust a disconnected pressure motor control with a vacuum pump and a compound gauge.

Range and Differential

Range is the span between a control's cut-in and cut-out points. *Differential* is the temperature difference between these points. For example, in a comfort-cooling system set to cut-in at 74°F and cut-out at 70°F, the range is 70° to 74°F, and the differential is 4°F (74° − 70°). The concept is identical in SI.

Range and differential are vital to setting operating controls. Why? Because if one tries to maintain exact temperature (inadequate differential) in the cooled space, short cycling may occur.

Adjusting range will alter both cut-in and cut-out temperatures, but not differential. The higher the range, the lower the load on the system. Markings on the adjusting screw may indicate which direction to turn to increase or decrease range.

Adjusting differential will change the cut-in or the cut-out point, but not both. Increasing the differential will extend the on and off cycles, reducing short-cycling. Because changing the differential changes the cut-in or the cut-out temperature, it also changes the range.

Finding Cut-In and Cut-Out Points

Use the following procedure to set a thermostat cut-in and cut-out for a reach-in refrigerator for a product that must be held between 37°F and 45°F:

Maximum permissible temperature:	45°F	7.2°C
Minimum permissible temperature:	37°F	2.8°C
Evaporator temperature differential:	8°F	4.4°C

Follow these steps:

1. Set the cut-in at the maximum permissible product temperature (45°F).

2. Find the control differential:

Maximum permissible temperature	45°F	7.2°C
– Minimum permissible temperature	– 37°F	– 2.8°C
	8°F	4.4°C
+ Evaporator temperature differential (ΔT)	+ 15°F	+ 8.33°C
Control ΔT	23°F	12.73°C

3. Subtract the control ΔT from the cut-in temperature to find the cut-out setting.

Cut-in temperature	45°F	7.22°C
– Control ΔT	– 23°F	– 12.78°C
Cut-out setting	22°F	–5.55°C

4. To set a pressure control, convert the cut-in and cut-out temperatures to pressure and adjust accordingly.

Thermostats that read evaporator temperature generally have a relatively wide differential because evaporators warm up faster than a cooled space or product during the off cycle.

Checking Operating Controls

The following four controls may affect motor performance: pressure motor control, thermostat, high-side cut-out, and oil-pressure safety. When diagnosing a balky system, make sure these controls are not improperly interfering with the motor. (If the controls are shutting down the system for a good reason, that problem must be fixed instead.)

Problems with operating controls can stem from leaking lines, broken bellows or springs, corroded points, maladjustment, or units that are out of level. Replace cracked mercury switches and corroded points (points can be temporarily dresses with sandpaper, but never with emery cloth). If an inspection does not reveal a problem, test a temperature-sensitive operating control by running the system and observing control operations, or by replacing the suspect control with a good one.

To check pressure controls, install the gauge manifold and run the compressor until the motor cuts in and cuts out. Compare these values with normal system values. You might also test cut-in and cut-out with gauges and a hand vacuum and pressure pump.

Refrigerant Control (Metering Device)

A refrigerant control (metering device) feeds liquid refrigerant into the evaporator at the desired rate and for the desired period of time. The metering device reduces evaporator pressure and separates the system's high-pressure and low-pressure sides. The common metering devices include the automatic expansion valve, the thermostatic expansion valve, the high-side float, the low-side float, and the capillary tube.

All metering devices except the high-side float and the capillary tube regulate the flow of refrigerant based on feedback about conditions in the evaporator and/or suction line. The high-side float controls the level of refrigerant in the receiver. The capillary tube is a fixed restriction to refrigerant flow—metering depends on nothing more than inside diameter and length. To see how metering devices are used in whole systems, see Chapter 8, "Whole Systems."

The following table compares some major features of different refrigerant controls:

Table 4-B: Refrigerant Controls

Metering device	Evaporator	Evaporator type	Motor control
Thermostatic expansion valve	Single or multiple	Dry	Temperature
Automatic expansion valve	Single	Dry	Temperature
Thermal-electric valve	Single	Dry	Temperature or pressure
Low-side float	Multiple	Flooded	Temperature or pressure
High-side float	Single	Flooded	Temperature or pressure
Capillary tube	Single	Dry	Temperature

Refrigerant controls are designed to deal with liquid refrigerant, not flash gas, which is refrigerant that has prematurely vaporized in the liquid line. Flash gas interferes with refrigerant metering and reduces system capacity. Prevent flash gas by using a heat exchanger to cool liquid refrigerant, and by minimizing restrictions in the liquid line.

Automatic Expansion Valve

The automatic expansion valve (AXV or AEV), also called the *pressure-controlled expansion valve*, meters refrigerant on the basis of low-side pressure. The valve tries to maintain constant pressure in the evaporator while the compressor runs. Because the evaporator never fills with liquid refrigerant, AXV systems are called "dry." AXVs are used with a temperature-sensitive motor control, and were common on brine or alcohol-ballasted coils with a relatively constant load. AXVs may read evaporator pressure with a bellows or diaphragm.

Three fluid pressures and two spring pressures combine to actuate the AXV. Referring to Figure 4-E, notice that suction pressure (F_1) and the needle-valve spring (F_2) push the valve closed, while liquid-line pressure (F_3), atmospheric pressure (F_4), and the adjusting spring (F_5) push it open. Changing the adjusting-spring pressure adjusts the valve to achieve the desired pressure in the evaporator or suction line.

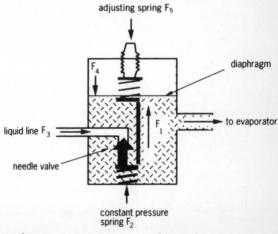

Closing forces:
F_1 evaporator (suction) pressure
F_2 constant (needle-valve) spring

Opening forces:
F_3 liquid-line pressure
F_4 atmospheric pressure
F_5 adjusting spring

Figure 4-E: Principles of the automatic expansion valve

The AXV works with the motor control to regulate evaporator pressure. As the valve meters refrigerant into the evaporator, suction pressure rises and the valve closes somewhat to hold suction pressure at the set point. When the motor-control sensing bulb detects adequate cooling in the suction line or cooled space, it signals the thermostat or the relay, depending on system size and control voltage, to shut off the motor. The compressor stops, raising the suction pressure and closing the AXV.

AXV capacity should match the load and the system. An undersized valve will starve the evaporator and reduce capacity. An oversized valve will feed excess refrigerant into the evaporator and may cause sweating or frosting on the suction line.

Some automatic expansion valves have a small groove in the seat so system pressure can balance during the off cycle. The groove is too small to affect the valve seal while the compressor runs, but large enough so the evaporator can fill with liquid refrigerant after the compressor shuts down. Balancing the load eases motor starting. If the AXV does balance pressures, an accumulator at the evaporator outlet may be necessary to prevent floodback to the compressor.

Installing and Adjusting

The AXV is usually used in small equipment, such as domestic comfort-cooling, vending machines, and air dryers. The liquid line is usually small enough to use a threaded fitting, although some have a soldered fitting. Follow these steps to mount and adjust an AXV:

1. Mount the valve at the evaporator inlet.

2. Attach the gauge manifold.

3. Charge the unit with the proper amount of refrigerant (charge level is critical with the AXV).

4. Start the unit and operate it for a few minutes to settle down.

5. Find the desired evaporator operating temperature, and convert it to pressure for the refrigerant.

6. Turn the adjusting screw until the suction gauge shows the desired suction pressure. Some valves have a pressure setting stamped near the adjusting screw. If so, move the pointer to the desired setting, then check the actual pressure with the gauge manifold.

7. Watch the system run through a few cycles, making sure it maintains the desired pressure without hunting.

Thermostatic Expansion Valve

The thermostatic expansion valve (TXV or TEV) is a very common and effective means of controlling refrigerant flow. The TXV, like the AXV, detects evaporator pressure. But the TXV also detects temperature (and sometimes pressure as well) at the evaporator outlet.

Evaporator pressure (F_1) on the valve diaphragm (see figure 4-F) and pressure from the adjusting spring (F_2) tend to close the valve. Pressure from the liquid line (F_3) and sensing bulb (F_4) tend to open it. The sensing bulb connects to the diaphragm by a capillary tube. When the evaporator is warm and the compressor is running, pressure from the bulb goes through the tube and presses the diaphragm, opening the needle valve so refrigerant will enter the evaporator. In an externally equalized TXV, an equalizing tube goes to the evaporator outlet, measuring suction-line pressure directly.

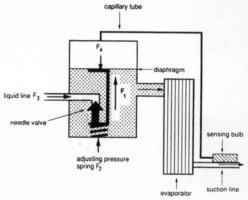

Closing forces:
F_1 evaporator (suction) pressure
F_2 adjusting spring

Opening forces:
F_3 liquid-line pressure
F_4 sensing-bulb pressure

Figure 4-F: Thermostatic expansion valve (internally equalized)

TXVs for large systems use flat seats rather than needle valves. For extremely large units, the valve may serve as a pilot for a second, larger valve that actually meters the refrigerant.

Superheat

A superheated gas is above saturation temperature for its pressure. In TXVs, superheat is the number of degrees the refrigerant warms between saturation conditions in the evaporator body and the evaporator outlet. The TXV sensing bulb detects outlet temperature and allows the valve to maintain constant superheat. A superheat setting of about 10°F (5.6°C) is common. The superheat setting may also be called the "superheat of the bulb over the evaporator."

Superheating of suction gas:

1. keeps the point of complete boiling away from the evaporator outlet, so liquid refrigerant cannot damage the compressor; and
2. evaporates all liquid refrigerant for peak efficiency.

Excessive superheat may:

1. overheat a hermetic compressor (which is cooled by suction gas); and
2. reduce capacity (because the area between the point of complete boiling and the evaporator outlet is warmer than saturation temperature).

Inadequate superheat may:

1. flood or starve the evaporator; and
2. cause short cycling, reducing efficiency, stressing components, and possibly allowing liquid slugs to reach the compressor. For more on superheat, see Chapter 9, Refrigerants.

TXV Operation

To understand the operation of a TXV more fully, let's watch one through a complete cycle. (See Figure 4-G.)

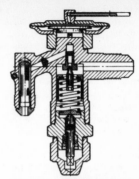

Figure 4-G: TXV cutaway view
Courtesy of Sporlan Division of Parker Hannifin, Inc.

1. The compressor is running and the TXV is feeding refrigerant to the evaporator. As the evaporator fills, pressure on the valve diaphragm rises, tending to close the valve. Meanwhile, the sensing bulb is cooling, reducing pressure that opens the valve.

2. With sufficient cooling, the valve closes. Leftover liquid refrigerant continues vaporizing in the evaporator, absorbing heat from the load. As the evaporator outlet and sensing bulb warm, pressure in the capillary tube from the sensing bulb increases, counteracting the adjusting spring and evaporator pressure that close the valve. The valve opens, allowing more refrigerant into the evaporator.

3. This open-closed cycle maintains the superheat and continues as long as the compressor runs. When the temperature or pressure control shuts down the motor, pressure rises in the evaporator, and the valve closes.

4. When the cooled space warms and the compressor starts, evaporator pressure drops. The TXV opens in response to lowered evaporator pressure and warming of the sensing bulb.

5. As the evaporator fills, suction pressure tends to close the valve, and the cycle continues.

Sensing Bulb

Four types of charges are used in TXVs: liquid (charged or cross-charged) and gas (charged or cross-charged). A "charged" bulb contains the system refrigerant. A "cross-charged" bulb contains a different refrigerant; the name reflects the "crossing" of the pressure-temperature curves of the system refrigerant and the sensor fluid.

These are characteristics of TXV charges:

1. A *liquid-charged* sensor contains the system refrigerant under pressure, so some liquid remains. The sensor's force on the valve equals the saturation pressure of the refrigerant at the sensing bulb. Because the charge is the system refrigerant, this sensor works at a wide range of temperatures and pressures. However, some evaporator flooding is possible when the compressor pulls down the system. This sensor is for evaporator temperatures ranging from −20° to 40°F (−28.9° to 4.4°C) and is common in air conditioner controls.

2. A *liquid cross-charged* sensor reduces hunting because suction pressure does not rise and fall as rapidly as bulb temperature. This charge is for evaporators running between −40° and 40°F (−40° and 4.4°C).

3. A *gas-charged* sensor does not respond to an increase in sensor pressure. However, when the sensor gets cold, the sensing gas condenses, reducing pressure and opening the valve. This charge is for evaporators running from 30° to 60°F (−1.1° to 15.6°C).

4. A *gas cross-charged* sensor can be adapted to virtually any system, at a wide range of operating temperatures. At operating temperatures, the sensor fluid is all vapor. A second type of gas cross-charged sensing element uses a combination of a noncondensing gas and a substance that adsorbs this gas. (In adsorption, the gas sticks to the surface of a solid substance without a chemical change.) At low temperatures, gas is adsorbed, reducing gas pressure. With warming, the adsorbed gas is released, so pressure rises.

External Equalizer

An external equalizer is a small tube connecting the TXV to the suction line near the sensing bulb. (See Figure 4-H.) The equalizer allows the valve to read pressure directly from the sensing bulb location rather than the evaporator inlet. This system allows precise superheat adjustment, especially in large evaporators (pressure drop above 4 psi, or 28 kPa) or systems with refrigerant distributors.

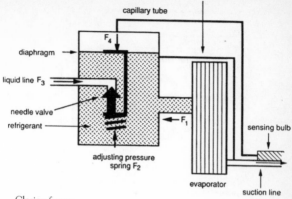

Closing forces:
F_1 equalizer or evaporator (suction) pressure
F_2 adjusting spring

Opening forces:
F_3 liquid-line pressure
F_4 sensing-bulb pressure

Figure 4-H: Thermostatic expansion valve (externally equalized)

We say a valve without an external equalizer has an "internal equalizer" because it detects evaporator pressure internally. Internally equalized TXVs are used on small systems with little pressure drop in the evaporator.

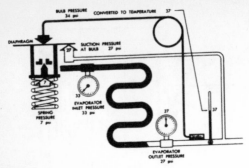

Closing pressure = 27 + 7 = 34 psi (suction pressure
  at bulb + spring pressure)

Bulb pressure needed to open the valve: 34 psi

Bulb temperature equivalent to 34 psi: 37°F

Saturated temperature equivalent to the evaporator
  outlet pressure: 28°F

Superheat: 9°F (Bulb temperature − saturated evaporator temperature)

Figure 4-I: Function of an external equalizer
Courtesy of Sporlan Division of Parker Hannifin, Inc.

Note that in Figure 4-I, the evaporator inlet pressure is 33 psi and outlet
pressure is 27 psi. The closing spring pressure is 7 lb.

With the equalizer, the closing spring pressure (7 lb.) and the evapor- ator
outlet pressure (27 lb. through the equalizer) combine to balance out the sensing
bulb pressure of 34 lb., creating a superheat of 9°F.

Without the equalizer, the closing spring pressure (7 lb.) and evaporator
inlet pressure (33 lb.) combine to a closing pressure of 40 lbs. This would
starve the evaporator, and a much higher superheat would be needed before
the sensing bulb would create 40 lbs. of pressure to open the valve. Such an
increase in superheat would also overheat the compressor.

To prevent oil from clogging the equalizer tube, the equalizer should
connect to the top of a horizontal suction line. If a control valve (such as an
evaporator pressure regulator) is in the suction line, the equalizer should be
between that valve and the evaporator. Otherwise, the valve would read the
effect of the pressure regulator, not evaporator pressure. If a TXV has an

equalizer fitting, the valve will only operate correctly if the equalizer is connected to the suction line. The equalizer line must never be capped or kinked.

Pressure Drop

A TXV needs to receive enough liquid refrigerant at sufficient pressure. Excess pressure loss in the evaporator can cause flash gas and interfere with TXV operation and system efficiency. Two types of pressure loss must be totaled before a TXV can be selected or its troubles diagnosed:

Static loss occurs when liquid refrigerant must be lifted to a metering device above the compressor. (See Table 4-C1.) *Friction loss* is due to elbows, tubing, evaporators, condensers, valves, and other components. Loss due to one of these restrictions (a refrigerant distributor) is shown in Table 4-C2. Friction loss can be calculated with information from valve and component manufacturers.

Table 4-C1: Liquid Line Pressure Loss

Refrigerant	Vertical Lift—Feet				
	20	40	60	80	100
	Static Pressure Loss—psi				
12	11	22	33	44	55
22	10	20	30	40	50
500	10	19	29	39	49
502	10	21	31	41	52
717 (Ammonia)	5	10	15	20	25

Table 4-C2: Liquid Line Pressure Loss—Distributor

Refrigerant	Average Pressure Drop Across Distributor
12	25 psi
22	35 psi
500	25 psi
502	35 psi
717 (Ammonia)	40 psi

Courtesy of Sporlan Division of Parker Hannifin, Inc.

Selecting a TXV

The TXV must be chosen on the basis of capacity, system refrigerant, and sensing-element charge. Manufacturers use a color-coding system to match valves to refrigerants. For example, yellow is often used to signify valves designed for R-12. Numbers or letters identify the charge in the sensing element.

An oversized TXV will cause erratic performance while an undersized one will starve the evaporator. TXVs are specified by the system engineer. Replacement valves should generally be exact duplicates of the old valve. When replacing a valve that cannot be identified, or that is incorrectly sized, the best procedure is to size the valve with a manufacturer's "Extended Capacity Chart," noting the following:

- *System load in BTU/hour or tons* (this may be less than the compressor's rated capacity).
- *Temperature of liquid entering the valve* (use a strap-on thermometer). Nominal valve ratings assume that the entering liquid temperature is 100°F. The extended capacity chart compensates for other entering temperatures.
- *Saturation temperature* in the evaporator.
- *Measured pressure drop across the valve* (see Pressure Drop, earlier) = inlet pressure – outlet pressure. Do not subtract suction pressure from head pressure.

The rated capacity of a valve is not a good indicator of its actual performance in an application. An extended capacity chart may show that a valve has more or less capacity than its nominal capacity. For example, a valve nominally rated at 2 tons may be big enough for a 3-ton system, while a 3-ton valve might flood the evaporator or operate erratically.

Installing a TXV

Follow these guidelines when installing a TXV:

- Install the TXV as close to the evaporator as possible in a location that can be serviced.
- Some valves must be insulated after installation.
- Some valves should not be located near the coil, because they require a warmer location.
- Install the valve body in the correct orientation.

- Allow no restrictions between the TXV and the evaporator, except for a refrigerant distributor. (See Chapter 5, "Components.")

- Gas-charged TXVs must be in a location warmer than the sensing bulb. Do not allow the gas-charged tubing to touch a cold surface other than the suction line, as this would cause vapor to condense in the tubing, cutting accuracy.

- Water can condense and freeze inside the flare nut connecting the TXV to the liquid line, possibly collapsing the line. Use special flare nuts. (See Chapter 7, "Pipe, Tube, Fittings, and Valves.")

Installing the Sensor Bulb

TXV performance depends on proper installation of the sensing bulb. Clamp the bulb to a clean, horizontal section of suction line near the evaporator outlet. (See Figure 4-J.) On small lines, the temperature is the same at the top and bottom of the line, so it can be clamped to the top. On lines larger than 7/8" OD, clamp the bulb at the 4 o'clock position to read average suction-line temperature. A bulb clamped below this might respond to the temperature of oil or liquid refrigerant instead of refrigerant vapor.

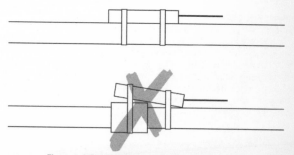

Figure 4-J: Sensor bulb installation—good and bad
Courtesy of Sporlan Division of Parker Hannifin, Inc.

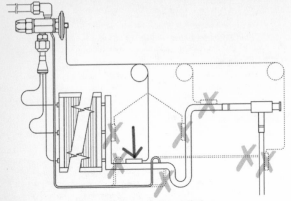

Figure 4-K: Sensor bulb installations
Courtesy of Sporlan Division of Parker Hannifin, Inc.

Sensor bulb location is critical. The arrow in Figure 4-K indicates proper mounting on the suction line. Make sure not to locate the bulb where refrigerant liquid can be trapped, as this liquid can vaporize and throw off the bulb reading. Steel pipe may need a coating of aluminum paint before the bulb is clamped. Protect the bulb from any airstream using a nonabsorbent insulator. If the bulb is submerged in water or brine, insulate the bulb with a pitch with a low melting point. If multiple TXVs are used on several evaporators, make sure each remote bulb measures superheat on the proper evaporator.

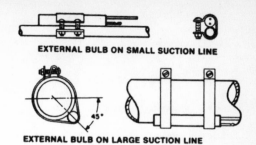

EXTERNAL BULB ON SMALL SUCTION LINE

EXTERNAL BULB ON LARGE SUCTION LINE

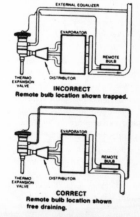

Figure 4-L: TXV sensor bulb location
Courtesy of Sporlan Division of Parker Hannifin, Inc

Measuring Superheat

When analyzing TXV operation, and before adjusting the superheat, you must determine the current superheat setting. The correct setting should be listed in literature for the valve. For an older valve, the usual practice is to set the superheat between 11° and 15°F (6° and 8.3°C).

To measure superheat:

1. Find the evaporator pressure. Install a compound gauge in the suction-service valve (or install the gauge manifold). If no service valve is available:

   a. Place a tee or tap in the TXV equalizer line and attach the gauge to it, *or*

   b. Braze a Shraeder valve in the suction line near the evaporator outlet, *or*

   c. If there is little pressure drop in the evaporator, subtract the inlet temperature from the outlet temperature and use this as the actual superheat. This method will always underestimate the actual superheat, but it may be accurate enough with a small pressure drop, *or*

   d. Use suction pressure (taken at the compressor) as evaporator saturation pressure. Due to pressure drop in the suction line, this technique will overestimate actual superheat.

   Errors resulting from techniques *c* and *d* will tend to be smaller in packaged and small systems than in large, built-up systems. For this example, assume that evaporator pressure is 35 psig (344.7 kPa).

2. Tape the sensing element of a refrigeration pocket thermometer or the thermocouple of a potentiometer to the suction line near the sensing bulb. Insulate this connection against ambient temperature. Write down the reading. For this example, use 50°F (10°C).

3. Convert suction line pressure to temperature with a pressure-temperature chart. Assume the system contains R-12. On the chart, look under the proper refrigerant and note that a saturation temperature of 35 psig equals 38°F (3.33°C). Subtract 38° from 50° to find the present superheat: 12°F (10°C − 3.33°C = 6.67°C). Thus:

Refrigerant R-12

Outlet temperature =	50°F	10°C
Evaporator pressure is 35 psig =	− 38°F	− 3.33°C
Superheat =	12°F	6.67°C

Adjusting Superheat

If a TXV is properly installed and in good working condition, superheat can be adjusted using the adjusting screw, which changes pressure on the adjusting spring. When the superheat is too high, the evaporator is starved of refrigerant. When it's too low, the evaporator gets too much refrigerant.

Proper adjustment requires small (approximately one-quarter turn) adjustments and plenty of patience. Assume the superheat is 15°F (8.33°C) and 10°F (5.56°C) is required. The manufacturer's installation slip should indicate the effect of one turn of the adjusting screw. If the slip is missing, turn the screw toward decrease one-quarter turn and wait at least 15 minutes for the system to stabilize (working faster will probably waste time in the long run). Remember that these adjustments will change evaporator temperature but not pressure. Take the suction-line temperature again, convert to pressure, and recalculate the superheat. Make further adjustments if needed after the system stabilizes. When the outlet temperature remains at 10° above TXV temperature (or whatever the target is), the superheat is correct.

The greatest stability is achieved when the temperature of the suction line remains as steady as possible while the system cycles on and off. This point is called the Minimum Stable Signal point, or MSS.

Repairing Expansion Valves

Both automatic and thermostatic expansion valves suffer similar problems. The following material applies in general to both types (except that AXVs don't have equalizers or sensing bulbs). (See Chapter 10, "Troubleshooting.")

These problems can affect expansion valves:

- Inaccurate superheat adjustment
- Lost charge in sensing bulb
- Poorly placed equalizer line (for example, in a liquid trap)
- Sticking due to dirt, moisture, or sludge
- Dirty liquid screen
- Flash gas in the liquid line (usually due to pressure drop)
- Undercharged system
- Excess pressure drop in evaporator
- Inadequate head pressure

To remove an expansion valve:

1. Attach the gauge manifold to the system.

2. Close the king valve (at the receiver outlet).

3. Pump down the system into the condenser, receiver, or a recovery apparatus, and shut off the compressor. (For more on pump-down, see Chapter 11, "Standard ACR Procedures.")

4. Purge refrigerant from the liquid line, down to about 0 psig.

5. Close the suction-service valve.

6. When the evaporator is warm, assume it is almost evacuated.

7. Disconnect and remove the expansion valve.

8. Cap the lines to keep them clean unless a new valve is immediately installed.

Some expansion valve problems can be repaired, but others indicate a need for replacement. Follow these guidelines:

1. A clogged screen is indicated by poor system performance, or sweating or frosting near the TXV. The valve must be removed or at least purged of refrigerant before service. Remove and inspect the screen. The best cleaning procedure is to use a safe solvent and a stiff brush. Air pressure will also remove dirt. Replace the screen before closing the valve. Do not operate an expansion valve without a screen in the liquid-line port.

2. The sensor bulb can be removed with a large pliers and a wrench. Replace with a new element with the proper charge and design. Very carefully unwind the capillary to avoid kinking. Be sure to make a good thermal seal between the sensor and the suction line.

3. Leaking bellows are difficult to repair. Replace the valve.

Low-Side Float (LSF)

A low-side float (see Figure 4-M) keeps a constant level of liquid refrigerant in the evaporator. The float pan floats on the liquid refrigerant and moves a needle valve that regulates refrigerant flow into the evaporator. As refrigerant evaporates, the valve opens and refills the evaporator. The float is used in a critical-charge system with a flooded evaporator (one that always contains liquid refrigerant).

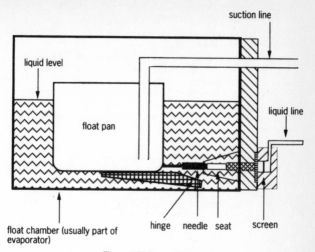

Figure 4-M: Low-side float

The LSF can be used with either a pressure- or a temperature-motor control, in systems with one or several evaporators. The liquid receiver must be large enough to hold all system refrigerant during a pump-down. An LSF will float on oil as well as refrigerant, so provisions must be made to return oil to the crankcase. With a pan-type float, the suction line reaches into the bottom of the pan to remove oil.

Installing and Servicing

Excess or insufficient cooling are both reasons to check the LSF. Too much cooling could signify that the float is stuck open, or the motor control is not shutting down the compressor when it should. Too little cooling indicates that the float may be stuck closed, or the charge is too low. But watch the charge carefully: Excess refrigerant in the evaporator can cause floodbacks.

The adjustment screw may be accessible outside the float chamber. If not, shut valves on both sides of the evaporator or float chamber, evacuate the chamber or evaporator, and adjust. Unfortunately, one cannot see the effect of the adjustment until the machine is recharged and operating. The needle valve of some low-side floats may be replaced without a pump-down with a replaceable cartridge that is factory-assembled and tested.

High-Side Float (HSF)

A high-side float (see Figure 4-N) controls a flooded system by operating a needle valve between the high and low sides of the system. The float can be located in a float chamber or a receiver. The HSF is commonly used with centrifugal compressors. As liquid leaves the vessel containing the float and enters the evaporator, the liquid level falls, and the float drops, closing the valve and stopping the flow. As more liquid refrigerant enters the float vessel, the float rises, the valve opens, and refrigerant resumes its flow into the evaporator.

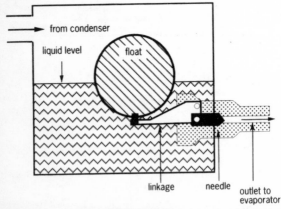

Figure 4-N: High-side float

The level of liquid refrigerant on the high side stays fairly constant, as does the pressure difference between the high and low sides. Liquid refrigerant is stored in the evaporator, making this a critical-charge system. The system can use a pressure- or a temperature-motor control.

Oil is less troublesome with the HSF than with the LSF because oil is likely to dissolve in the liquid refrigerant. However, the evaporator needs an oil return line to the compressor to prevent oil from gathering and starving the compressor of oil.

Installing and Servicing

The float should be located as close as possible to the evaporator inlet. If the float must be installed far from the evaporator, a weighted valve near the metering device may need to be installed to prevent flash gas in the line from the float to the metering device.

High-side floats in high-tonnage centrifugal compressors are installed in the casting of the condenser or evaporator. Otherwise, mount the float horizontal in both directions and check that the float moves freely.

Dirt can clog the needle valve or damage the valve seat. To repair the valve, the charge usually must be removed. With a high-temperature refrigerant and an evaporator that operates at a vacuum, bring system pressure up to atmospheric pressure before starting the repair.

Capillary Tube (as Metering Device)

A capillary tube (cap tube) with an accurate inside diameter can serve as a constant throttle on the flow of liquid refrigerant. Five factors determine flow through the tube: length, ID, configuration, operating temperature, and pressure difference from end to end.

A capillary tube has two big advantages: it has no moving parts and it balances pressure during the off cycle. The charge is critical. An undercharged system may run constantly, while the suction line will frost on an overcharged system. As with the TXV, the operation can be assessed by measuring superheat, although the tube cannot be adjusted. Use a thermostatic motor control because the cap tube does not compensate for sudden load changes.

Small-diameter tubes can clog. Although larger tubes have reduced this problem, the tubes must be longer to compensate for reduced resistance. A filter or filter-drier at the inlet can prevent clogging and vapor lock (a reduction in capacity caused by flash gas inside the tube).

Installing and Servicing

Although capillary tubes are simple, bending, kinking, freezing, and obstruction can reduce the effective size or cause refrigerant to gather in the condenser, raising head pressure. If this occurs, one may also see:

- Some frost on the evaporator
- A cool condenser
- The compressor cycling on overload

If plugging is suspected, start the system and listen near where the capillary tube enters the evaporator. If a hissing sound is not heard, the tube is plugged. Warm the tube with a hot rag. If it opens, ice was the problem.

Here is an alternative way to check a cap tube metering device (see Figure 4-O):

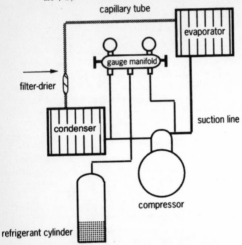

Figure 4-O: Checking flow through a capillary-tube metering device

1. Hook up the gauge manifold with both its valves closed.
2. Crack the service valves off the backseats to get a reading.
3. Hook a service drum to the middle opening of the manifold to provide some pressure.
4. Open both gauge manifold valves.
5. Disconnect the cap tube at the flare near the filter-drier and pull it away.
6. Open the drum valve to pressurize both sides of the system.
7. Hold a hand at the disconnection. If refrigerant is not flowing from both sides, the side without flow is plugged.

Some obstructions can be cleared from cap tubes. Use a cap-tube cleaner to force refrigerant or oil through the tube. Or force pressurized carbon dioxide opposite the direction of refrigerant flow.

If the tube must be replaced, make sure to use the proper size and length of tube. (See Table 4-D.) Protect the new tube from kinking and other damage during installation. Do not cut the cap tube with a tubing cutter, as this can crimp the ID. Instead, cut it partway through with a hacksaw and bend back and forth to finish the break. Capillary tubes are usually brazed into place. Some cap-tube connectors deform when tightened, so replace the connectors when installing a new tube. The cap tube may be fastened to the suction line for cooling. (See Figure 4-O.) Take care not to solder it shut or allow solder into the tube.

Table 4-D: Capillary Tube Specifications

100 ft. Coil Prod. No.	Diameter	
	I.D.	O.D.
122	0.026	0.072
110	0.031	0.083
111	0.036	0.087
112	0.042	0.093
113	0.044	0.109
123	0.049	0.099
114	0.050	0.114
124	0.054	0.106
115	0.055	0.125
125	0.059	0.112
116	0.064	0.125
117	0.070	0.125
118	0.075	0.125
119	0.080	0.145
120	0.085	0.145
121	0.090	0.145

Table 4-D: Capillary Tube Specifications (continued)

For 2), 3), and 4): Condensing Temperature: 130°F for R-22; 125°F for R-12 and R-502. Length indicated is per circuit.

1) Freezers

Low Temp. Compressor	−10°F Evaporator	−10°F Evaporator		0°F Evaporator	
H.P.	Refrigerant	BTUH	Cap. Tube	BTUH	Cap. Tube
0.5	12	2700	95″ #115	3350	69″ #115
0.5	502	2700	45″ #112	3300	80″ #114
0.75	12	4100	80″ #116	5200	60″ #116
0.75	502	4050	45″ #114	5100	50″ #115
1	12	4900	70″ #116	6200	60″ #117
1	502	4800	60″ #115	6100	78″ #116
1.5	12	6900	105″ #119	8800	72″ #120
1.5	502	6800	60″ #116	8700	55″ #117
2	12	10700	70″ #121	13300	50″ #117(2)
2	502	10600	80″ #119	13200	85″ #121

2) Refrigerators

Med. Temp. Compressor		0°F Evaporator		+10°F Evaporator		+20°F Evaporator		+30°F Evaporator	
H.P.	Ref.	BTUH	Cap. Tube	BTUH	Cap. Tube	BTUH	Cap. Tube	BTUH	Cap. Tube
0.5	12	2850	90" #115	3600	80" #125	4100	60" #125	4800	68" #116
0.5	502	2800	100" #114	3550	63" #114	4050	75" #124	4750	52" #114
0.75	12	4260	57" #125	5300	90" #117	6550	55" #117	7200	95" #119
0.75	502	4200	48" #114	5250	75" #125	6500	72" #116	7150	57" #116
1	12	5300	90" #117	7100	95" #119	8600	62" #119	10000	65" #116(2)
1	502	5250	48" #115	7050	60" #116	8550	64" #117	9950	60" #118
1.5	12	9500	50" #119	11500	75" #117(2)	14000	102" #119(2)	16800	70" #119(2)
1.5	502	9400	45" #117	11400	63" #119	13900	80" #121	16700	50" #111
2	12	10000	65" #116(2)	12000	68" #117(2)	15000	90" #119(2)	17500	60" #119(2)
2	502	9900	40" #117	11900	57" #119	14900	78" #121	17400	56" #117(2)
3	12	16000	76" #119(2)	19500	90" #121(2)	24000	52" #121(2)	27000	105" #121(3)
3	502	16600	50" #121	19400	43" #117(2)	23800	58" #119(2)	26800	59" #110(2)

Table 4-D: Capillary Tube Specifications (continued)

3) Coolers

High Temp. Compressor		+20°F Evaporator		+30°F Evaporator		+40°F Evaporator	
H.P.	Ref.	BTUH	Cap. Tube	BTUH	Cap. Tube	BTUH	Cap. Tube
0.5	12	3800	70" #125	4500	85" #116	5300	90" #117
0.5	502	4200	68" #124	5030	53" #115	6000	86" #116
0.5	22	4200	94" #123	5030	70" #114	6000	48" #124
0.75	12	5800	75" #117	6950	105" #119	8200	70" #119
0.75	502	6300	76" #116	7550	50" #116	9000	51" #117
0.75	22	6300	70" #124	7550	53" #115	9000	83" #116
1	12	7400	92" #119	9000	115" #119	10800	70" #121
1	502	8075	56" #117	9650	67" #118	11500	64" #119
1	22	8425	98" #116	10050	62" #116	12000	68" #117
1.5	12	10900	62" #121	13600	110" #119(2)	16200	71" #119(2)

1.5	502	12300	52" #119	14500	77" #121	17500	44" #121
1.5	22	12650	61" #117	15000	60" #118(2)	18000	83" #116(2)
2	12	16000	75" #119	19500	84" #121	23200	82" #119(3)
2	502	16500	51" #121	19700	65" #118(2)	23500	67" #119(2)
2	22	16850	72" #119	20100	80" #121	24000	55" #121
3	12	21000	102" #119(3)	31300	80" #119(3)	31300	80" #119(4)
3	502	24500	75" #120(2)	29350	71" #121(2)	35000	44" #121(2)
3	22	25275	52" #117(2)	30200	60" #118(2)	36000	56" #119(2)
4	12	28700	100" #119(4)	35700	58" #119(4)	43000	62" #119(5)
4	502	33000	52" #121(2)	39400	65" #120(3)	47000	63" #121(4)
4	22	33700	50" #116(3)	40250	62" #116(4)	48000	68" #117(4)

Capillary Tubes in Other Controls

A capillary tube can also be used to connect to a sensor on a controlled device, such as in an externally equalized TXV. Capillary tubes can fail if mistreated. Follow these guidelines:

1. Minimize vibration and flexing to avoid metal fatigue. Do not route the tube across vibrating surfaces. Controls mounted directly on the compressor should vibrate with the compressor. A vibration coil can minimize movement on capillaries that run between a stationary component and the compressor.

2. Almost all capillary tubes will sense the coldest surface they touch. Unless a special capillary tube is available, make sure the tube does not pass through temperatures colder than the area to be sensed.

3. Form extra capillary tubing in a coil with a minimum diameter coil of 3" (7.5 cm). Secure the coil so it does not rub against itself.

4. Install a soft grommet to prevent abrasion where a tube goes through a partition.

5. Do not bend or stretch the tube more than necessary, as this will work-harden it.

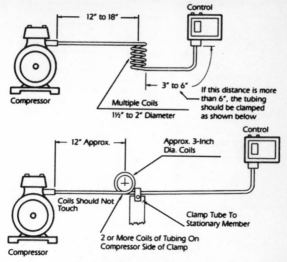

Figure 4-P: Mounting capillary tubes
Courtesy of Invensys Controls Americas

Follow these guidelines when using a capillary tube to sense temperature in specific locations:

1. To measure the temperature of a liquid, submerge at least 4" (10 cm) of the tube in the liquid.

2. To sense evaporator temperature, secure at least 6" (15 cm) of the tube to the evaporator. (See Figure 4-P.)

3. To sense the temperature of an air stream, make an air coil with at least 18" (45 cm) of tube.

4. To sense the temperature of a close-fitting well, form at least 10" (25 cm) of tube into a bulb and make sure it makes direct contact with the well.

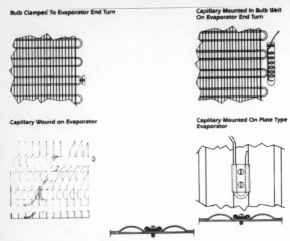

Figure 4-Q: Mounting sensing bulb on evaporator
Courtesy of Invensys Controls Americas

SAFETY CONTROLS

Compressors need protection from any foreseeable source of trouble. Compressors are designed to pump compressible vapor; pumping uncompressible liquid can break pistons or valves. Thus, all compressors need *floodback safety devices* to prevent liquid refrigerant from entering through the suction line. To prevent motors from running during conditions that endanger the motor, compressor, or other components, designers use a *high-pressure cut-out*, a *low-pressure cut-out*, *internal relief valve*, *motor thermostat*, and an *oil safety switch*. These switches are called "limits" because they prevent the system from operating outside safe limits. Smaller systems usually have a smaller group of limits. For more on motor safety, see Chapter 6, "Motors."

Floodback Safety Devices

Several devices can prevent liquid from entering the compressor:

A *suction-line accumulator* is a tank where liquid refrigerant can settle. (See Chapter 5, "Components.")

A *heat exchanger* between the liquid line and the suction line vaporizes any liquid refrigerant before the compressor. (See Chapter 5, "Components.")

An *electric heater* on the suction line can be controlled by a thermostat. When the line is cold enough to indicate the presence of liquid refrigerant, the heater turns on.

A *temperature sensor* in the suction line may be connected to an alarm or a compressor shut-off switch. A fast-acting sensor, such as one based on a thermistor, is best.

Testing Safety Controls

Check safety controls on large units at least once a year during routine maintenance. The general testing procedure is to force the system into the unsafe condition, then check that the switch works. But be careful—this may put the system in danger!

> NOTE: For high-pressure and low-pressure cut-outs: The bellows and the capillary or ¼" copper tube leading to the bellows in the high-pressure and low-pressure cut-outs are subject to oil logging (filling with oil). A self-draining hookup will allow oil to drip from the tube during the off cycle, improving accuracy. The control should be mounted above the connection for the same reason, and the lines should never connect to the bottom of the tubes. (See Figure 4-R.) A large-diameter capillary tube, combined with proper installation, can reduce oil logging.

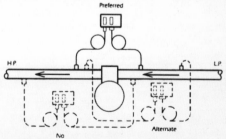

Figure 4-R: High- and low-pressure cut-out installation
Courtesy of Invensys Controls Americas

High-Pressure Cut-Out

The high-pressure cut-out (HPCO) shuts off the compressor when head pressure exceeds the limit, usually about 20% above normal operating pressure. (See Table 4-E.) The cut-out prevents dangerous pressure in the system and motor overloading. The cut-out has a bellows connected to the high side of the system. When high-side pressure exceeds the limit, the bellows pushes a plunger to shut off current to the compressor.

In systems with an air-cooled condenser, fan failure or condenser blockage can raise head pressure. In water-cooled condensers, excess head pressure indicates loss of cooling water or clogged or fouled condenser tubes.

Both automatic and manual resetting cut-outs are available. Manual resets are preferred because repeated cycling on the high-pressure control can damage the compressor. However, automatic reset can help during unattended operation and prevent product deterioration. Some controls may be set to automatic or manual reset during installation.

Table 4-E: Limit Settings for High-Pressure Cut-Out

Refrigerant	Water-cooled		Air-cooled	
	psi	kPa	psi	kPa
R-12	150–160	1138–1206	250	1827
R-22	260–270	1896–1965	400	2861
R-500	190–200	1413–1482	300	2172
R-502	280–290	2034–2103	450	3206

The cut-out pressure can be high on air-cooled equipment, so observe all safety precautions when testing a HPCO:

1. Install the gauge manifold and crack the discharge service valve off the backseat to get a gauge reading.

2. *Air-cooled condenser:* shut off the condenser fan or block the air flow. *Water-cooled condenser:* shut off the water supply by closing a valve and/or stopping the pump.

3. Start the compressor and let pressure build up until the cut-out opens and stops the compressor. Keep one hand on the disconnect and an eye on the head pressure in case the cut-out does not work. Do not allow system pressure to exceed safe levels!

4. Compare the cut-out point to the manufacturer's specifications.

Low-Pressure Cut-Out

The low-pressure cut-out (LPCO) shuts down the compressor when suction pressure drops below the set point. The cut-out can be used as a safety and/or operating control.

As a safety factor, the LPCO protects a hermetic compressor and motor (which are cooled by suction-line refrigerant) from overheating due to hot, low-density gas. Low suction pressure increases the pumping ratio, leading to overheating and breakdown of oil or refrigerant. Because less gas enters the cylinder during each intake stroke, low suction pressure also raises the compression ratio and decreases the compressor output. Low suction pressure is usually due to inadequate refrigerant level or a restriction in the suction line.

The LPCO is tapped into the suction side of the compressor. Some LPCOs have an automatic reset, but manual resets are better because tripping an LPCO can mark big system trouble. Ideally, the situation should be investigated before returning the system to service, but an automatic reset may be better for a system that cools perishables. The LPCO may incorporate a time delay to prevent premature tripping.

To test the LPCO:

1. Install the gauge manifold and run the system for a few minutes.

2. Shut the suction-service valve and note the pressure when the unit stops. (The pressure might drop quickly, so watch the gauge closely.)

3. If the LPCO is also an operating control, check the setting by comparing the pressure to the desired evaporator temperature with a P-T chart. If the LPCO is only a safety control, refer to system specifications or the compressor manufacturer's literature for the proper setting.

Oil Pressure Cut-out

The oil pressure cut-out (OPCO) is a pressure-differential limit switch generally found on large units with forced lubrication. The OPCO is wired in series with the starter holding coil, which supplies current to the compressor motor. The OPCO shuts down the compressor when oil pressure is dangerously low and may fail to lubricate. The oil pump must pump against low-side pressure, so oil-pump pressure must be higher than this pressure. The cut-out compares these two pressures and shuts down the compressor when oil pressure drops too low. (See Chapter 5, "Components.") Manufacturers should specify the oil pressure differential, but in general, a differential below 10 psi (69 kPa) may endanger the compressor.

The shutoff may be done by a solid-state device or a bimetallic strip. The limit should be set to allow a brief delay while oil pressure returns to normal (see below).

In an oil pressure limit (see Figure 4-S), separate bellows measure crankcase pressure and oil-pressure, and the net pressure is transferred to the differential pressure switch (**A**). Normally, switch **A** is open, so no current flows through heater **B**. Switch **C** stays closed, allowing current to flow to the starter holding coil (**D**).

If oil pressure drops, switch **A** closes and current reaches the heater (**B**), which warms the bimetallic strip (**E**). If element **E** stays warm long enough (reflecting sustained low oil pressure), it bends and releases the pressure holding switch (**C**) closed. This opens the circuit to the holding coil and shuts down the motor. If pressure returns to normal before the contacts open, the heating circuit opens and the bimetallic strip cools, preventing a compressor shutdown due to a brief drop in oil pressure. The limit switch may need to be reset manually after it trips.

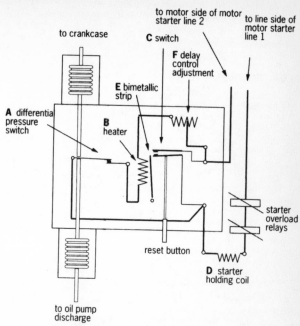

Figure 4-S: Oil pressure cut-out (shown in cut-out position)

Adjust the time delay by changing the position of the potentiometer in the delay control adjustment (F). Raising the resistance reduces current to the heating element, so the bimetallic element will warm more slowly. A usual time delay is 90 to 120 seconds between oil pressure dropping and compressor shutdown.

To check the delay from oil pressure loss to motor cut-out, and overall OPCO operation:

1. Shut off the compressor's main disconnect.
2. Disconnect the run windings from the load side of the starter. Remember their hookup for reassembly.

3. Take a watch and start timing when the disconnect is reclosed. The starter should pull even though the compressor will not run.

4. After a short time the starter will drop back out if the OPCO is working correctly. This time is the delay setting.

5. Open the main disconnect and reconnect the wires.

Internal Relief Valve

If the high-pressure cut-out fails, the internal relief valve prevents overpressure by routing refrigerant from the high side to the low side. The location varies according to system design, although the relief is commonly found inside the discharge service valve.

Check the relief when the low-pressure cut-out is inspected. If suction pressure rises quickly after the LPCO shuts down the compressor, discharge pressure is probably reaching the suction side through the internal relief. Some reliefs reseat themselves—in which case suction pressure should stop rising when the relief reseats. Rupture-disk reliefs must be replaced if they blow.

Motor Thermostat

Motor thermostats, also called winding thermostats, are buried in the windings of large motors. Since you cannot cause the motor to overheat, you must test this thermostat indirectly. First test if it's intact, using a continuity meter. Then disconnect the motor thermostat from the control circuit and check that it is actually wired in (some have been disconnected and offer no protection). Make this check by trying to run the system with the motor thermostat disconnected.

When a motor thermostat opens after overheating, it will reclose automatically, but due to the mass of the motor, this might take some time. During the cooling period, check the motor for opens, shorts, and grounds. (See Chapter 6, "Motors.") If nothing is found, and the motor still does not run after it has cooled, look for a second set of contacts (low-voltage wires) in the motor control box. These may be connected to a second thermostat in the windings. Connect these wires to the control circuit and try to restart the motor. If it still does not run, or there is no second thermostat, consult the motor's manufacturer. Because it is difficult or impossible to measure motor temperature directly, look for signs of poor cooling or excessive current draw when troubleshooting a motor that has shut down due to overheating.

5

Components

Beyond compressors and controls, modern ACR systems require a variety of other components. Some, such as the evaporator and condenser, are in all vapor-compression systems, while others, like fans, heat exchangers, and oil-control systems, are only needed in certain situations.

CONDENSER

The condenser is the high-side component where hot, high-pressure refrigerant gas loses its latent heat of condensation to the environment. Having lost this heat, the gas condenses into a high-pressure liquid that goes to the metering device. Due to various inefficiencies, refrigerant in an open-system condenser must dispose of about 1.25 times as much heat as it gained in the evaporator. Hermetic-system condensers must also dispose of motor heat.

The basic design goals of a condenser are to remove maximum heat with minimum cost, complexity, and size. Many types of condensers are used, but the two basic categories are water-cooled and air-cooled.

Water can quickly remove a lot of heat, so the condenser can be small. Water-cooled condensers are more economical when cheap, suitable water is available. However, water may be scarce or chemically unsuited, and scale, fouling, freezing, and corrosion can damage water-cooled condensers. Although air-cooled condensers must be larger, they do not suffer from these water-related problems. In a combination air-and-water condenser, cooling normally is done by air, but water is used when ambient air is too warm.

Fins, wires, or plates are usually fastened to condenser tubing to increase the surface area and speed heat disposal. Fans or pumps are often used to move the condensing medium. These enhancements increase the subcooling of the refrigerant and rate of heat transfer, without increasing condenser size.

Air-Cooled

Air-cooled condensers dispose of heat to the air. The condenser must be engineered to work in the hottest ambient conditions, when heat transfer is slowest and cooling load is highest. Air circulates across a "static" condenser by convection alone. A fan blows air across a "forced" condenser to speed heat removal. Because the cooling is so much faster, practically all large condensers are forced. In open systems, this fan may be powered by the compressor motor or crankshaft. Hermetic systems need a separate fan motor. Shrouds raise fan efficiency by directing all air flow past the condenser tubes. Good heat transfer requires a clean condenser surface.

Double condensers are sometimes used to cool the compressor head. After hot discharge gas cools in the first condenser, it is piped through the cylinder head, picking up heat. The gas then condenses in the second condenser and travels to the receiver. Outdoor air-cooled condensers in cold weather present a special design challenge. (See Chapter 8, "Whole Systems.")

Water-Cooled

If water is available and suitable for a condenser, a water-cooled condenser may be best, because it can remove heat faster. If the same water cools the compressor and the condenser, it should reach the condenser first, so the refrigerant gets maximum cooling.

Water velocity should be 7' to 10' per second. A faster flow will strip away the oxide coating that protects copper tubing from corrosion; slower flows may allow scaling or fouling.

Water-system components, such as solenoid, modulating, or hand valves, should be fitted with a stand-pipe and an air pocket to prevent water hammer. Do not locate solenoid or pressure-operated valves between the condenser and the drain—place them between the water supply and the condenser. If water pressure is higher than condenser operating pressure, install a pressure-reducing valve in the condenser water supply.

The basic types of water-cooled condensers are *shell-and-tube*, *shell-and-coil*, and *tube-within-a-tube*. The first two also serve as receivers and are quite similar in design.

Shell-and-Tube and Shell-and-Coil

A shell-and-tube condenser is a large cylinder with a water manifold at each end. Water circulates through the large cylinder. Hot refrigerant vapor enters the inlet manifold, flows through the cooling tubes, and exits the discharge manifold.

The shell-and-coil style is similar, but the refrigerant flows through coiled tubes, not straight ones. Due to their shape, the coils must be cleaned with chemicals, not brushes.

Tube-Within-a-Tube

In this condenser, also called "tube-in-tube," the outer tube contains refrigerant and the inner tube contains water. The fluids flow in opposite directions, so the cold, entering water contacts the refrigerant just before the refrigerant enters the receiver, ensuring maximum cooling to the refrigerant. The wall between the two fluids is shaped to maximize heat transfer. This condenser design is too small to store refrigerant, so it cannot serve as a liquid receiver, and it's easy to overcharge. Overcharging reduces the space available for heat transfer, and can cause erratic cooling.

Cooling Tower and Evaporative Condenser

Heat from a water-cooled condenser may be transferred to the surroundings through a cooling tower or an evaporative condenser.

1. In a *cooling tower*, condenser water is sprayed through a blast of air. Some designs rely on the wind created by the spraying itself; others use fans. The evaporating water carries away the latent heat of vaporization. The cooler, liquid water that remains drips to the bottom and returns to the condenser for reuse. Chemicals may be needed to control rust, algae, fungus, and disease-causing organisms.

   During operation, condenser heat prevents a cooling tower from freezing. In a cold climate, an idle tower can freeze in winter unless it is drained or has an electric heater.

2. An *evaporative condenser* also uses evaporation to remove heat. Condenser water flows through a heat exchanger that is under a spray or drip of water. Fans blow air across the condenser to speed evaporation. If scale builds up, it can be seen.

Water Problems and Treatment

Water-cooled condensers are subject to corrosion, scale, fouling, and microbial problems.

Corrosion, the oxidation of metal, can degrade metal and cause leaks or failure. (See Chapter 2, "Energy, Electricity, and Cooling Cycles.")

Scale is the deposition of alkaline material, chiefly calcium carbonate (lime) and magnesium compounds, inside a tube or container. The compounds that form scale are often dissolved in water; they only cause problems when they precipitate from the water. The rate of scale formation depends on acidity. Since the biggest culprit, calcium carbonate, is much more soluble in acidic water, it precipitates slower in acidic water. Scaling is also affected by water temperature, the concentration of the alkaline compounds, and the presence of some other chemicals. To control scale, reduce the concentration of the alkaline chemicals, boost water acidity (although this may speed corrosion), make mechanical changes (such as speeding up the water flow), and treat the water with scale-preventing chemicals.

Fouling is the deposition of other substances on vessel walls. Fouling can result from loosened corrosion particles, dirt, masses of microbes, and other materials. The following factors increase the rate of fouling:

- Contaminated water
- Corrosion
- Slow water flow
- High temperature
- Microbes in the water

To prevent fouling, keep the cooling water clean during startup, filter the water during operation, and use antifouling compounds.

Microbial growth results from the multiplication of single-celled organisms such as algae and bacteria. The primary problem, slime formed of mats of microbes, can interfere with water flow and insulate the surface, slowing heat transfer. If pathogens such as the bacteria that cause Legionnaire's disease are present, microbes can also cause disease.

Microbe growth requires the presence of:

- Atmosphere—either oxygen or carbon dioxide.
- Nutrients—such as hydrocarbons.
- Temperature—slime organisms thrive between 40°F and 150°F.

Warning signs of microbes include rotting wood, slime, and corrosion (which some microorganisms accelerate). Microbes can be chemically controlled, but it's best to identify them first. Three types of chemical agents may control or kill microbes.

1. *Oxidizing biocides*, such as chlorine or bromine, are effective against a wide array of organisms.
2. *Non-oxidizing biocides* may work if oxidizing biocides don't.
3. *Biodispersants* do not kill microbes, but they can loosen films and mats, making them easier to flush or scrape away.

CRANKCASE HEATER

Large compressors, especially those operated in low ambient temperatures or subject to frequent on-off cycles, are often fitted with crankcase heaters, either at the factory or in the field. The heater warms the crankcase, driving dissolved refrigerant from the oil. If the crankcase is the coldest part of the system, refrigerant will migrate there and mix with the oil. Oil absorbs more refrigerant when cold, but when the compressor starts and pressure drops, the oil-refrigerant mix boils, depriving the compressor of lubrication.

The heater may be set to operate whenever the compressor is off, or it may respond to a thermostat that runs it as needed. In comfort-cooling systems, turn on the crankcase heater at least 4 hours before spring startup.

DEFROST SYSTEM

Frost is a potential problem with most dry evaporators. Humidity will freeze and form frost crystals on a cold coil. Coils that run just below freezing will develop clear ice as humidity in the air condenses, then freezes. Frost:

- reduces heat transfer to the evaporator;
- withdraws moisture from air in the cabinet, increasing dehydration; and
- clogs passages, causing mechanical damage.

The following factors increase the severity of frosting:

- Cold operating temperature
- High relative humidity in the cooled space
- Frequent opening of doors to the cooled area
- Drafts across open cases

Defrost controls must operate the defrost cycle as often as necessary, and for as long as necessary, while avoiding excessive defrosting, which reduce comfort, storage quality, and energy efficiency. A mechanical, electric, or electronic device can set the timing and duration of the defrost cycle.

Defrost can be started and stopped based on evaporator pressure, temperature, time of day, or elapsed time. Defrost controls may compare the temperature of air entering and exiting the evaporator by sensing temperature, air flow, or low-side pressure. A ΔT of 20° to 30°F (11° to 17°C) will generally trigger the defrost cycle. These sensors—often thermistors—also restore the normal cooling cycle when the ΔT returns to normal, showing that the frost has melted.

Pressure-operated switches (or low-side pressure sensors) can also terminate the defrost. In many cases, a timer is a fail-safe that starts the defrost cycle if the normal triggering mechanism fails. Defrost timers may (1) be wired in series with the compressor motor (so it registers running time), or (2) start a defrost cycle at the same time every day. (See Chapter 8, "Whole Systems.")

The defrost control may perform some or all of these functions:

1. Operate solenoid valves in hot-gas defrost systems
2. Shut off evaporator fans to prevent warming of stored products
3. Shut off or operate the compressor
4. Close a circuit to energize defrost-heater elements in the evaporator
5. Heat the receiver so it does not act as a condenser during the defrost cycle

In large systems, controls may affect several motors, fans, and valves. Different evaporators may be shut off at different times. Programmable timers, used to control multiple system functions, are usually repaired and adjusted by specialists.

EVAPORATORS

In the evaporator, refrigerant absorbs heat from the cooled space and evaporates, or boils. Evaporators that cool air are commonly called *coils*, *blower coils*, or *cooling coils*; evaporators that cool water are called *chillers*.

Pressure drops as liquid refrigerant passes through the metering device into the evaporator. As dictated by the gas laws, temperature also drops. The ΔT between the boiling refrigerant and the surroundings causes the refrigerant to absorb the latent heat of vaporization, which drives further boiling. During this change of state, the refrigerant remains at its saturation pressure-temperature for the evaporator pressure. Depending on the application, the evaporator can remove sensible heat (by cooling the load) and/or latent heat (by dehumidifying air).

The rate and nature of refrigerant flow in the evaporator is determined by the:

- Metering device
- High-side pressure
- Compressor drawing on the suction line
- Length, inside diameter, and configuration of the tubing
- Viscosity of the refrigerant

The amount of cooling in a dry evaporator will depend on the:

- quantity of air blown past the coil,
- dry- and wet-bulb temperatures of the air,
- saturation temperature of the refrigerant, and
- coil surface area.

Evaporators are rated by heat removed (in BTUs) per degree of temperature difference (ΔT). If the evaporator will operate at 10°F ΔT, multiply the specification BTUs by 10 to find the rated capacity of the evaporator in that application. (In SI, ΔT in degrees Celsius × rating in joules = expected evaporator capacity.)

Although a high ΔT allows the use of a smaller evaporator, condensation or freezing on the coils increases along with ΔT, so a high ΔT greatly reduces the relative humidity of the cooled space. (See Table 5-A.) In meat and produce cases, for example, low relative humidity will cause ugly, expensive shrinkage. Thus, a small ΔT is often best for fresh-food installations, even though this increases evaporator size. A small ΔT has another benefit. Because the suction gas is relatively cool and dense, the compressor pumps more efficiently.

Table 5-A: Relative Humidity and Evaporator ΔT

For evaporators in a temperature range of 25°F to 45°F

Desired Relative Humidity	ΔT (coil to air in cooler)
90%	8°F to 12°F
85%	12°F to 14°F
80%	12°F to 16°F
75%	16°F to 22°F

Proper superheat adjustment can prevent excess liquid refrigerant in the evaporator, which could flood back to the compressor. (See Chapter 4, "Controls.")

Refrigerant must flow fast enough through the evaporator to circulate the oil and to scrub oil and refrigerant droplets from tube walls (these droplets can slow heat transfer). A large pressure drop, caused by many bends, small tubing diameter, or even (ironically) excess refrigerant velocity, will slow the vapor, cause oil logging, and cut performance. Several tubing circuits may be needed to obtain the correct refrigerant capacity and prevent pressure drop and oil logging.

Evaporator Types

The two basic categories of evaporator are wet ("flooded") and dry ("direct expansion"):

Some liquid refrigerant is always present in a *flooded* evaporator, which chills water flowing through or past the evaporator tubes or coils. A high- or low-side float is the metering device. Instead of a receiver, refrigerant may be pumped down to the evaporator during service. Wet systems are usually large.

Most refrigerant is in vapor or droplet form in a *dry* evaporator, which cools air with plates, fins, or coils. The metering device must supply only enough refrigerant to create the desired temperature, without flooding the evaporator. The metering device may throttle down or shut off during the off-cycle. Dry-evaporator tubing may be an integral part of the cabinet wall.

Static or Forced Coil

Static evaporators, which are rare, use convection to move air in the cooled space past the evaporator. Forced-air evaporators ("blower coils"), which use a fan to circulate air across the coils, are more common because the evaporator can be smaller. Without special measures like a slow air speed or a small ΔT between evaporator and cabinet, the fan can cause rapid drying. If the evaporator fan motor is not running, check it with the VOM. Bypass the switch to see if the fan is receiving power. Some fans are self-oiling, while others need occasional oiling.

The blower may run continuously or be controlled by evaporator or cabinet temperature. Because blower coils tend to be compact, with narrow passages between the fins, they can frost up easily.

Frosting Evaporator

This evaporator has no provision for defrosting, so the equipment must be shut down occasionally for manual defrosting, using external heat. Frosting evaporators that run near the freezing point may defrost without additional heat if they warm up enough when the compressor shuts down.

Nonfrosting Evaporator

Non-frosting evaporators operate down to 33° to 34°F (.5° to 1°C). At these temperatures, little frost builds up, and the mild frost that does will quickly melt when the compressor stops. Baffles may be used to collect condensate and keep it out of the cabinet. These evaporators maintain a high relative humidity in the cabinet, and thus can store produce with little desiccation.

Defrosting Evaporator

Defrosting evaporators operate at temperatures that cause frost to accumulate, but the coils are warmed upon compressor shutdown, so frost melts. The temperature rise may be caused by a hot-gas defrost system, electric heating elements, or another means of warming the coil interior or exterior. This system leaves air within the cabinet relatively humid and aids food preservation. The installation needs good drainage or else melted frost will puddle at the bottom and refreeze when the unit cools again. Defrosting evaporators come in many styles. They are especially useful when evaporator temperature is low or the fins are tightly spaced.

FANS

Fans are used to cool air-cooled condensers and to force conditioned air through ductwork. Fans are classified by application and design:

Classification	Design
Exhauster	Inlet duct only
Booster	Inlet and discharge ducts
Blower	Discharge duct only

The two major categories of fans used in cooling systems are *axial* (or *propeller*) and *radial* (or *centrifugal*). Either type may be powered by direct- or belt-drive. Large, slow fans are more likely to be driven by belts.

Axial fans force air parallel to the fan axis, or shaft. They are best suited to moving large air flows against low resistance. Axial fans are lighter and smaller than comparable centrifugal fans. *Tube axial fans* are mounted in a cylinder. *Vane axial fans* are mounted in a cylinder, with vanes to guide the air flow. Axial fans are used to cool condensers, humidifiers, and cooling towers.

Centrifugal (radial) fans push air perpendicular to the shaft, using a housing to direct the outflow. Air enters this housing, or scroll, near one fan-shaft bearing. Centrifugal fans can push air against large resistance, so they are often used to force air through ductwork.

Fans are specified by:

Volume: cubic feet of air per minute (cfm) handled at specified outlet conditions

Total pressure: the rise in pressure between inlet and outlet

Velocity pressure: the pressure created by the velocity of the air flow

Static pressure: total pressure minus velocity pressure

Fan inlet area: the inside area of the fan inlet

Fan outlet area: the inside area of the fan outlet

Fan noise: a function of tip speed, blade shape and number, and blade angle. For building occupants, fan noise also depends on duct design and construction. In any given installation, the higher the air speed, the louder the fan noise.

When selecting a fan, consider:

- Nature of the load
- Cfm required
- System resistance to flow
- Mounting arrangement
- Type of drive needed
- Tolerable sound level

FILTER-DRIER

Moisture can freeze and clog a system. Moisture and contaminants in a system can combine with refrigerants and oil to form sludge, acid, and varnish that clog valves and damage compressors, bearings, and motors in hermetic units. Refrigerants and oil can break down if discharge gas gets too hot. Metal particles, including solder, can also interfere with system operation. For all of these reasons, filter-driers are an essential part of many systems.

Do not rely on the filter-drier alone to keep the system clean.

1. *System design* should prevent overheating and include ways to remove contaminants.
2. *Installation procedures* must minimize entry of moisture and dirt.
3. *Operating procedures* should prevent contamination with a safe discharge-gas temperature.

Filter-driers combine an absorbent chemical, such as activated alumina or silica gel, with a screen or filter. The filtering and drying functions may also be performed by separate components. Filter-driers are chosen based on system operating temperature, refrigerant type, degree of contamination, allowable pressure drop, bursting pressure, and ability to trap liquid and solid contaminants. Flow ratings are measured on clean systems. Because flow declines as dirt accumulates, the filter-drier should start out slightly oversized, so it will still work after dirt starts to accumulate.

Absorbed moisture is less damaging than moisture in the system that is not absorbed by the refrigerant, and halocarbon refrigerants have different capacities to absorb moisture. Manufacturers specify maximum moisture levels for the various refrigerants. Thus, a drier used, for example, with R-502, must be larger and more effective than one used with other refrigerants.

Install liquid-line filter-driers in the direct flow of the system, so dirt or moisture doesn't plug or damage the refrigerant control. If the liquid-line filter-drier causes too much pressure drop, flash gas may appear at the metering device. (See Table 5-B.) To catch low-side contaminants, suction-line filter-driers may be placed in a bypass, where the full flow of vapor can still reach the compressor unimpeded. Get the system ready to receive the filter-drier before opening the package. Evacuate and dry the connecting lines and connect it quickly to minimize moisture entry. A filter-drier can be used temporarily to clean a system, especially after a burnout.

A filter-drier can offer a window into the system, since it may contain:

- a sight glass for checking refrigerant level;
- service connections for recharging the system or checking pressure drop from one side to the other; and
- a moisture indicator.

Table 5-B: Maximum Recommended Pressure Drop for Suction-Line Filter-Drier

Refrigerant	Permanent Installation				Temporary Installation			
	R-22 & R-502		R-12		R-22 & R-502		R-12	
Pressure	psi	kPa	psi	kPa	psi	kPa	psi	kPa
Air-conditioning	3	20.7	2	13.8	8	55.2	6	41.4
Commercial	2	13.8	1.5	10.3	4	27.6	3	20.7
Low temperature	1	6.9	0.5	3.5	2	13.8	1	6.9

Courtesy of Sporlan Division of Parker Hannifin, Inc.

MOISTURE INDICATOR

A moisture indicator monitors the moisture level in the liquid line. Although the indicator does not give exact readings, it does show whether the level is safe or not. Excess water can cause many problems, such as icing of metering devices, rust, corrosion, refrigerant decomposition, and sludge in the oil. Some refrigerants, such as R-21 and R-22, are much better at dissolving water than others, like R-12. Refrigerant also dissolves less water when cold, so a cold system with R-12 is much more prone to icing than a warm system using R-22, and would thus need greater protection against moisture. A filter-drier may be used to remove moisture, but a moisture indicator is a good safety precaution.

Moisture indicators have a reversible chemical that indicates "wet" or "dry" as conditions change in the liquid line. Some indicators must be matched to particular refrigerants, while others are more generic. Temperature greatly affects the reading. An indicator might read "dry" at both 75°F (24°C) and 125°F (52°C), even though the higher reading actually means the refrigerant contains two or three times more moisture. For this reason, knowing the approximate temperature will help interpret the reading. Moisture-indicator manufacturers provide color scales to help assess the reading in terms of temperature and system refrigerant. Because many moisture indicators absorb more moisture when cold, a moisture indicator may read "normal" when cold but "wet" when warm. If so, the drier element is probably waterlogged and due for replacement.

Installing and Servicing

Connect a moisture indicator in the liquid line where it will receive a positive flow of refrigerant. On a large system, the indicator may be installed in a bypass, which ideally should be parallel to the main line and connected by 45° fittings. Keep the indicator cool during brazing.

Because indicators may pick up moisture from the air, it may read "wet" just after installation. Wait a few hours before trusting a new indicator.

If a lot of water enters the refrigerant and dissolves the indicating salts, the sensing element or the whole indicator may need replacement. Too much oil in the refrigerant may also damage the indicator. After a hermetic motor burnout, wait 48 hours after restart before installing a moisture indicator so the filter-drier can remove acid from the system and protect the indicator. Dye-type leak detectors and dehydrating additives, such as methyl alcohol, may also interfere with the indicator.

HEAT EXCHANGER

A heat exchanger mounted between the suction line and the liquid line can move heat from the liquid-line refrigerant to the suction vapor. The exchanger simultaneously superheats the suction vapor and subcools the liquid line. A heat exchanger (see Figure 5-A) can increase operating efficiency, especially in medium-and low-temperature systems.

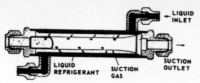

Figure 5-A: Heat exchanger
Courtesy of Mueller Industries, Inc.

A heat exchanger:

1. *reduces flash gas* (the sudden change of liquid to gas) in the liquid line. Flash gas can reduce metering-device capacity, damage the metering device, and cause pressure drop, excessive noise, and erratic operation.

2. *regulates suction gas temperature to the optimum level to prevent floodback.*

3. allows the *TXV to take full advantage of the evaporator,* without worrying about floodback.

4. warms the suction gas to *reduce sweating* on the suction line.

The heat exchanger can be a manufactured device or can be fabricated by soldering or taping the suction and liquid lines together. Whatever the design, the device should allow full fluid flow in both lines. Some systems skip the heat exchanger and get subcooling by blowing air across the liquid line.

A heat exchanger can cause trouble in a hermetic or semihermetic system if it warms the suction gas enough to reduce cooling to the compressor and motor. To ensure cooling in hermetic or semihermetic systems, set the TXV to accurate (not excessive) superheat, and insulate the suction line so the suction gas stays cold on its way to the compressor.

Liquid Line

The liquid line, on the high side of the system, connects the condenser, receiver (if used), and metering device. The line is commonly copper tubing connected with brazing, soldering, or flared fittings. The liquid line may contain valves, a filter-drier, and a moisture indicator. Liquid lines that run through warm areas may need insulation to keep the refrigerant cold.

Oil return is seldom a problem because oil mixes well with liquid refrigerant, so the oil is carried by the refrigerant, even at low velocity. In any case, the liquid line should be large enough to prevent pressure drop and flash gas. A system with a great deal of vertical lift in the liquid line must be designed to accommodate the resulting static pressure loss.

LUBRICATION AND OIL CONTROL

Refrigerant oil is required to prevent metal-to-metal contact in compressor bearings, between the piston and cylinder wall, and elsewhere. The oil must withstand temperatures in the cylinder head and flow through the system without congealing in the coldest sections. Compressor manufacturers designate the proper oil for their machines, and their suggestions should be followed closely. Under proper conditions of cleanliness and temperature, oil will lubricate for an indefinite period. In large systems, use a drier element to neutralize acid and perform annual acidity tests on the oil, to help ensure proper lubrication without needless oil changes.

Oil must lubricate compressors and hermetic motors at all operating pressures and temperatures. Liquid oil is soluble in liquid refrigerant, but the vapors are less able to dissolve in each other. Oil can present three types of problems:

1. Oil can break down and lose its ability to lubricate, especially at high discharge temperature or in a dirty system. Filter-driers can reduce acidity and contamination.

2. Oil loses some lubricating capacity when diluted by refrigerant. The problem may be caused by oversized expansion valves, inadequate superheat, or incorrect piping.

3. Excess oil in the system, often caused by an oversized suction line, may reduce crankcase lubrication, clog the metering device, and reduce efficiency by 5 to 15%.

Excess system oil can cause these problems:

Table 5-C: Troubleshooting Excess Oil

Component	Problem
Condenser	Coats walls, reducing heat transfer and volumetric efficiency; may alter condensing temperature
Filter-drier	Plugs filter or screen; may coat dessicant

Component	Problem
Metering device	Forms gummy deposits; in expansion valves may restrict the orifice, may alter evaporator pressure, cause hunting, or lead to unneeded replacement; clogs capillary tube
Evaporator and suction line	Reduces volumetric efficiency and heat transfer; interferes with sensing bulb accuracy; increases ΔT between on and off cycles; may rob compressor of oil
Heat exchanger	Insulates walls, interfering with ability to subcool and superheat refrigerant
Compressor	Liquid oil may return as slugs, causing hydraulic jack; may overload motor; low oil may reduce lubrication

Net Oil Pressure

Because the oil pump outlet is inside the crankcase:

net oil pressure = pump outlet pressure − crankcase (suction) pressure.

An oil pressure cut-out registers net oil pressure and allows startup during brief periods of low pressure. If suction pressure is below atmospheric pressure, net oil pressure is greater than pump outlet pressure. Net oil pressures in the range of 30 to 40 psi (207 to 275 kPa) are normal, although many systems work on pressures as low as 10 psi (69 kPa).

Oil Systems for Compressors

Reciprocating compressors use two types of lubrication systems:

1. In the *splash system*, the crankshaft splashes oil, which flows through channels to the main bearings. Bearings may be noisy because the system produces a small oil cushion.

2. In the *pressure system*, a gear-driven oil pump in the crankcase forces oil into channels in the connecting rods, main bearings, and piston pins. This system does a better job of quiet lubrication, but at higher initial cost. The pump needs an overload relief to prevent dangerous pressures. An oil pressure cut-out is a safety switch that monitors oil pressure and shuts down the compressor if pressure drops below a safe level.

Rotary compressors require a film of oil on the cylinder, blades, and roller. Some machines propel the oil by the sliding action of the blades, called a slide valve; others use a pump.

Centrifugal compressors operate at high speed and may have elaborate oil control systems, with a pump, separator, reservoirs to lubricate bearings during coast-down, filter, relief valve, and an oil cooler.

Helical compressors need oil to cool, seal, and silence the rotors; they generally have a forced lubrication system. A positive displacement pump may operate independently of the compressor, ensuring complete lubrication at startup. Oil is separated, piped to a sump, cooled, and delivered to bearings and ports for injection into the compression chamber. A sump heater prevents oil dilution during the off-cycle.

> TIP: When starting a system for the first time, a certain amount of oil will likely migrate and reduce the level in the crankcase. Adding oil once is normal during a startup, but a need to continually add oil is not.

Promoting Oil Return

Oil in direct expansion evaporators is swept back to the compressor by the flow of refrigerant; the amount returned depends on oil viscosity and refrigerant velocity in the evaporator. In horizontal lines, a velocity of about 700' (214 m) per minute is sufficient; in vertical lines, about 1,500' (457 m) per minute may be needed.

To increase oil return in dry evaporators:

- slope the suction line toward the compressor;
- install a trap to prevent slugs of liquid from reaching the compressor; and
- ensure adequate refrigerant velocity in the suction line by making it big enough but not too big.

Remember that high-viscosity oil (as measured in evaporator conditions) is more difficult to return, and that oil gets more fluid if it dissolves a great deal of refrigerant. (Oil with no refrigerant is about as thick as molasses at 0°F (−18°C.) The amount of refrigerant dissolved in the oil varies according to pressure and temperature conditions in various parts of the evaporator and the nature of the two fluids.

Due to viscosity, oil return is difficult in low-temperature evaporators. High compression ratios also decrease oil return, because the suction gas is less dense. In both cases, suction-line velocity is especially important.

Oil is not swept back to the compressor in a flooded evaporator, so the system needs an oil return line. In some systems, a special chamber is connected to the evaporator to boil refrigerant from the oil before the oil returns to the compressor. (See Chapter 10, "Troubleshooting.")

Three devices are used in industrial systems to control oil: an *oil separator*, an *oil-level regulator*, and an *oil reservoir*. Other elements, such as oil strainers and valves, may be needed to complete the system. Oil test kits are also used to detect damaging acidity in oil.

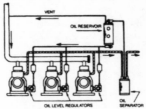

Figure 5-B: Oil control system
Courtesy of AC&R Components, Inc.

Oil Separator

An oil separator is a container in the discharge line containing a series of baffles or screens. As the oil-bearing refrigerant passes through, it turns corners and collides against the baffles, and the fog of oil forms drops that drip down to a sump. In the sump, sludge and contaminants settle out and a magnet may gather ferrous particles. When sufficient oil has gathered in the sump, it opens a float valve and returns to the crankcase, propelled by oil pressure in the separator. Oil separators are usually found on large and low-temperature systems, and are mandatory on ammonia systems.

Installing and Servicing

Follow the compressor manufacturer's recommendations when sizing and installing oil separators. (See Figure 5-C.)

In addition, consider these suggestions:

- Install close to the compressor outlet.
- Mount in the proper orientation, usually vertical.

- The small oil-return line must connect to the proper location on the compressor (the oil-filler plug or an oil regulator on the compressor may have a fitting). Do not install a shut-off in the return line.

- Do not install the separator near something that could cool it, like a fan or evaporator, as this will interfere with separation. Separators in areas colder than the evaporator may need a strap heater to prevent refrigerant from condensing in them.

- If the separator is below the condenser, route the discharge line above the condenser and pitch it downward so refrigerant that condenses in this line will drip to the condenser, not the separator.

- Increase the oil charge in the system to account for the amount held in the separator sump.

- Clean or replace the separator after a compressor burnout.

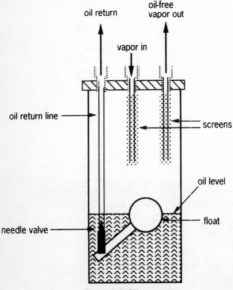

Figure 5-C: Oil separator

In operation, the oil-return line should alternate hot and cold. Hot shows that the float valve is open and oil is returning to the crankcase. Cold shows that oil has stopped flowing when the valve closes. Look for the following:

- If the line remains hot, the float may be stuck open due to malfunction or a dirty needle. If the float is operating, the compressor may be pumping too much oil.

- If the return line is always cold, refrigerant may be condensing in an overly cold separator, and possibly causing foaming or other problems in the crankcase. To correct, heat the sump (to drive out refrigerant) and insulate the outside of the separator. Or put a permanent heater on the separator.

Oil Reservoir

An oil reservoir stores oil so the crankcase has the proper level under all operating conditions. The reservoir has tubing connections to (a) the oil separator, (b) an oil-level regulator at each crankcase, and (c) the suction line (to prevent high-side pressure from damaging the reservoir. A sight glass on the side of the reservoir shows the oil level. A float and a needle valve inside the reservoir control oil level, so the regulator can add oil to the crankcase when it's low.

For gravity flow of oil, install the reservoir about 6' above the regulators. Add oil to the reservoir by closing the valve on the line to the separator; reopen the valve after filling. The outlet valve on the reservoir can be used to drain oil from the system.

When starting a new system, fill the reservoir to the upper sight-glass port since some oil will be absorbed by the refrigerant. After about 2 hours, recheck the oil level and refill to the upper port. Repeat two days later, by which time the system should be balanced. Do not add more oil unless the level falls below the lower sight glass.

If a new oil-control separator is installed on an existing system, it will withdraw some oil that is already in the system. Don't fill the reservoir to the upper sight glass; instead, fill to the lower glass, wait a day, then adjust the level.

Oil Level Regulator

An oil regulator mounted on each crankcase may control oil level with a float-controlled valve. The regulator should have a sight glass for checking oil level. Some regulators can be adjusted while the system runs, others require a shutdown. In parallel-compressor systems, a small equalization tube can balance pressure in all crankcases, even if some compressors are shut down, to reduce or prevent oil siphoning from idle compressors.

A regulator is mounted to the three-hole sight-glass opening on the side of a compressor. An adaptor may be needed to fit a particular bolt pattern. The oil line connects from the oil reservoir to the regulator. With a shut-off valve, one unit can be serviced while the rest of the system runs.

For oil to flow, the oil reservoir needs positive pressure toward the regulator. A pressure valve on the reservoir may be used to regulate pressure. A gravity feed may work if the reservoir is high enough. With satellite compressors, provide a higher pressure to force oil to flow to all compressors. Charts from regulator manufacturers should serve as a guide in setting an adjustable regulator.

Oil Test Kit

Acid in a system usually is picked up in oil, so testing oil acidity can assess system contamination. A particular oil test kit must be used with a specific refrigerant; using one with the wrong refrigerant will give a false reading. Old oil may be too cloudy to see the indicator color clearly, so some test kits allow for a technician to separate a clear solution from the oil before testing.

After testing the oil, make the necessary repairs: replace filter-drier elements, refrigerant, or oil as indicated. If the moisture indicator did not show excess moisture, the indicator may need servicing or replacement because system moisture is a primary cause of oil acidity.

MUFFLER

A muffler reduces the transmission of discharge noise from the compressor to the piping. A muffler is usually a cylinder that encloses baffle plates. Because noise level can be difficult to predict, a bit of trial and error is required to find the most effective way to control noise in a particular installation. Some mufflers are adjustable. Low-pitched noise travels farther than high-pitched noise.

Both the volume and density of gas flow through the muffler affect muffler performance. In general, mufflers tend to be more effective if they create a large pressure drop.

Mufflers are usually placed inside hermetic units. Good vibration isolation is also important in controlling noise from compressors (see Vibration Absorber, later). To prevent the building from becoming a resonator for system noise, hang pipes without direct contact with the building.

Pump, Water

Centrifugal or reciprocating water pumps circulate condenser water, chilled water, or brine in ACR systems. Pumps also circulate the fluids in absorption machines. Many types of motors can power these pumps, so long as they match the system specifications.

A *centrifugal pump* uses a rotating impeller to accelerate the fluid by centrifugal force, acting much like a centrifugal compressor. The pump must be primed, by submersion or another method, before operation. Because this pump has no pistons or other positive-action parts, it cannot pump against much resistance, but it can pump large quantities of water. A single-stage pump will operate against about 100 lbs. of pressure.

If the head exceeds the pump's capacity at a given operating speed, the pump will just churn water.

Due to its simple design and scarcity of moving parts and close tolerances, centrifugal pumps are economical and common. The pumps can be placed in the pipe line and supported by the pipe, or connected to a branch.

Many types of *reciprocating pumps* are available, but due to their complexity, they are seldom used unless the piping has high resistance.

Receiver

The receiver, or liquid receiver, is a vessel that stores liquid refrigerant on the high side of some systems. Some receivers are built into the condenser. Receivers (see Figure 5-D) are common in low-side float and expansion-valve systems but not in high-side float or capillary-tube systems.

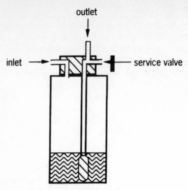

Figure 5-D: Liquid receiver

A receiver:

- eliminates the need for an exact refrigerant charge;
- helps prevent flash gas by allowing subcooling of liquid refrigerant;
- is handy for storing refrigerant during service; and
- holds refrigerant during automatic pumpdowns, defrosting, and when some evaporators are shut off.

If the cooling cycle includes a partial pumpdown, the operating control will close a solenoid valve at the receiver outlet, and the compressor will pumpdown into the receiver until the low-pressure cut-out opens. The refrigerant will remain in the receiver until the next on-cycle starts when the liquid-line solenoid valve opens, admitting refrigerant to the evaporator. (See Chapter 8, "Whole Systems.")

Valves on both sides of the receiver can shut it off for service. Sight glasses may be fitted to monitor refrigerant level in the receiver. Some receivers include two petcocks instead. When the charge is correct and the compressor is running, liquid refrigerant will flow from the lower petcock and vapor from the upper one.

To prevent over-pressure in a receiver, a pressure- or temperature-sensitive safety device must be connected to a vent line to the outside.

REFRIGERANT DISTRIBUTOR

Refrigerant distributors (see Figure 5-E) feed refrigerant from a thermostatic expansion valve (TXV) to different parts of a large evaporator or to several evaporators. The tube from the TXV to the distributor is connected by soldering, brazing, a flared fitting, or a flange. The distributor has two to twenty-four or more female fittings that connect to the evaporator. Poor distributor design or installation can cause the TXV to hunt, reduce evaporator performance, and send floodbacks to the compressor.

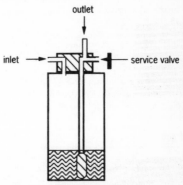

Figure 5-E: Refrigerant distributor
Courtesy of Sporlan Division of Parker Hannifin, Inc.

When brazing the outlet tube connections, heat the distributor uniformly and allow the body to cool slowly to avoid cracking. After brazing, disassemble the distributor and inspect. If this is impossible, use a probe wire to be sure all the branches are clear of solder (a pressure test will not reveal plugged tubes). When soldering a distributor to a TXV, direct the heat away from the valve and do not overheat the joint. Test the system for leaks before operating. It's not recommended that some distributor outlets are plugged, but if necessary, they can be plugged symmetrically.

REFRIGERANT-LEVEL CONTROL

A refrigerant-level control may be found on receivers, intercoolers, surge drums, or other places where liquid refrigerant can gather. Some of these controls merely signal when the level is incorrect. Others will automatically add or withdraw refrigerant as needed.

SIGHT GLASS

A sight glass, usually in the discharge line before the metering device, will allow for a diagnosis of problems such as low charge or excessive moisture. A steady stream of refrigerant in the glass while the unit runs indicates a sufficient charge. See-through glasses have two openings, so a flashlight can be shone from the opposite side to get a better view.

If possible, mount the sight glass downstream of a filter-drier. If there is a restriction in the filter-drier, bubbles will appear in the sight glass, but the bubbles can also indicate a low charge.

Some sight glasses incorporate a moisture indicator that turns color when the refrigerant is too moist. Moisture indicators are temperature-dependent and may take up to 8 hours to give an accurate reading after system conditions change.

An *electronic sight glass* can clamp on a line to detect bubbles by ultrasound. This device emits a noise when it detects bubbles and can be left in place temporarily or permanently. Charge can also be assessed on liquid receivers with two petcocks.

SUCTION LINE

The suction line completes the circuit by returning refrigerant from the evaporator to the compressor. The suction line is at low pressure and low temperature, so it's usually insulated to prevent sweating and save energy. Some systems exchange heat between the suction and liquid lines, to increase superheat and/or subcooling.

Suction-line pressure-drop can significantly raise evaporator temperature, especially at low temperatures. For example, if R-12 with no pressure drop was running at $-40°F$ ($-40°C$), a drop of 2 psi (13.8 kPa) would raise the temperature to $-32°F$ ($-35.6°C$). Thus any restrictions (such as filter-driers or bends) should be designed and installed to minimize the restriction and pressure drop.

The suction line must be designed to help oil return from the evaporator to the compressor. A reverse trap in the top of the suction riser should be used to prevent oil from returning down the riser to the evaporator. Slugs of oil that reach the top of the riser must fall into the suction line beyond the reverse trap so they can return to the compressor.

The double-riser suction-line system (see Figure 5-F) is used only with capacity-controlled compressors. The larger riser has about twice the capacity of the smaller riser. During full-load operation, both risers carry refrigerant. If a slug of oil forms in the lower trap (or accumulator), it is pulled up the large line as usual. When the compressor unloads, there is no longer enough velocity to pull the slug of oil up the larger line, and slugs in the trap will close the line. However, the small line will allow oil and refrigerant to return to the compressor.

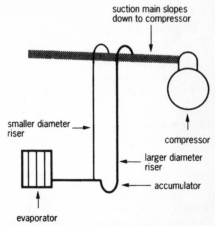

Figure 5-F: Double riser-suction line with accumulator

A p-trap at the bottom of a vertical suction line can promote oil return. Some manufacturers say a p-trap enables good oil return with vapor velocities as low as 160' per minute. Depending on vapor velocity, the oil can return as a mist, a rippling film, or a colloidal dispersion.

SUCTION-LINE ACCUMULATOR

A suction-line accumulator is a small reservoir used to prevent slugs of liquid refrigerant from reaching the compressor. The accumulator is generally, but not always, located inside the cabinet. The typical accumulator has an outlet at the top so only vapor can return to the suction line. The unit should be sized according to the system design and capacity, evaporator temperature, and refrigerant.

Suction-Line Pressure Alarm

The low-pressure cut-out may include an alarm to announce that suction pressure has risen too high, meaning the evaporator is too warm. The alarm may have a delay to allow defrosting. When the delay is energized, the timer waits a certain period—commonly 45 to 60 minutes—before sounding the alarm.

Vibration Absorber

The suction and discharge lines can transmit vibration from the compressor to other cooling system components and the building. This vibration can cause noise, damage tubing, and cause leaks in refrigerant lines and capillary tubes in controls. (See Chapter 4, "Controls.") Compressors should be fitted with a vibration absorber, or stress relief.

On a small system with small, soft-copper refrigerant lines, the vibration absorber may be simply a coil of tubing. Flexible metallic hose, with an ID at least as large as the connected tubing, is better for larger systems. This section of tubing may be terminated by flanges or threaded male ends. Refrigerant traveling too quickly along the convoluted inner diameter of the absorber may cause whistling.

In a larger system, elbows can be used for vibrations absorbers, as shown in Figure 5-G, or use special vibration absorbers for the purpose. These absorbers are not designed for compression or extension, so they should be oriented parallel to the crankshaft. Improperly mounted absorbers will resist the compressor's rocking instead of flexing. For maximum vibration control, place two absorbers in each line, to account for horizontal and vertical movement. Do not stress, compress, or twist the absorbers during installation.

Figure 5-G: Vibration absorber (stress relief) in compressor piping
Courtesy of American Standard

6

Motors

Electric motors are used to drive the vast majority of compressors and fans in cooling systems. Although motors are usually reliable, they do suffer from troubles that originate elsewhere. For example, a burnout, the ultimate form of motor trouble, may result from contamination or the failure of a limit switch. True motor trouble, on the other hand, is not something the average cooling system technician is trained or equipped to handle. Nevertheless, to pinpoint trouble and correct problems in motor circuits and controls, it helps to understand the principles of motor operation and troubleshooting.

The degree of service performed also depends on the system configuration. Motor compressors in small hermetic systems must be replaced after a motor failure, although controls located outside the hermetic housing can be repaired in the field. Motors in large hermetic and semihermetic systems may be replaced in the field.

Electric motors convert electrical energy into magnetic energy and then kinetic energy. The rotation results from repeated attractions and repulsions between electromagnets located in the motor housing and induced magnets on the rotating part. Practically every motor used in a commercial cooling system operates on alternating current because AC's wave-shaped magnetic field induces a current in conductors, even if the field and conductor are not moving in relation to each other. (See Chapter 2, "Energy, Electricity, and Cooling Cycles.")

Electric motors have two basic parts: the *stator* (or the *housing* or *field*) and the *rotor* (or *armature*) which spins on a shaft inside the housing. (See Figure 6-A.) When electricity passes through the stator windings, they become an electromagnet whose field strength rises and falls with the AC waves. This induces a current in the rotor, causing it to become a second magnet. The motor would not rotate if the opposite poles were positioned next to each other, so motors are designed so the magnetic fields can never rest in this condition. Pushed by magnetic attraction and repulsion, the rotor spins, and the magnetic fields shift position to cause further attraction or repulsion.

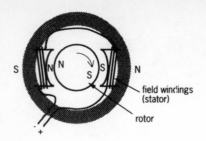

Figure 6-A: Elementary electric motor

As the AC wave increases in strength at the start of each half of its cycle, the induction of magnetism in the rotor lags slightly. By the time the rotor is fully magnetized, the stator is already starting to change polarity due to the change in the AC wave, so the fields can never line up with north opposite south.

Electric motors can respond to changes in demand. As the rotor slows under increased load, more current is induced in the rotor, strengthening its magnetic field and also the motor's output.

The simplest AC motor has a single magnet in the field windings and is called a two-pole motor. Each change of the AC wave causes half a revolution of the rotor. Thus, a two-pole motor running on 60 Hz (60 cycles per second) current rotates 60 times per second, 3,600 revolutions per minute. This is termed synchronous speed, although motors actually "slip" behind synchronous speed, generally to about 3,450 rpm. A four-pole motor (with two magnets in the field windings) operates at half this speed because each reversal of the AC produces 1/4 turn of the rotor. Synchronous speed for a four-pole, 60 Hz, motor is 1,800 rpm and the normal running, or "operational," speed is 1,750 rpm. Four-pole motors are common in compressor drives.

NAMEPLATE INFORMATION

All electric motors should have a nameplate listing:

- *Required voltage and frequency, in volts and hertz.* 1 Hz = 1 cycle per second.

- *Service factor.* Describes the motor's ability to handle overload. A motor rated 1.0 cannot sustain an overload without dangerous overheating; one rated 1.15 can handle a 15% continuous overload.

- *Locked rotor kVA.* The number of kilovolt-amperes drawn when the rotor is locked or starting. Used for troubleshooting.

- *Time rating.* How long the motor can run without overheating. A "continuous" rating indicates no time limit.

- *Frame size.* Used primarily to size a motor for installation.

OVERLOAD AND OVERHEAT PROTECTION

Motors must be protected from two related conditions: overloading (an excess current draw for any reason), and overheating (which can result from overload or other reasons). Overloading and overheating can cause melted contacts, burned insulation, and burnout. Motors are protected against these perils with fuses or circuit breakers (to prevent overload) and temperature-sensors coupled with shut-offs (to prevent overheating).

Each motor circuit needs a motor overload protector—a circuit breaker or fuse—which may be part of another device, like a switch or controller. The starting relay, for example, may offer overload protection in the form of a bimetal strip and a resistance heater. Excess current will warm the heating element, heating and bending the bimetal strip, and opening the circuit.

Each compressor motor must be on a separate circuit, so a problem elsewhere does not shut off the motor. The National Electric Code requires a circuit disconnect within sight of the motor control. This disconnect must disconnect the motor *and* the control from all ungrounded supply wiring. It may be part of the overload protective device.

A *fuse* or *circuit breaker* must be on every electric circuit to protect against excess current. To prevent motor damage, the protector must trip under a sustained current more than about 25% above rated amperage. Unlike normal circuit breakers, this protector must permit a temporary overload because motors draw up to 600% of the running current during startup. A time-delay fuse allows a brief excess current, but might not open quickly enough during a true overload. A current-limiting fuse puts a ceiling on amperage, but does not blow. Circuit breakers are better than fuses because they can be reset after tripping. If the protection device is correctly sized but continually blows, there is trouble in the circuit. Do not install an oversized breaker or fuse; correct the problem in the circuit.

Overheating can result from inadequate refrigerant in hermetic systems, poor air flow near the compressor in open systems, a locked rotor, or excess head pressure during startup. Motor temperature in general should not exceed 72°F (40°C) above room temperature—or about 150°F (66°C). The motor cooling system should receive attention during routine maintenance.

A *bimetallic overload device* senses temperature or current and opens a circuit if the value exceeds a safe limit. These devices may be buried in the motor windings in hermetic systems—a system called "internal overload protected." The protector should have a snap action so it opens the points quickly to prevent arcing.

A *thermistor* is an electronic device that senses motor temperature and shuts off current to the motor relay. As temperature rises, resistance increases in a "positive temperature coefficient" thermistor. Resistance decreases with temperature rise in a "negative temperature coefficient" thermistor. (See Chapter 4, "Controls.")

START-WINDING RELAY

Until an electric motor nears operating speed, it does not have the normal cycle of attraction and repulsion from the main windings. The attraction-repulsion during startup comes from the start winding, which is energized by the start-winding relay.

The relay is mounted outside hermetic housings for easy service. In open-drive equipment, a centrifugal switch may replace the starting relay. This governor-type device, mounted on the motor shaft, cuts off start-winding current when the motor nears operating speed.

To troubleshoot, either test the relay according to the manufacturer's instructions or replace it with a good one. A motor-starting relay tester can be used if it is available, or the current can be tested in each part of the relay to diagnose the trouble. When replacing a relay, make sure to reconnect the wires to the correct terminals. Masking tape and a marking pen are handy for labeling wires.

Three types of starting relays (see Figure 6-B) can energize the start winding on hermetic and semihermetic systems:

1. A *current relay* is a magnetic switch that senses current in the run winding. This current is highest when the rotor is stationary or rotating slowly, both indications that the motor is starting. The relay stays closed and energizes the start winding whenever the run-winding current is above the setting. When the run-winding current falls, a weight or a spring overpowers the magnet, and the switch shuts off the start winding.

2. A *potential relay* is a magnetic switch that senses voltage in the start winding. As the motor gains speed, start-winding voltage increases, strengthening the relay's electromagnet. At the set point, the relay opens and current to the start winding is shut off. Because the relay contacts are closed during the off cycle, there is no danger of arcing across the points during startup.

3. Various types of *electronic relays* can control current to the start winding by sensing motor voltage. These relays replace current and potential relays. For servicing, see the manufacturer's instructions.

a) current relay position in circuit

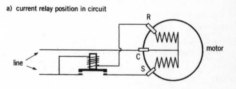

b) potential relay position in circuit

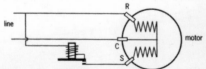

a) Current relay position in circuit, in off position
b) Potential relay position in circuit, in run position

Figure 6-B: Starting relays

CONTACTOR AND MOTOR STARTER

A contactor is an electromagnetic relay (solenoid switch) used to make and break electric circuits. In contrast to a start-winding relay, a contactor handles the full line voltage to the motor. Using a contactor eliminates the need to route large currents or voltages to the motor control, cutting costs and increasing safety. When the control circuit in the contactor is closed (in response to a signal from a thermostat or another control), the contactor's electromagnet pulls the armature to close the contacts. The motor circuit remains closed as long as the control energizes the contactor.

A motor starter contains the relay described above, as well as other elements, such as overload protectors, disconnects, and whatever else is required to operate a large motor in a complex system.

ENCLOSURES

Four types of motor enclosures may be used for open (nonhermetic) motors, depending on the application:

- An *open* motor is cooled by air circulating over the windings. It's used in cool locations without much dust or moisture.
- In dusty conditions, *totally-enclosed, fan-cooled* motors may be visible, with a double shell and a fan to circulate air between the inner and outer chambers.
- *Splashproof* motors are suited to outdoor installations because they are protected from rain.
- *Explosion-proof* motors are totally enclosed and used in an explosive atmosphere.

BEARINGS

Motors require quiet, efficient shaft bearings for proper operation. Ball bearings can carry a large load but need proper care. The following conditions can shorten bearing lifespan:

- Rapid rotation
- Excess load
- Dirt
- Overheating due to dirty, old, or wrong-grade oil
- Overly tight belts
- A pulley rubbing against a bearing
- Improper drive alignment

Bearings on open motors are lubricated with:

1. *Wicks* that hold lubricant against the shaft, and are oiled with the correct nondetergent, medium-viscosity oil about twice a year. A wick may plug if it is singed, dirty, or lubricated with sludgy oil.

2. A *slip ring* that dips into a pocket of oil to lubricate a bearing.

3. *Oilless bearings,* made of porous bronze impregnated with oil at the factory, that should not need service. Tolerance in oilless bearings is very tight and a bearing may get noisy with wear. These bearings are most effective when the shaft is rotating continuously; they wear quicker with frequent cycling.

Bearing Installation

Bearings must be installed correctly, or they will never do their job. Do not drop bearings, as they are brittle. Prevent contamination by keeping the bearing, hands, and the work area clean. Some ball bearings must be replaced in pairs.

Press out bearings with special tools, taking care to protect the motor endplates. Before installing the rotor, ream the bearing to the correct alignment with a special reamer. Support and align the shaft during installation to prevent pitting of the races.

Do not remove the rust-preventative coating from new bearings; it's compatible with bearing grease. Use the correct grade of grease, but do not overfill, which can cause overheating. Use a tube of grease to lube sealed bearings (a grease gun can create enough pressure to dislodge the seals).

Severely worn bearings can allow the rotor to contact the stator. If this is heard when the motor runs, service the bearings immediately. Motor damage can quickly follow.

SINGLE-PHASE MOTORS

Single-phase motors are most common in fractional-horsepower applications. Because these motors depend on the spinning rotor to produce the continual magnetic attraction and repulsion, they need a separate start winding to start the rotor spinning and get it spinning in the right direction. The start (or auxiliary) winding is wired to repel the rotor when the motor is at rest, usually by exerting a magnetic field that is out of phase with the run-winding field. Once the motor reaches about two-thirds of synchronous speed, the start winding shuts off and the run winding takes all the current.

Single-phase motors are generally described by the starting and running methods, as in "capacitor-start, induction-run." An induction-run motor depends on the field to induce magnetism in the rotor.

The most popular single-phase motors for refrigeration systems are the split-phase; the capacitor-start, induction-run; and the permanent split capacitor. The capacitor-start, capacitor-run motor is sometimes used on large systems.

A capacitor-start produces good starting torque, but starting capacitors cannot dispose of heat, so they must not be substituted for running capacitors. A great deal of heat builds up in run capacitors, but they are built to dump this heat.

A *split-phase* motor has a start winding with high resistance and low inductance, which alters the phase of the current in the start winding. These windings are physically located in a place that will provide a weak starting torque. To reverse direction, reverse the main and start windings. A centrifugal switch or starting relay shuts off the start winding when the motor reaches about 75% of synchronous speed. The motor is suitable to systems that balance pressure during the off cycle, such as those with a capillary tube metering device or an unloader on the compressor. (See Figure 6-C.)

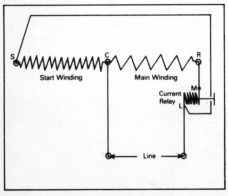

Figure 6-C: Split-phase motor

The *capacitor-start, induction-run* motor (see Figure 6-D) is probably the most popular single-phase motor for ACR systems. The capacitor, wired in series with the start winding, causes the motor to act like a two-phase motor during startup. These motors produce high starting torque, and many are adaptable to 120V and 240V.

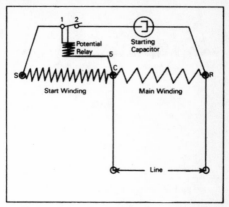

Figure 6-D: Capacitor-start, induction-run motor

The *permanent split-capacitor* (PSC) motor has low starting torque, so it must be used with systems that balance pressures during the off cycle. No relay is used; both start and run (main) windings are energized whenever the power is on. A running capacitor is wired between the terminals of the main and start windings; there is no starting capacitor. The motor requires a relatively stable line voltage. Low supply voltage can cause overheating, so a thermal protection device is needed. (See Figure 6-E.)

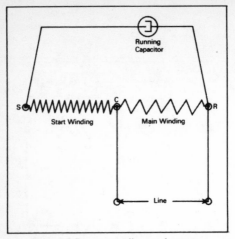

Figure 6-E: Permanent split-capacitor motor

The *capacitor-start, capacitor-run* motor is used in large hermetic systems. A potential relay controls power to the start windings. During startup, both the start and run windings receive current through capacitors. This two-phase motor is very efficient and has a high starting torque. (See Figure 6-F.)

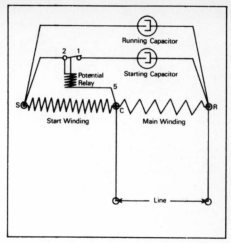

Figure 6-F: Capacitor-start, capacitor-run motor

THREE-PHASE MOTORS

Three-phase motors are used in larger compressors and fans because they have a higher power factor and greater efficiency than single-phase motors. In addition, they require no start winding because some magnets are always in a position to repel each other.

Most three-phase motors run on 208V and above. Because of the complicated nature of the wiring, it is best to have a qualified electrician hook them up. Swapping any two leads of the connection will reverse the rotation. Many three-phase motors can be adapted from 220V or 440V by changing the connections. Figure 6-G shows two common wirings: wye (star) and delta.

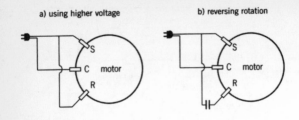

a) using higher voltage

b) reversing rotation

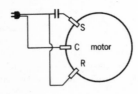

c) using a capacitor in the start winding

Figure 6-G: Three-phase diagram

The current is supplied by a heavy-duty relay with three contacts. The motor starter housing may contain the overload protection device. Most three-phase motors are protected by a circuit breaker that controls all three hot leads to the motor. If fuses are the protection, each fuse will regulate a single phase of the current. If one fuse blows, the motor may run on the remaining two phases, but this may overload the motor. A "phase-loss monitor" can be used to detect this situation. If a loss of phase in a fuse-protected motor is suspected without a phase-loss monitor, test each phase with a voltmeter. Show full line voltage between each pair of input wires.

Three-phase motors that draw the full line current are said to have "across-the-line starting." This can pull a starting current up to 650% above full-load current, which may dim lights and reduce voltage to other equipment. For these reasons, some utilities restrict across-the-line starting.

Part-winding start may be used to reduce current surge at startup, but this also reduces starting torque. See below for a testing procedure for voltage of three-phase motors.

Testing Voltage and Amperage

The voltage imbalance between the three legs of a three-phase motor should not exceed 2% when calculated with this formula:

100 × the sum of the deviations of each voltage reading from the average (make the sign positive) divided by twice the average voltage.

For a motor rated at 208V, with legs reading 211V, 206V, and 205V, the calculation is:

$$\text{Average} = 211 + 206 + 205 = 622/3 = 207.33$$

$$\frac{(211 - 207) + (207 - 206) + (207 - 205)}{2 \times 207.33} \times 100 = \frac{7 \times 100}{414.66}$$

$$= 700/414.66 = 1.69\%. \text{ This is within the 2\% guideline.}$$

If the voltage balance is unacceptable, notify the electric utility before the motor is damaged.

Amperage on all lines should also be close to each other. If one leg is out of line with the others, either unbalanced voltage or a winding imbalance is present. Either check the voltage with the procedure above or:

1. Mark each supply wire and write down its amperage.
2. Disconnect the supply wires from the terminals and reconnect to different ones.
3. Measure amperage with the same load as when the problem was spotted.
4. If the high-amp reading stays with the same line, the problem is with the supply. If the high amperage remains with the same terminal, the winding is at fault.

MOTOR TROUBLES

Motors can suffer mechanical or electrical damage. A motor with major problems must be replaced, or repaired or rebuilt by a specialist. However, an air conditioning and refrigeration technician should be able to diagnose and repair simple motor problems. For overall system troubleshooting, refer to Chapter 10, "Troubleshooting."

When assessing motor problems, first check the safety and operating controls and the operating conditions. Many external factors—such as excessive cycling, a blown capacitor or fuse, or a faulty operating control—can interfere with operation.

Then read the motor nameplate. Check that the electric power has the proper frequency, voltage, amperage, and phase. Voltage must be within 10% of the nameplate value. Check for loose or undersized wires or overloaded circuits, or inadequate power supply to the building. Read the actual voltage with a voltmeter while the unit runs, if it will run. Hook up an ammeter—amperage should only exceed 120% of nameplate value during startup. Excessive current draw indicates overload or other difficulties.

Identifying Terminals

If work is being done on a motor that does not identify terminals for start winding (S), run winding (R), or common (C), test the impedance across each pair of terminals with an ohmmeter:

- Highest resistance: R to S
- Lowest resistance: C to R
- Resistance C to S plus C to R equals R to S:

$$\begin{array}{r} \text{Resistence } C - S \\ + \text{ Resistance } C - R \\ \hline \text{Resistance } R - S \end{array}$$

Winding Problems

Motor windings can have three types of problems:

- *Grounds* are insulation failures between a winding and the motor frame. A ground will generally cause motor failure.
- *Shorts* are internal insulation failures that cause part of the winding to be bypassed. The motor may run, but will not reach full power. A short will increase current draw, decrease power, and cause overheating. Resistance in the winding will be below specification.
- *Opens* are incomplete windings that block the current and generally cause motor failure. Opens show up as infinite resistance in the winding (measure with an ohmmeter).

Motor Diagnosis

After confirming that the motor is not being shut down by operating or safety controls, let the motor cool down—it may be responding to overload or overheat protection. If the cooled motor does not work, check for grounds, shorts, or opens, using a meter (steps 1 and 2, below) or a homemade tester. (See Alternate Motor Test, following):

1. *Check for grounded windings.* Connect one lead of an ohmmeter to the housing and the other lead to each winding terminal in turn. Resistance should be off the scale of a standard ohmmeter. A better test for grounds requires a megohmmeter, because some grounds will not show up without a very high test voltage.

> CAUTION: Use caution with a high voltage. Refer to the manufacturer's literature or use these guidelines: A hermetic motor of 1 hp or less should have at least 1 million ohms resistance. Larger motors should have at least 1,000 ohms per volt. (Grounds are more likely to arise in a warm motor, so run the motor for a few minutes before testing.)

2. *Check operating and locked-rotor volt-ampere draw.* Use an ammeter-voltmeter to measure current draw, and compare to nameplate values. If a wattmeter is available, measure the wattage draw during startup (1 second only) and during running. Starting wattage should be much higher than running wattage. If both readings are similar, the motor is locked or has other problems.

Alternate Motor Test

Some motor diagnostic tests can be made without a meter. Prepare a simple continuity tester by assembling a 25-watt bulb and socket, a pair of test leads, and a standard 120V plug as shown in Figure 6-H. (Use care; the test leads will carry 120V current.)

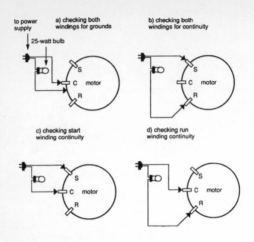

S = start winding terminal
R = run winding terminal
C = common terminal

Figure 6-H: Alternate motor test with continuity meter

3. Disconnect the motor from the circuit and connect the leads to the:

   a. *start* terminal and a clean, rust-free section of *housing*. If the bulb lights, find and repair an internal ground.

   b. *start* and *run* terminals. A light indicates intact windings. If the bulb stays dark, connect the leads to the start and common terminals.

   c. *start* and *common* terminals. A light indicates an intact start winding.

   d. *run* and *common* terminals. A light indicates an intact run winding.

Testing and Replacing Capacitors

The capacitor is a common source of motor trouble. The capacitor creates a slight "delay" in the current, usually to create a temporary second phase for the start winding. Some motors use starting and running capacitors, while others use only a starting capacitor. Test a capacitor with a capacitor tester, or just replace the suspect capacitor with an identical new one. Capacitors may connect with solder or screw terminals.

When replacing a capacitor, do not use an undersized capacitor. Follow these guidelines if the identical item is unavailable:

- The *voltage rating* must be at least as high as the original.
- *Starting capacitors* must have 100 to 120% of original capacitance.
- *Running capacitors* must have 90 to 110% of original capacitance.
- *Do not substitute* a starting capacitor for a running capacitor, as starting capacitors cannot dispose of heat rapidly enough.

For capacitors in parallel, each replacement must have a voltage rating at least as high as the original. For series capacitors, the total voltages of the replacement capacitors must equal the originals.

To find the total capacitance of *series capacitors*:
$$Ct = C1 + C2$$

To find the total capacitance of *parallel capacitors*:

$$C_1 = \frac{C_1 C_2}{C_1 + C_2}$$

> **CAUTION:** A capacitor can hold its electric charge after the power is turned off. Be sure to discharge a capacitor by attaching a 100,000-ohm resistor across the terminals. Older wet-type capacitors, which are designed for continuous duty on running windings, may contain a toxic chemical called polychlorinated biphenyl (PCB). Do not open such a capacitor. If it is dripping fluid, do not touch or breathe the fumes. Dispose of wet capacitors in accord with local environmental regulations.

Starting a Stuck Hermetic Compressor

Some units will not start even though the motor and controls are in good condition. This may occur if the unit has been idle for a long time or is overcharged. First check for motor or control problems as suggested above. Then use one of these methods to start the motor:

a. Connect a power line to the motor terminals, bypassing the starting relay.

b. *Briefly* connect a higher-voltage source to the motor terminals. (See Figure 6-Ia.)

c. Wire a capacitor in series with the run winding to run the motor backward. Connect the circuit for only 2 seconds. (See Figure 6-Ib.)

d. Install a capacitor in the start winding as shown in Figure 6-Ic.

e. Use a hermetic analyzer to move the motor. Consult the instructions for the device for the exact hookup.

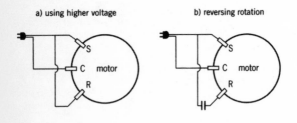

a) using higher voltage

b) reversing rotation

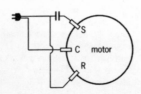

c) using a capacitor in the start winding

Figure 6-I: Starting a stuck motor (apply current for 2 seconds maximum)

Motor Drives

Compressors and fans are driven by motors through belts and pulleys, or by shafts connected by a flexible or rigid coupling. The system of belts and pulleys, or of shafts and couplings, makes up a "drive" or a "motor drive." We'll take up belt drives first.

Belts

Most flexible belts for motors are made of layers of fabric, rubber, and cord, formed into the desired shape. The most common type is the V-belt, which tapers to fit the pulleys, also called sheaves. The power is transmitted because belt tension forces the V shape into the pulley slot. Either standard or narrow V-belts are used in ACR. Synchronous belts, with teeth engaging notches in the pulley, are used when the driven equipment needs exact timing.

Single belts may flip over when asked to transmit power above their capacity. Multiple (compound) belts can transmit more power, but be sure to match the belts—each must get the same tension and carry an equal share of the load. When one belt wears, replace the entire set.

Shafts for fractional-horsepower motors are commonly 1/2", 5/8", or 3/4" diameter. Pulleys are fastened to the shaft with a key secured by a set screw. The "driver" pulley on the motor spins the "driven" pulley on the compressor or fan. Most drives allow the motor to run faster than the load, increasing torque and allowing the machinery to operate at optimum speed.

A sheave may be simple (one belt per sheave), compound (several belts per sheave), or variable pitch.

When the width of the slot on a variable-pitch sheave is altered, the effective diameter is changed, and thus the speed of the driven pulley.

Belts must be sized correctly. Belts are described by outside length and width, either with letters or inches. "A" width belts are up to 17/32" (1.35 cm) wide. "B" width belts are 1/2" (1.27 cm) to 11/16" (1.75 cm) wide.

Belt Safety

Belt drives are dangerous! Heed these precautions when working around a belt drive:

1. Turn off the power and lock the switch. Check that the equipment is in safe condition before starting work.

2. Wear safe clothing. Do not wear neckties, loose sleeves, or other clothing that can catch in a belt.

3. Keep the area around the drive clear of debris and clutter. Floors must be dry and free of oil.

4. Keep drive guards in place except when working on a drive. A proper guard encloses the drive completely, allows good ventilation, has access panels for inspection, is easily removed and replaced, and protects the drive from weather, damage, and debris as necessary.

Determining Driven Speed

Pulley sizes may need to be changed to make a compressor run better, or to match another load to a motor. Diameter and speed are related in this formula:

$$D_r \times R_r = D_n \times R_n$$

D_n = diameter of driven pulley
D_r = diameter of driver pulley
R_n = speed (rpm) of driven pulley
R_r = speed of driver pulley

Belt Inspection and Analysis

To inspect a belt:

1. Shut down the power switch and tag it: "Down for maintenance. Do not turn on power." Lock the switch open.

2. Remove the guard and inspect it for wear or damage. Clean grease and crud off the guard for good ventilation.

3. Notice the temperature. If a belt is too hot to touch just after the drive is shut down, the belt has problems. Find and correct the source of overheating before returning the drive to service.

4. Inspect the belt. Mark a starting point and work around, looking for cracks, nicks, frays, cuts, or unusual or uneven wear. Replace belts with excessive wear, cuts, or missing teeth.

5. Check alignment (see below).

6. Inspect other parts of the drive: motor and pulley mounting, and housing.

Aligning a Belt

To prevent premature wear, instability, turnover, and failure, belt drives must be in good alignment, with the shafts parallel and the pulleys in one plane. (See Figure 6-Ja.) A belt can have angular misalignment and/or parallel misalignment. (Misalignment can also result from a damaged or improperly mounted pulley.)

1. Detect *angular misalignment* with a long straightedge (use a tape measure, string, or straight board on a long drive). In general, pulley alignment should be within 1/10" per foot (8.4 mm per meter) of span between the pulleys. Correct by loosening the mounting bolts and rotating one piece of equipment as needed. Then tighten the mounting bolts and check for parallel misalignment. (See Figure 6-Jb.)

2. To check for *parallel misalignment*, hold the straightedge against both pulleys and check that it touches in four places. (See Figure 6-Jc.) Correct misalignment by loosening pulley mounting screws and sliding the pulley as needed.

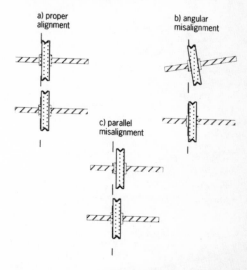

a) Aligned
b) Angular misalignment
c) Parallel misalignment

Figure 6-J: Belt alignment

Installing and Tensioning a Belt

Belts must be properly tensioned. Overtight belts will cause compressor seals to leak, and prematurely wear sheaves, bearings, and belts. Loose belts will slip, heat up, and fail. New belts will stretch slightly, so manufacturers recommend installing them a bit tighter than normal. Always check and re-tension a new belt after 4 to 24 hours of operation.

After inspecting alignment, use this procedure to *replace and tension a belt:*

1. Check the number on the belt to order a replacement. If the number can't be read, measure the outside length with the belt in place. (Measure the belt section later or gauge the sheave to find the section.)

2. Loosen the motor mount and slide the motor toward the compressor to slack the belt.

3. Remove the old belt without prying.

4. Install the proper sized belt. Replace all belts on a multiple drive so they will pull evenly.

5. Slide the motor back into position. Rotate the belt(s) by hand to seat in the pulleys. Check and adjust alignment as described above.

6. Check tension by deflecting the belt at the midpoint between the pulleys. A belt tension gauge can be used, but most mechanics deflect the belt by hand and check that it moves slightly, but without much slack. Use this rule of thumb: 10 lb. (4.5 kg) of force should deflect a belt about 1/2" (1.3 cm).

7. Tighten motor-mounting bolts to the proper torque.

8. After 4 to 24 hours of operation, recheck and readjust belt tension.

Couplings

Flexible couplings are a second common method for connecting motors to compressors. If flexible couplings are poorly aligned, leaking seals or other problems may be visible. Use care to align the coupling to the manufacturer's tolerances. (See Figure 6-K.) Because the compressor is usually fixed by its piping, it is best to align the motor, not the compressor, by adding or subtracting shims from the motor mounting.

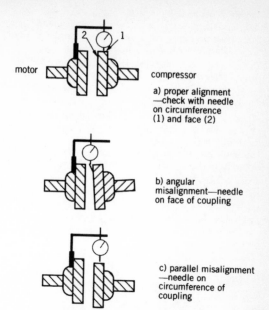

motor

compressor

a) proper alignment
—check with needle
on circumference
(1) and face (2)

b) angular
misalignment—needle
on face of coupling

c) parallel misalignment
—needle on
circumference of
coupling

Figure 6-K: Aligning flexible coupling

In general, flexible couplings must be align within .004" (0.1 mm) in each direction, although many manufacturers specify a closer alignment. Use jack screws to align a large motor. To make a jack screw, cut a hole for a bolt in a piece of plate steel and weld a nut to it (or drill and tap the hole). If jack screws are not available, move the motor with a pry bar or jack and tighten the mounting screws while reading the dial gauge.

Assemble all tools: wrenches, shims, dial indicator, and jack screws. Then use this procedure (and some patience) to *align a flexible coupling*:

1. Mount two jack screws to each motor foot, one to push the motor sideways, the other forward and back.

2. Disassemble the coupling, but do not remove flanges from the motor shaft or the compressor shaft.

3. To check *parallel alignment*, mount the dial indicator to the motor flange. Rest the feeler button on the circumference of the compressor flange. Spin the compressor flange and read every 90° of rotation. If the readings are equal, parallel alignment is good.

4. To correct parallel misalignment, loosen the mounting bolts and move the jack screws. Keep a record of alignment and adjustments.

5. Retighten the mounting bolts and recheck the circumference with the dial gauge until it reads equal all the way around.

6. When parallel alignment is good, check the *angular alignment*. Rest the feeler button against the face of the compressor flange and spin the flange. If the reading varies, angular misalignment is present. Loosen the motor mount screws and add or remove shims to level the motor. Be careful: dirt under the shims can throw off the adjustment.

7. When angular alignment is good, recheck parallel alignment, with the jack screws still positioning the motor. When both alignments are correct, tighten the mounting and remove the jack screws.

8. Reassemble the coupling and run the compressor for a while. After the coupling warms up, disassemble and recheck both readings. Make further corrections if necessary.

7

Pipe, Tube, Fittings, and Valves

Pipe, tube, and fittings are the sinews that join the components of air conditioning and refrigeration systems. This section covers the major varieties of pipe and tube, fittings, and valves.

PIPE AND TUBE

Although "pipe" and "tube" are often used interchangeably, in this manual *tubing* is material that is not threaded. Pipe is material, primarily iron or steel, that is joined with threads. However, we'll also use *pipe* for the welded steel pipe used in ammonia systems. In ACR work, most tubing is copper, although steel, stainless steel, and plastic are also used. For tubing procedures, see Chapter 1, "Tools, Equipment, and Materials."

Copper

Copper tubing is classified by method of manufacture:

1. Hard (hard-drawn) tubing is stiff because it is not annealed after drawing. Anneal hard tubing before flaring or bending, and use fittings for bends and connections.
2. Soft tubing is annealed after drawing and is more workable, so it can be flared, swaged to make a joint without a coupling, or bent. Soft tubing needs more support on long runs.

Although hard ACR tube is best for cooling system work, soft tubing may be used in liquid and suction lines that must be flexible, as in transport refrigeration. It is also used in capillary tubes, which must be shaped during installation.

Age, hammering, and bending will "work harden" soft copper, making it too brittle for bending or flaring. To anneal work-hardened (or hard-drawn) tubing, heat it to a dull red and allow it to cool.

Copper tubing is also classified by use:

1. *Plumbing (nominal-size)* tube, has an actual OD 1/8" (.32 cm) larger than nominal size. Plumbing tube includes water tube and drain-waste-vent tube.

Water tube, used for water supply, is available in hard or soft temper. Water tube may be connected by flaring or soldering. Soft tubing is sold in 25' and 50' (7.62 and 15.24 meter) coils. Hard tubing is sold in 20' lengths. The inside diameter is close to, but not exactly the same as, the nominal size.

Water tube is made in three wall thicknesses:

- Type K: heavy wall (used where corrosion is expected)
- Type L: medium wall
- Type M: light wall

Drainage (DWV—Drain-Waste-Vent) tube is used for drains and vent lines. The minimum size is 1¼" (3.175 cm). DWV has a thin wall, is not for pressure applications, and comes in hard temper only.

2. *Air conditioning and refrigeration* (ACR) tube is identified by OD, which equals actual outside diameter. Manufacturers color-code ACR cartons with crimson. Most ACR tubing is made hard in Type L—medium wall.

ACR is sold in 20' (6.01 m) lengths. To allow the construction of clean cooling systems, pipe factories clean, dry, and fill the tube with nitrogen to prevent oxidation, then cap it to prevent contamination and corrosion in storage. Keep the ends sealed in storage and while working. The nitrogen will be diluted, but this is better than nothing. When brazing ACR tubing, purge the lines and fill them with nitrogen to prevent oxidation inside the system, which can cause scale problems.

Work ACR tubing with the same techniques used for hard plumbing tube. However, annealing the tube before bending or flaring will cause corrosion, nullifying the benefit of using clean, evacuated tube. Therefore, it is best to change directions with fittings, not bending.

Table 7-A: Dimensions and Properties of Copper Tube

Line Size O.D.	Type	Diameter OD In.	Diameter ID In.	Wall Thickness In.	Surface Area Sq. Ft./Lin. Ft. OD	Surface Area Sq. Ft./Lin. Ft. ID	Inside Cross-section Area, Sq. In.	Lineal Feet Containing 1 Cu. Ft.	Weight Lb/Lin. Ft.	Working Pressure Psia
⅜	K	0.375	0.305	0.035	0.0982	0.0798	0.0730	1973.0	0.145	918
	L	0.375	0.315	0.030	0.0982	0.0825	0.0779	1848.0	0.126	764
½	K	0.500	0.402	0.049	0.131	0.105	0.127	1135.0	0.269	988
	L	0.500	0.430	0.035	0.131	0.113	0.145	1001.0	0.198	677
⅝	K	0.625	0.527	0.049	0.164	0.138	0.218	660.5	0.344	779
	L	0.625	0.545	0.040	0.164	0.143	0.233	621.0	0.285	625
¾	K	0.750	0.652	0.049	0.193	0.171	0.334	432.5	0.418	643
	L	0.750	0.666	0.042	0.193	0.174	0.348	422.0	0.362	547
⅞	K	0.875	0.745	0.065	0.229	0.195	0.436	331.0	0.641	747
	L	0.875	0.785	0.045	0.229	0.206	0.484	299.0	0.455	497

Table 7-A: Dimensions and Properties of Copper Tube (continued)

1⅛	K	1.125	0.995	0.065	0.295	0.260	0.778	186.0	0.839	574
	L	1.125	1.025	0.050	0.295	0.268	0.825	174.7	0.655	432
1⅜	K	1.375	1.245	0.065	0.360	0.326	1.22	118.9	1.04	466
	L	1.375	1.265	0.055	0.360	0.331	1.26	115.0	0.884	387
1⅝	K	1.625	1.481	0.072	0.425	0.388	1.72	83.5	1.36	421
	L	1.625	1.505	0.060	0.425	0.394	1.78	81.4	1.14	359
2⅛	K	2.125	1.959	0.083	0.556	0.513	3.01	48.0	2.06	376
	L	2.125	1.985	0.070	0.556	0.520	3.10	46.6	1.75	316
2⅝	K	2.625	2.435	0.095	0.687	0.638	4.66	31.2	2.93	352
	L	2.625	2.465	0.080	0.687	0.645	4.77	30.2	2.48	295
3⅛	K	3.125	2.907	0.109	0.818	0.761	6.64	21.8	4.00	343
	L	3.125	2.945	0.090	0.818	0.771	6.81	21.1	3.33	278
3⅝	K	3.625	3.385	0.120	0.949	0.886	9.00	16.1	5.12	324
	L	3.625	3.425	0.100	0.949	0.897	9.21	15.6	4.29	268
4⅛	K	4.125	3.857	0.134	1.08	1.01	11.7	12.4	6.51	315
	L	4.125	3.905	0.110	1.08	1.02	12.0	12.1	5.38	256

With copper fittings made to fit both nominal size and ACR tube, there is a potential for confusion. This problem can be avoided by always ordering and naming fittings, lines, and devices by OD only.

Long runs of tubing must be designed to accommodate the thermal expansion of copper. Otherwise, the tubing assembly may break, buckle, leak, or damage the building structure. A temperature rise of 50°F (27.8°C) will expand a 100' (30.5 m) tube by 0.57" (1.45 cm), while a 100°F (55.6°C) rise will expand it by 1.06" (2.69 cm). Long lines need expansion joints if the tube temperature will vary much. The expansion joint can be a loop of tube (horizontal in a suction line so oil can return) or another method that allows the tube to flex.

Steel

Ammonia systems require standard-weight, black steel pipe. Connections are generally welded, using extra-heavy black steel fittings. Steel pipe is described by ID (inside diameter). Stainless steel tubing (often no. 304) is required for some food-processing applications, such as in the brewing and dairy industries.

Plastic

Plastic tubing is restricted by limitations on working temperature and pressure. Plastic tubing may be used for cold-water lines and water-cooled condensers. Polyethylene is the most common type of plastic tubing. Use black plastic tubing outdoors, where the pigment can block damaging ultraviolet light. Manufacturers will supply information on how well products resist oil, refrigerant, and other chemicals. Codes commonly restrict where each type of plastic tubing can be used.

PIPING DESIGN

A good piping design will help a system operate safely, efficiently, and under control. Pipe and system design is the province of engineers, but a few pointers will help technicians install and service equipment. The size of fittings at the compressor do not indicate the size of piping needed, since pipe size depends on many factors that the compressor manufacturer cannot know.

The piping and components in an ideal refrigerant system must meet the following goals:

Economical on energy and refrigerant—Energy should be conserved. Systems with excess refrigerant are hard to control and operate erratically. Systems with too much capacity tend to short-cycle, reducing equipment life.

Minimum noise—Undersized pipe leads to high refrigerant velocity, which creates noise.

Controlled in all demand states—The system must be able to handle minimum and maximum expected loads.

Minimal pressure drop—Pressure drop reduces capacity and wastes energy. However, enlarging the suction line to reduce pressure drop may slow refrigerant and reduce oil return to the compressor.

Observe the guidelines in Figure 7-A when installing copper tubing:

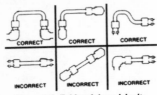

Figure 7-A: Tubing do's and don'ts
Courtesy of Imperial Eastman

- *Minimize straight-line connections*, especially in short runs. Symmetric piping systems are easier to install.
- *Support long pieces of tube*. Bolt heavy parts, including valves and fittings to prevent metal fatigue.
- *Inspect tube before installation* to check that it meets specifications in terms of diameter, wall thickness, and composition.
- *Make square cuts*, then deburr rough ends.
- *Leave sufficient straight tube* at the end of a bend (at least twice the length of a flare nut). Tubes must align to the center line of fittings.

TUBING INSULATION

Insulation is essential for reducing energy loss from refrigerant tubing and cooled spaces. Insulation is rated by "R-factor," a measure of how well an inch of material resists the passage of heat. The higher the R value, the greater the insulation value. To calculate the R rating of several layers of material, add the R values of each layer together. Cabinet manufacturers are responsible for insulating the cabinet, but cooling system technicians may be responsible for insulating the tubing.

Tubing insulation is used to reduce warming (and energy loss) and sweating (which can damage tubing, fittings, or adjacent areas) of cold refrigerant and water lines. Tubing insulation should be chosen after considering the operating temperature, chemicals in the operating environment, cost, ease of installation, ability to withstand moisture, and ability to conform to the tubing configuration.

Tubing insulation is described by material, ID, and wall thickness. Wall thickness ranges from about 1/4" (.63 cm) to 1" (2.54 cm). Heavier thicknesses are used where there is a larger ΔT between the tubing and the environment.

Some materials are designed to be used outdoors, with the proper coating, while others can be used underground. Special shapes of insulation may be available for covering fittings. Consult the manufacturer for detailed instructions on using tubing insulation.

The following two basic types of tubing insulation are used in the trade:

1. *Fiberglass* is supplied in 3' (92 cm) pieces that are split length- wise, with glue on the joining surfaces. Cover fittings with loose fiberglass, then apply a plastic preformed shroud on top. Fiberglass is harder to place over fittings than closed-cell foam. Wear a mask or respirator to prevent irritation from fiberglass fibers.

2. *Closed-cell foam* is sold in sheets, cylinders, and tape. Sheets are used to insulate flat areas, such as ducts. Cylinders are used for tubing. Some cylinders are sold preslit, with adhesive on the slit that is sealed after the cylinder is placed on the tubing. Insulation tape is handy for covering tight areas and fittings, although you can also miter cylindrical insulation to cover simple fittings like elbows.

Elastomeric material is easy to slip on and can slip over smaller fittings, such as elbows and 45° elbows. For larger fittings, use prefabricated coverings. If the insulation does not cover the entire assembly, seal gaps between the insulation and the tubing or fitting with adhesive. Closed-cell foam absorbs practically no water, resists solvents and other chemicals, and provides some protection against physical damage. In extremely humid areas, a waterproof wrapping may keep the insulation dry. Observe operating temperature restrictions.

> CAUTION: Adhesives used with these insulations are toxic, so work with adequate ventilation. Adhesive vapor is flammable, so keep flame and sparks away. The adhesive may set off an electronic leak detector, so do all leak testing before gluing the joints.

INSTALLING CLOSED-CELL FOAM

Use this procedure to cut and install elastomeric insulation to tubing in a new installation:

1. Cut the material slightly longer than the tubing lengths. Make a square cut to get a good seal with adjacent insulation.
2. Slip the insulation over the length. Glue its lengthwise mating surface.
3. Assemble the tubing.
4. Slide the insulation back from the fittings to be brazed or soldered and clamp it out of the way.
5. Make the connections without overheating the insulation.
6. After the connection is cool, remove the clamps and slide the insulation back into position.
7. Insulate the fitting.
8. Use the manufacturer's adhesive to seal all insulation joints.

To install elastomeric insulation on an *existing system:*

1. Cut the material slightly longer than the tubing lengths, using a square cut to permit a good seal between sections.
2. Slit the lengths and slip them over the tubing.
3. Insulate the fittings, using prefabricated pieces if available or by mitering standard pieces.
4. Apply sealant to all joints and slits in the insulation and press together.

FITTINGS

Fittings are used to connect adjacent lengths of tubing and pipe. In ACR work, most fittings connect with brazing or flaring, although threads are used on water pipes and small pipes. As mentioned earlier, larger ammonia systems use welded steel fittings.

Copper fittings are available in short-, medium-, and long-radius configurations. In cooling system work, long radius is best because it presents lower resistance to fluid flow, and a smaller pressure drop. Wrought fittings resist pressurized refrigerant vapor better than cast fittings.

A vast number of fittings are made for various applications, with a standard terminology for describing fittings and reducing confusion. The safest procedure is to always specify fittings by OD. (See Table 7-B.)

Table 7-B: Common Fitting Varieties

Class	Use	Common varieties	Sample identification	Comments
Extension or joining	Connect same-size pipe or tube	Coupling	⅞-inch OD solder coupling	Two female ends.
		Nipple	¾-inch by 4inch nipple	Connects fittings—has two male ends. From "close"—all threaded, to 6 inches.
	Removable connection of tube or pipe	Union	⅞-inch OD solder union	Both ends are sweat fittings; also available with one sweat, one threaded.
Reducing or enlarging	Connect different size pipe or tube	Reducing coupling	⅞-inch OD solder by ⅝-inch OD solder coupling	
	Connects threaded pipe to sweated tube	Adaptor	⅞-inch OD solder by ¾-inch pipe thread (NPT)	
Directional	Change direction of a pipe	Elbow (ell)	⅞-inch OD solder ell	Elbows come in three radii—short, medium or long. Long-radius should be used in refrigeration

				because they cause less pressure drop.
		Street elbow	7/8-inch OD solder street ell	Has one male end and one female end.
	Connects two sizes of tube	Reducing elbow	7/8-inch OD solder by 5/8-inch OD solder ell	
	Makes a 45° bend	45° elbow	7/8-inch OD solder 45°	Also made in street variety.
Branching	Join three or more tubes at one point	Tee	7/8-inch OD solder tee (all tubes same size)	
	Three tubes, two tube sizes	Reducing tee	7/8-inch OD by 5/8-inch OD (reducing tee with constant run)	Specify the run first and then the branching size.
	Three tubes, three tube sizes	Reducing tee	7/8-inch OD by 5/8-inch OD by 7/8-inch OD	Specify the two run sizes first and then the branching size.
Shut off or closing	Closes end on tube or pipe	Cap	7/8-inch OD cap	Female.
	For threaded only	Plug	3/4-inch plug	Male.
Flange	Connects pipe to equipment	Flange	2-1/8-inch OD solder flange	Specified by pipe OD.

MANY OTHER FITTINGS ARE AVAILABLE, FOLLOWING THIS GENERAL NOMENCLATURE.

ELBOWS, TEES, UNIONS AND 45° CAN BE USED AS SOLDER-TO-THREAD ADAPTORS. TO SPECIFY, YOU MUST DESCRIBE WHICH END IS SOLDERED AND WHICH IS THREADED. FOR EXAMPLE, 7/8-INCH OD SOLDER BY 3/4-INCH MPT (MALE PIPE THREAD).

NOTE: FOR PURPOSES OF THIS MANUAL, TUBE IS CONNECTED BY SOLDERING OR BRAZING; PIPE IS CONNECTED BY THREADS OR WELDS (FOR AMMONIA SYSTEMS).

1. *Flare fittings* are often used with soft copper, in relatively small sizes (usually under 3/4" [1.9 cm] OD) The flare must be a 45° flare, not the 37° flare used in other trades. Flare fittings are described by the tubing OD, not the thread size: a 1/4" OD flare nut connects 1/4" OD tubing to 1/4" OD flare fitting. Fitting nuts have hexagonal flats that are turned with a standard open-end wrench.

   In cold connections, capillary action can draw water between the flare nut and the tubing. (See Figure 7-B.) If this water freezes, it can compress and destroy the tube. Alleviate this problem by 1) drilling through the flare nut, 2) using a flare nut with built-in water passages, or 3) using a special, short flare nut, which has no room for frost.

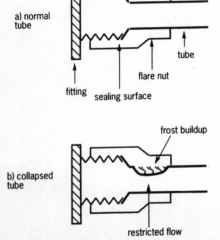

Figure 7-B: Flared tube collapsing under frost

2. *Threaded fittings* in refrigeration work are used mainly for water lines and the smaller sizes of ammonia piping. Threaded fittings have either coarse or fine thread.
   • *Coarse thread* is called pipe thread (NP, or National Pipe).

- *Fine thread* is found on Society of Automotive Engineers (SAE) fittings, which is also called National Fine (NF).

  Fittings are described by the tubing OD and thread, such as: 1/4" NP.

3. *Capillary fittings*, also called *solder, sweat,* or *wrought fittings,* are soldered or brazed to tubes. Capillary fittings are named because the filler metal flows into the joint by capillary action. These fittings are strong, easy to join, and virtually leakproof if installed properly. A tight joint requires just enough room for the filler metal to flow, so a precise gap between the fitting and the tubing must be maintained during brazing or soldering.

4. *Compression fittings* can connect plastic tubing to copper tubing. (Because polyethylene is soft, tighten these fittings gently. Polyethylene fittings are uncommon in ACR systems.)

5. *Quick-connect fittings* allow field connection of factory-charged systems without purging and charging the lines. A precharged system using these connectors would include an evaporator, a compressor, a condensing unit, and the tubing to connect them. Everything is precharged, and the suction line is ready-insulated. The quick-connect couplings have diaphragms that seal the tubing during storage and setup. A knife in each coupling cuts the diaphragm as the coupling is quickly engaged. Do not cut long tubes; this would allow air to enter. Make a horizontal coil of the excess tube (especially in a suction line, to promote oil return).

Pressure Drop

Fittings restrict fluid flow, causing pressure drop and reducing system efficiency. Minimize the number of fittings in a system, and choose fittings that allow maximum flow. When engineers design piping systems, they use a technique called "equivalent length of pipe" to determine how much restriction each fitting or component will add to the total restriction. They assume that each fitting has a resistance to fluid flow equal to that of a certain length of same-diameter tube.

To determine the total resistance of a piping circuit, an engineer simply adds the length of all straight runs to the equivalent length of pipe of all fittings. A line sizing table gives pressure drop per 100' of a particular pipe size. (See Table 7-C.) Pressure drop in complicated fittings, such as solenoid or pressure-regulating valves, should be listed in manufacturer's literature.

In practice, many engineers use a compensation factor based on experience instead of equivalent length of pipe. Thus, they might assume that a standard 100' run would have 20% to 30% restrictions, making it equivalent to 120' or 130' of straight pipe. Shorter, more complicated layouts require a higher compensation factor. Although equivalent length of pipe data primarily concerns engineers, the calculation may help if a compressor that is too small for a system is suspected.

Table 7-C: Equivalent Length of Pipe for Common Fittings

OD, In. Line Size	Globe Valve	Angle Valve	90° Elbow	45° Elbow	Tee Line	Tee Branch
½	9	5	.9	.4	.6	2.0
⅝	12	6	1.0	.5	.8	2.5
⅞	15	8	1.5	.7	1.0	2.5
1⅛	22	12	1.8	.9	1.5	4.5
1⅜	28	15	2.4	1.2	1.8	6.0
1⅝	35	17	2.8	1.4	2.0	7.0
2⅛	45	22	3.9	1.8	3.0	10.0
2⅝	51	26	4.6	2.2	3.5	12.0
3⅛	65	34	5.5	2.7	4.5	15.0
3⅝	80	40	6.5	3.0	5.0	17.0

Liquid- and Suction-Line Sizes

Engineers use pressure-drop tables to size liquid and suction lines. Technicians, who are responsible for installing the designs, do not ordinarily need these tables. A simpler table listing line-carrying capacity (see Table 7-D) is enough to make a rough check of liquid- and suction-line sizes. Find the system refrigerant in the top row and the system BTU/hour in the left column. Read across from the BTU/hour column to find liquid-line size. Find the suction-line size under the proper temperature heading.

To do the above check, you must know the system capacity in BTU/hour (tons × 12,000 = BTU/hour). The capacity of a new system can be found in the specifications. For old systems, check the rating of the expansion valve, read the compressor nameplate, or track down literature for that model of compressor.

The liquid line should be somewhat oversized if the exact capacity is not listed on the chart. If the suction line is not listed for the exact capacity, go down in size a bit to speed up the suction line and ensure oil return.

Table 7-D: Carrying Capacity of Pipe

Btu. Per Hour	Refrigerant 12			Refrigerant 22			Refrigerant 502		
	Liquid Line	Suction Line		Liquid Line	Suction Line		Liquid Line	Suction Line	
		5°F	40°F		5°F	40°F		5°F	40°F
3,000	¼	½	½	¼	½	½	¼	½	½
6,000	⅜	⅝	⅝	⅜	⅝	⅝	⅜	⅝	⅝
9,000	⅜	⅞	⅝	⅜	⅞	⅝	⅜	⅞	⅝
12,000	⅜	1⅛	⅞	⅜	⅞	⅞	⅜	⅞	⅞
15,000	⅜	1⅛	⅞	⅜	1⅛	⅞	⅜	1⅛	⅞
18,000	⅜	1⅛	⅞	⅜	1⅛	⅞	⅜	1⅛	⅞
21,000	½	1⅛	1⅛	½	1⅛	1⅛	½	1⅛	1⅛
24,000	½	1⅜	1⅛	½	1⅛	1⅛	½	1⅛	1⅛
30,000	⅝	1⅜	1⅛	½	1⅜	1⅛	⅝	1⅜	1⅛
36,000	⅝	1⅜	1⅛	⅝	1⅜	1⅛	⅝	1⅜	1⅛
42,000	⅝	1⅝	1⅜	⅝	1⅜	1⅜	⅝	1⅜	1⅜
48,000	⅝	1⅝	1⅜	⅝	1⅝	1⅜	⅝	1⅝	1⅜

Table 7-D: Carrying Capacity of Pipe (continued)

54,000	⅝	1⅝	1⅜	⅝	1⅝	1⅜	⅝	1⅝	1⅜
60,000	⅞	1⅝	1⅜	⅝	1⅝	1⅜	⅞	1⅝	1⅜
72,000	⅞	2⅛	1⅝	⅞	1⅝	1⅜	⅞	1⅝	1⅜
96,000	⅞	2⅛	1⅝	⅞	2⅛	1⅝	⅞	2⅛	1⅝
108,000	⅞	2⅝	2⅛	⅞	2⅛	1⅝	⅞	2⅛	1⅝
120,000	⅞	2⅝	2⅛	⅞	2⅛	1⅝	⅞	2⅛	1⅝
150,000	1⅛	2⅝	2⅛	⅞	2⅛	2⅛	1⅛	2⅛	2⅛
180,000	1⅛	2⅝	2⅛	1⅛	2⅝	2⅛	1⅛	2⅝	2⅛
210,000	1⅛	3⅛	2⅛	1⅛	2⅝	2⅛	1⅛	2⅝	2⅛
240,000	1⅜	3⅛	2⅝	1⅜	2⅝	2⅛	1⅜	2⅝	2⅛
300,000	1⅜	3⅛	2⅝	1⅜	3⅛	2⅝	1⅜	3⅛	2⅝
360,000	1⅜	3⅝	2⅝	1⅛	3⅛	2⅝	1⅜	3⅛	2⅝
420,000	1⅝	3⅝	3⅛	1⅜	3⅛	2⅝	1⅝	3⅛	2⅝
480,000	1⅝	4⅛	3⅛	1⅝	3⅛	3⅛	1⅝	3⅝	3⅛
540,000	1⅝	4⅛	3⅛	1⅝	3⅝	3⅛	1⅝	3⅝	3⅛
600,000	1⅝	4⅞	3⅛	1⅝	4⅛	3⅛	1⅝	4⅛	3⅛

TO CONVERT BTU PER HOUR TO TONS OF REFRIGERATION—DIVIDE BY 12,000.
SUCTION TEMPERATURE, CONDENSING MEDIUM, COMPRESSOR DESIGN AND MANY OTHER FACTORS DETERMINE HORSE-POWER REQUIRED FOR A TON OF REFRIGERATING CAPACITY. CONSULT ASHRAE HANDBOOK.

Courtesy of Mueller Industries, Inc.

VALVES

A wide variety of valves are used in cooling systems. Refrigerant piping requires shut-off, solenoid, and three-way valves. Heat pumps use a four-way valve. Water-cooled condenser systems and chiller distribution systems also have plumbing valves.

> TIP: It is a good idea to "crack" a valve open when opening it for the first time: open it one-quarter turn or less, then immediately close it. Cracking protects against unexpected rushes of pressure in a system with very high pressure or a malfunctioning valve.

Valves can be categorized as low resistance (gate, ball, plug, and butterfly) or high resistance (globe or angle). In addition, valves are described by the following important aspects:

1. *Flow characteristic* is the relationship between valve handle position and flow rate. The characteristic can be varied by altering the actuator mechanism or the internal valve mechanism. In *linear flow* characteristic, each turn of the handle produces the same increase in flow. In *quick-opening* characteristic, the first turn opens the valve more than the second turn, and so on. Quick-opening is useful for on-off valves.

2. *Rangeability* is the ratio of maximum controllable flow to minimum controllable flow. The higher the rangeability, the better the control of low flows, and the higher the price.

3. *Tight shut-off* is the ability to close with virtually no leakage. Single-seated valves have better shut-off than double-seated valves.

4. *Cavitation* is the creation of bubbles in a valve due to pressure drop after a restriction (flash gas is a type of cavitation). The repeated formation and implosion of bubbles after they reach higher pressure causes tiny shock waves that can fatigue and ruin the valve.

5. *Maximum fluid pressure and temperature* are rated by the manufacturer to reflect all aspects of valve construction. The nominal body rating is not reliable for this purpose because some components of the valve may be weaker than the body.

6. *Pressure drop* is the difference between upstream and downstream pressure.

Valve Construction

Valves have four basic types of construction:

1. A *single-seated valve* is capable of tight shut-off, although it needs more control force than a double-seated valve. Single-seated valves may have a diaphragm inside the valve body and between the stem and the seat so turning the stem will not open the valve when there's a vacuum in the line.

2. A *double-seated valve* is designed to minimize closing force and maximize opening area. However, it does not shut off as well as a single-seated valve.

3. A *three-way mixing valve* has two inlets and one outlet. The stem regulates the proportion of inlet A to inlet B.

4. A *three-way diverting valve* has one inlet and two outlets. The stem regulates flow to either or both outlets. An example is a compressor service valve.

Check Valve

Check valves (see Figure 7-C) allow fluids to flow in only one direction. They are used to prevent a backflow of refrigerant in hot-gas defrost cycles and during compressor shutdowns. Damaged check valves may fail to reseat and make a hammering sound.

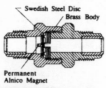

Figure 7-C: Check valve

Condenser Pressure Regulator

A condenser pressure regulator (also called a *holdback valve*, a *head pressure control*, a *limitizer*, or a *condenser limiter*) maintains high-side pressure so enough pressure drop will occur at the metering device. The valve can be damaged by pressure fluctuation and should be protected by being located at the condenser outlet, not at the inlet.

The condenser pressure regulator helps maintain head pressure during low ambient temperatures. The valve can be set to nearly fill the condenser with refrigerant, thus reducing the area available for condensing during these conditions. (See Chapter 8, "Whole Systems.")

Crankcase Pressure Regulator (CPR)

This modulating valve (also called the *suction pressure regulator*) limits the supply and pressure of refrigerant to the crankcase, to limit compressor loading during motor startup. The valve (see Figure 7-D) responds only to outlet (suction) pressure from its position in the suction line near the compressor. The valve remains closed as long as crankcase pressure is above the valve setting. When the compressor lowers the crankcase pressure (after a defrost cycle or a normal off cycle), the valve opens and admits suction gas to the crankcase, but only after the motor has finished starting. When the compressor shuts down, pressure in the compressor rises and the valve closes.

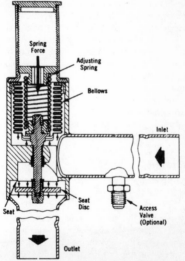

Figure 7-D: Crankcase pressure regulator
Courtesy of Sporlan Division of Parker Hannifin, Inc.

Three factors influence the choice of a crankcase pressure regulator:

1. Design suction pressure
2. Maximum allowable suction pressure
3. Pressure drop across the valve

An equal amount of inlet pressure is exerted on the top of the seat disk and on the bellows so the valve can be controlled by the relationship between the adjusting-spring pressure and the outlet pressure on the bottom of the seat disk. This allows the valve to modulate crankcase pressure.

Evaporator Pressure Regulator (Two-Temperature Valve)

This valve controls pressure and temperature in the warmer evaporator(s) of a system with several evaporators, and is especially useful if the evaporators run at different temperatures. The regulator prevents the compressor from creating excessive vacuum in the warmer evaporator. The valve balances pressure among several evaporators running at the same temperature but with different loads, and also maintains pressure during minimum load.

Most evaporator pressure regulators (also called *two-temperature*, *constant-temperature*, or *pressure-reducer valves*) are installed in the suction line of the warmer evaporators. These valves close the suction line when evaporator pressure drops below the set point. A second type of regulator is located in the liquid line of the warmer evaporator. This valve uses a solenoid to shut off refrigerant supply when the evaporator reaches operating temperature. It is opened by electricity and closed by pressure.

Pressure-Operated

Pressure-operated two-temperature valves use a bellows or diaphragm to detect pressure in the warm evaporator. (See Figure 7-G1.) This valve has two basic varieties:

1. A *metering-type valve* throttles the opening in the suction line in response to pressure variation in the evaporator. A spring is the only adjustment mechanism. Because the valve has no differential, it responds directly to pressure without any lag. In larger systems, this valve uses a solenoid to open and close a pilot line because the pressure differential is too small to move the sealing faces. (See Figure 7-G2.)

2. The *snap-action valve* opens and closes without intermediate steps. The valve is commonly used with fixtures with similar temperatures or in systems that defrost each piping circuit.

Repairing Pressure-Operated Two-Temperature Valves

Pressure-operated two-temperature valves can have four types of problems. The valve may:

- Leak past the seat, reducing temperature in the warmer evaporator. This can also be due to maladjustment, but if a valve that has not been adjusted recently is no longer preventing low temperature, it is probably leaking.

- Stick closed. This is indicated by a warm evaporator when the other evaporators are cooling properly. A clogged screen can cause the same symptoms.

- Be out of adjustment. Readjust by turning the adjusting nut 1/2 turn at a time and monitoring the results for 15 minutes.

- Have frosted bellows. Frosted valves cannot work smoothly. Move the valve to a warmer location and/or coat it with grease to inhibit frost.

A shut-off and a gauge opening in the suction line are great conveniences for repairing a pressure-operated two-temperature valve. Use the opening to measure pressure in the suction line while making adjustments. Use an electrical meter to test an electronic pressure-regulating valve; consult the manufacturer for details.

Temperature-Operated

Temperature-operated two-temperature valves use a sensing element to detect air or surface temperature in the warmest cabinet. These valves come in two categories:

1. a. The sensing bulb is connected by capillary tube to the valve bellows. The overall mechanism is similar to a thermostatic expansion valve. Cooling the bulb causes the plunger to close the suction line. As the evaporator warms, increasing pressure in the capillary tube forces the bellows to open the valve, allowing the compressor to again pull down evaporator pressure and temperature. Thermostatic valves are modulating valves that can throttle the opening.

1. b. An electronic version of the thermostatically operated two-temperature valve contains a solenoid-operated valve to modulate the suction pressure. A line from the high-side may provide actuating power to the valve. (See Figures 7-G.) Several electronic two-temperature valves can be controlled by a panel board, which can, in turn, accept input from a defrost timer.

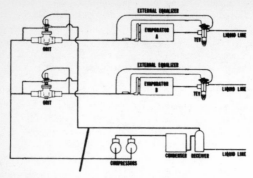

1) Pressure-operated, modulating-type, two-temperature valve, shown with parallel compressors. The pilot line reads suction pressure.

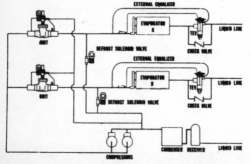

2) Temperature-sensing, solenoid-operated valve with hot-gas defrost.
"ORIT" means "open on rise of temperature"
"SORIT" means "solenoid-open on rise of temperature"

Figure 7-E: Pressure-operated two-temperature valve in system
Courtesy of Sporlan Division of Parker Hannifin, Inc.

2. A solenoid two-temperature valve is connected to a thermostat in the cabinet, near the metering device (See Figure 7-E2). Unlike other two-temperature valves, this valve shuts off refrigerant supply to the evaporator. The motor runs as long as any fixture needs cooling. As each evaporator reaches proper temperature, a separate solenoid valve shuts off refrigerant supply. When all fixtures are properly cooled, the motor shuts off. The solenoid is normally closed. When the temperature rises, the thermostat energizes the solenoid coil, and the valve opens. A check valve in the suction line keeps out high-pressure gases from other evaporators.

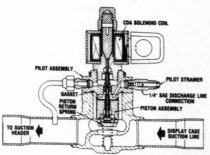

Figure 7-F: Fluid in the pilot line helps operate this two-temperature valve. Pilot-operated two-temperature valves are used on any system with a large pressure difference between inlet and outlet.

Courtesy of Sporlan Division of Parker Hannifin, Inc.

Temperature-operated two-temperature valves face the same type of troubles as thermostatic expansion valves: pinched capillary tubes, poor contact between the sensor and the evaporator, loss of sensor charge, frosted bellows, and maladjustment. Repairs should address the problem at hand.

Heat Pump Four-Way Valve

A heat pump uses a four-way valve to switch operation between heating and cooling. The valve directs the hot gas to the proper heat exchanger, according to the system's job at the moment, and also directs hot gas to de-ice the outside heat exchanger in winter.

The slide in the four-way valve shown in Figure 7-G1 is moved by a pressure difference controlled by the solenoid-operated pilot valve. The pilot valve is connected to the suction line and sometimes also the discharge line. If the four-way valve has bleed holes in the slide, it need only be connected to the suction line. An electric signal causes the pilot valve to direct suction to either side of the main-valve's slide.

Because the body of the main valve contains discharge pressure, the slide moves, causing discharge to reach the correct heat exchanger. At the same time, the slide connects the suction to the other heat exchanger.

Diagnosing Problems

A few quick checks can help isolate problems in a four-way valve:

1. *Check tube temperature.* The compressor discharge line and the line between the valve body and the heat exchanger that is serving as condenser should be hot. The suction line and the line from the current evaporator to the four-way valve should be cold. The two capillaries from the pilot valve to the valve body should be about as warm as the valve body.

2. *Inspect for damage.* Check for pinches or other problems in the capillaries. Inspect the valve body for dents, deep scratches, or signs of overheating during installation.

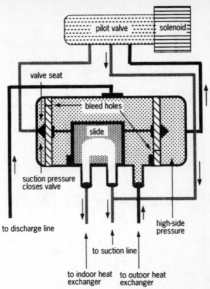

Figure 7-G1: Heat pump four-way valve in cooling mode. Discharge gas goes to the outdoor heat exchanger; the indoor heat exchanger is connected to the suction line.

3. *Check electrical supply to the pilot valve coil.* The valve may require energy during heating or cooling, depending on system design. Pilot valves that are energized during cooling will also be energized during defrost. A click should be heard when the valve is energized.

4. *Check system charge.* Undercharge can cause malfunction.

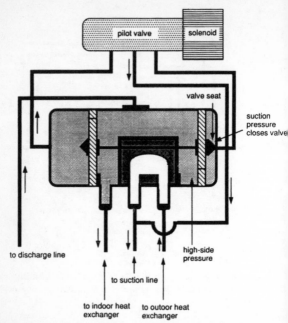

Figure 7-G2: Heat pump four-way valve in heating mode. Discharge gas goes to the indoor heat exchanger; the outdoor heat exchanger is connected to the suction line.

Even if the pilot valve operates, the four-way valve may still fail due to dirt in a bleeder hole. De-energize the solenoid, increase the head pressure, and reenergize the solenoid to blast out the dirt. If this fails, disassemble the valve and wash it. Use air pressure to check operation before reinstalling. Add a strainer in the tube feeding the valve.

If the pilot tubes are plugged, raise the head pressure and operate the valve a few times. If this fails, replace the valve. If the valve starts to reverse but cannot complete the stroke, check the operating pressures and charge. A valve with smaller ports may be needed.

Pressure Limiter

A pressure limiter is a safety that prevents evaporator pressure from exceeding an upper limit. The limiter is used in special applications, such as one compressor feeding several evaporators running at different temperatures (as in freezers and refrigerators running on a single compressor).

Relief Valve

A relief valve opens when pressure or temperature in a vessel exceeds safe levels due to fire, electrical or control problems, or any other reason. Dangerous pressure can build up quickly in components that are flooded with liquid refrigerant. Flooding can occur even in vessels that normally contain a large percentage of vapor (such as receivers, flooded evaporators, and liquid-line driers with a bypass). These vessels are also subject to explosive forces from thermal expansion.

A relief-valve setup should:

- be suitable to the refrigerant and have enough capacity to meet the code (Valves are rated by cfm or pounds per minute discharge rate.);

- have a discharge tube that meets code requirements for length and inside diameter; and

- not be discharged during installation or pressure testing of the system.

The relief valve is usually installed on a receiver, although it may be located on a condenser or a flooded evaporator. All relief valves should connect to lines that vent the escaping refrigerant to the outdoors. In ammonia systems, however, the relief should be piped to a water tank to absorb the ammonia and prevent its escape.

The National Refrigeration Code and many local codes require relief valves in ACR units above certain capacities. ANSI/ASHRAE standards require that pressure-relief devices be capable of protecting against over-pressurization. Sizing of pressure relief devices is given in the *American Society of Mechanical Engineers Boiler and Pressure Code Refrigeration Handbook*, which states:

- No device is required on a pressure vessel with a capacity of 3 cubic feet (85 liters) or less if the inside diameter is less than 3" (7.62 cm).

- Devices with internal gross volume of 3 cubic feet or more require protection. These devices may not use fusible plugs for protection.

- A pressure vessel with a capacity of at least 10 cubic feet (283 liters) requires a three-way valve connected to two pressure relief valves, each of which is large enough to vent the system by itself.
- No stop valve is permitted between the relief valve and the vessel, except in systems with multiple reliefs.
- In such a case, the stop valve may not be installed where it could shut off all relief valves.

1. *Fusible plugs* contain a compound that melts when the receiver temperature exceeds a safe level. When the plug melts, all the refrigerant escapes to the air.

2. A *rupture-type device* (or *rupture disk*) usually contains a disk of silver set to rupture when pressure exceeds the rating. Disks may be rated from 175 to 1,000 psi (1,310 to 6,997 kPa). Rupture disks should be chosen to blow at 50% above static system pressure or 100% above pulsating system pressure. Rupture disks may be used on vessels of any size.

3. A *spring-loaded (pop) valve* has springs that counteract system pressure. The advantages are low cost, simplicity, high discharge capacity, and the ability to reclose after the pressure drops, thus saving some refrigerant. The difference between opening and reclosing pressure is called "blowdown." Closing pressures may be 10% to 20% below opening setting. After adjusting the valve to the desired setting, wire the valve seal tight to prevent tampering. Spring-loaded valves are affected by back pressure in their discharge line; do not install a rupture disk at the outlet of a spring-loaded relief.

4. *Diaphragm-type spring-loaded relief valves* use an indirect linkage, so system pressure pushes on the diaphragm, not directly on the valve. The action is little affected by back pressure, and this valve may discharge into the low side of the system, saving refrigerant in case of an overpressure. A diaphragm valve has a relatively high initial cost and lower discharge capacity than a comparable pop valve.

5. A *three-way valve connected to two relief devices* is required on larger vessels. The valve allows for placement of one relief in service and removal of the other for inspection or repair. Normally, the three-way valve has one relief in service and the other in reserve.

Foreign matter hampers valve reseating after discharge, but filters or screens are not permitted between the vessel and the relief. Relief valves may need cleaning, repair, or replacement after discharge. A periodic maintenance program is recommended for a relief system, with regular replacement of rupture elements and the return of relief valves to the manufacturer for inspection and resetting.

Service Valves

Service valves are used in diagnosis, repair, recharging, and other service operations. Both one- and two-way valves are used. One-way valves, which open and control the flow between two ports, can shut off parts of the system to remove or repair components. An example is the king valve at the condenser outlet. Two-way valves have one inlet and two outlets. Either or both outlets can be open to the inlet, depending on the valve setting. Examples are the discharge- and suction-service valves. (See Figure 7-H.)

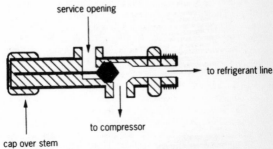

service opening

to refrigerant line

to compressor

cap over stem

Figure 7-H: Three-way suction-service valve (shown backseated)

Use protective caps and plugs to protect the valve stem area from contamination. Service valves are mounted at the suction and discharge ports on compressors in open and some hermetic systems. The valves are fully open when the system is running normally. Most service valves are the "backseating" types—meaning that the valve is seated against the rear seat in operating position. This helps prevent leaks through the valve packing.

Service valves are sometimes found on the receiver, where they can be used to isolate refrigerant during repair or system pumpdown. Other possible locations include the liquid line or suction line.

In a system without service valves, a line-piercing valve for service operations may be installed. These valves clamp to the line, pierce the tubing, and allow installation of a gauge manifold or charging hose. Some clamps have a positive stop to prevent over-piercing. After service, close the valve and leave it in place.

Using a Service Valve

To use a service valve, remove the cap, loosen the packing nut one full turn, and clean and oil the valve stem. Then crack the nut about 1/8 turn. This will prevent a rush of fluid, which could damage gauges, flush excess oil, or cause injury. Do not crack the valve with a ratchet wrench, as the valve may have to be closed quickly. Oil the hose threads before fitting them to the valve. When finished, seat the valve and retighten the packing nut, then replace the cap. If severe corrosion of the valve is anticipated, fill the valve body with the system oil before refitting the cap.

Solenoid Valves

Solenoid valves are magnetically operated valves that work by remote control. The valve can be a shut-off or a three-way valve. In a solenoid, wires are wound around a core to make an electromagnet. Inside the coil is a plunger made of a magnetic material, usually iron. When electricity flows through the coil, the magnet attracts the plunger and pulls it toward the center of the coil. When the current is removed, the plunger responds to other forces, such as a spring, fluid pressure, or gravity. (See Figure 7-I.) To increase opening force, the plunger has some free travel before it contacts the valve stem.

The plunger in a solenoid valve is connected to the valve needle or another apparatus that controls flow. A solenoid valve may be normally open (NO) or normally closed (NC). An NO valve is open when power is off, and closed when power is on. The reverse is true of a NC valve. In some valves, a manual stem may operate the valve if electric current is absent.

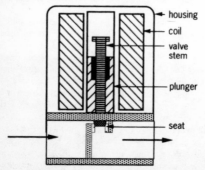

Figure 7-I: Normally closed solenoid valve (shown closed)

In small systems, a simple, direct-acting solenoid valve may work if the magnet is strong enough to move the valve. In large systems, a pilot-operated solenoid valve is often used: The solenoid closes a pilot valve, which causes discharge pressure to pressurize a diaphragm that closes the main valve.

Solenoid valves should be selected based on:

- The fluid in the system
- Operating temperature
- Pipe capacity
- Maximum operating pressure differential (inlet pressure—outlet pressure)
- Electrical control system (AC or DC, hertz, and voltage)
- Valve maximum pressure (must be above system working pressure)

When installing a solenoid valve, pay attention to the flow-direction arrow on the body. A strainer is helpful for keeping the valve clean. When brazing, keep the valve body as cool as possible by using a low flame and draping wet rags or chill blocks over the valve. Do not over-torque the valve during assembly.

8

Whole Systems

Air conditioning and refrigeration systems are more than individual components—they are systems that must work together. In this chapter, we deal with typical systems. We explain the absorption cycle and then discuss common variations on the vapor-compression system. We describe defrost systems, the pumpdown cycle, and cold-weather operation; give hints for selecting and installing components; and conclude with information on estimating, installing, and servicing comfort-cooling and commercial refrigeration as entire systems.

ABSORPTION CYCLE

The absorption cycle uses heat instead of mechanical compression to energize the cooling cycle. Absorption systems usually have two interconnected loops: one for the absorber and one for the refrigerant. The absorber loop runs from the generator through the separator and the absorber and back to the generator. The refrigerant loop runs from the generator through the separator, condenser, evaporator, absorber, and back to the generator.

The two major absorption systems use (1) ammonia as the refrigerant and water as the absorber, or (2) water as refrigerant and lithium bromide as the absorber. Table 8-A lists operating conditions for these systems:

Table 8-A: Pressure-Temperature in Absorption Systems

Component	Pressure-temperature ammonia		Pressure-temperature lithium bromide	
Generator	290 psi 290°F	2103 kPa 143°C	1.5 psia 210°F	10.34 kPa 99°C
Condenser	290 psi 122°F	2103 kPa 50°C	1.5 psia 115°F	10.34 kPa 46.1°C
Evaporator	52 psi 36°F	462 kPa 2.2°C	29.6" Hg 40°F	1.1 kPa 4.4°C
Absorber	52 psi 190°F	462 kPa 87.8°C	.15 psia 105°F	1.03 kPa 40.6°C

Heat for the boiler can come from steam, fossil fuels, cogeneration, or, occasionally, electricity. Ammonia systems typically operate at pressures up to

400 psi (about 2,800 kPa), so welded steel is the preferred construction material. Ammonia reacts with copper, which cannot be used in components or tubing.

Ammonia-water absorption systems are used in comfort-cooling and refrigeration. The lithium bromide-water system works at very low temperatures and pressures and is used primarily in industrial applications. Both systems have similar actions and components, although the details vary by manufacturer and application.

Capacity control is simple. A thermostat senses the temperature of the chilled air or water leaving the evaporator. As temperature drops toward the set point, heat is gradually reduced at the generator, so a weaker solution is pumped from the concentrator to the absorber. This weaker solution can absorb less refrigerant vapor from the evaporator, so less warm-vapor refrigerant goes to the condenser.

Terminology

Understanding the unique language of absorption systems (see Figure 8-A) will be helpful.

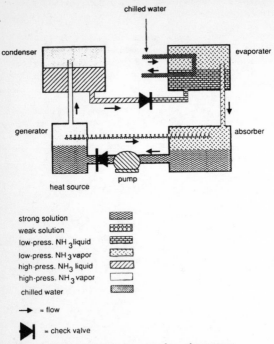

Figure 8-A: Ammonia-water absorption system

Components

Absorber—The low-side vessel where low-pressure refrigerant vapor dissolves in the strong solution of absorber. Some heat of dissolving is dissipated to the surroundings or the cooling water.

Condenser—The high-side vessel where refrigerant condenses, losing the heat of condensation to the surroundings.

Evaporator—The low-side vessel where liquid refrigerant evaporates, cools the load, and flows to the absorber.

Generator—The high-side vessel where the strong solution is heated and forced to the separator. Also called the *boiler*.

Separator—The high-side vessel where refrigerant vapor is liberated from the weak solution. High-pressure refrigerant flows as a vapor toward the condenser; a weak solution of absorbent flows toward the absorber. The separator may be a part of the generator or a different component.

Solution pump—An optional device that moves strong solution from the absorber to the generator. The pump divides the high and low sides. Several pumps may be used.

Fluids

Ammonia—A toxic, nonflammable chemical used as refrigerant, with water as the absorber.

Hydrogen—A light, insoluble, flammable gas that increases the boiling of ammonia. It's found in a circuit between the evaporator and the absorber in some water-ammonia systems, but not in lithium-bromide systems.

Lithium bromide—A nonflammable, stable substance used as the absorber, with water as refrigerant. It is corrosive in contact with air, and damages the eyes, skin, and mucus membranes.

Strong solution—Solution of cool absorber with great (strong) ability to absorb refrigerant. Flows from the absorber to the generator.

Weak solution—Solution of refrigerant and absorber with little (weak) ability to absorb refrigerant. Flows from the generator to the absorber.

One way to understand the absorption cycle is to compare its components with those of the vapor-compression cycle. (See Table 8-B.) A fundamental difference is that the absorption cycle has far fewer moving parts than the vapor-compression cycle, and it may operate at uniform pressure throughout the system. In other words, although we talk of "high" and "low" sides, they don't always exist.

Table 8-B: Absorption Versus Vapor-Compression Cycles

Cycle	Energy Source	Energy Input to	Heat Removed at	Refrigerant
Vapor-compression	Electricity	Compressor	Compressor and condenser	Halocarbon or ammonia
Absorption	Fuel, steam, or electricity	Generator (boiler)	Absorber and condenser	Ammonia or water

Water-Ammonia Cycle

This system cycles solutions of water (the absorber) and ammonia (the refrigerant). The water dissolves ammonia at low temperatures; at higher temperatures the ammonia comes out of solution. Absorption cycles have two interlocking loops of fluids: one for ammonia, the other for water. A third loop sometimes contains hydrogen gas. The system disposes of unwanted heat from the absorber and the condenser.

The cycle begins in the generator, also called the boiler, where a cool, strong solution of ammonia in water is heated and driven by convection to a separating device. As the solution warms, it becomes a weak solution (warm liquids dissolve less gas). In the separator, the ammonia leaves solution. When it enters the condenser, the ammonia loses the heat of condensation to the condensing medium and condenses, just like refrigerant vapor in the condenser of a vapor-compression system. The liquid ammonia enters the evaporator after passing through a liquid trap that keeps hydrogen gas in the evaporator and out of the condenser.

In the evaporator, the liquid ammonia enters an atmosphere with a high concentration of hydrogen. According to Dalton's law of partial pressures, the total gas pressure is the sum of the pressures of hydrogen and ammonia. Therefore, even though total pressure on the ammonia may be the same as elsewhere in the system, it is low enough for the ammonia to evaporate. This evaporation cools the gas, and more heat migrates from the surroundings, causing evaporation to continue, as in the vapor-compression cycle.

As the ammonia gas warms and evaporates, it travels to the absorber. A stream of weak solution from the separator is cooled in the absorber (or on the way to it) and gains ability (becomes a strong solution) to absorb vapor. The heat liberated during absorption is dumped to the surroundings. After the ammonia is absorbed, the strong solution flows back to the generator to repeat the cycle. Because hydrogen is virtually insoluble in water, it passes through the absorber and returns to the evaporator, flowing in the opposite direction as the refrigerant.

Some systems have a pump to create a high side (generator and condenser) and a low side (absorber and evaporator). The pump circulates strong solution from the absorber to the generator. A check valve, liquid trap, or another means is used to maintain the pressure difference: high side, 200 to 300 psi (1,482 to 2,172 kPa); low side, 40 to 60 psi (379 to 517 kPa).

The hydrogen loop is closed by a liquid trap at the entrance to the evaporator, and at the absorber because hydrogen cannot dissolve in water. Hydrogen occurs only between the evaporator and the absorber. The higher the hydrogen pressure, the colder the boiling ammonia.

Lithium Bromide-Water Cycle

In this system, water is the refrigerant and lithium bromide is the absorber. With a very low system pressure, the water boils in the evaporator at a very cold temperature. Lithium bromide systems can be used in heating-cooling equipment as well as industrial refrigeration. In other respects, the cycle parallels the water-ammonia cycle, except that water is the refrigerant instead of the absorber. The absorber and the condenser are cooled by water, which generally is piped to a cooling tower and recycled.

The higher the concentration of lithium bromide, the thicker the solution will be. Lithium bromide can crystallize. While crystals interfere with operation until they dissolve, they are unlikely to harm the equipment. Each manufacturer has its own method of preventing crystallization; so make sure to understand the one being used. Octyl alcohol is sometimes added to the charge to act as a wetting agent to reduce surface tension. A lithium bromide system can use two pumps to move the solutions and create a high and a low side.

Safety

Ammonia-water systems operate under pressures as high as 400 psi. Ammonia is toxic, making it hard to breathe, and it harms eyes and skin. Hydrogen is highly flammable. Follow these hints:

- Be especially cautious about leaks.
- Never cut or drill into the piping.
- Check the gas pipes supplying fuel to the generator. Use soapsuds, not a flame, to check for gas leaks.
- Check the flame safety valve by smothering the flame and waiting for the shut-off valve to close. If it does not close promptly, repair or replace the shut-off.
- Place ammonia systems outdoors to prevent leaking ammonia from injuring people. For more on ammonia safety, see Chapter 9, "Refrigerants."

TYPES OF VAPOR-COMPRESSION SYSTEMS

Many system types can be built around the components of a vapor-compression (or "mechanical") refrigeration system. These systems can be classified as "self-contained," with all components housed within a single enclosure, or "remote" ("split"), with the major components in several locations.

Another important classification for systems concerns the housing for the compressor and motor. (See Table 8-C.) In "open" systems, the motor drives the compressor by a coupling or belt. "Semihermetic" systems place the motor and compressor inside a gasketed housing that may be opened for service. A "hermetic" system (see Figure 8-B) houses these two components inside a single vessel that cannot be opened. The motor and compressor must be replaced together if either fails.

Table 8-C: Categories of Vapor-Compression Systems

System Type	Advantages	Disadvantages
Open	Accessible for service; adaptable	Crankshaft seal likely to leak and must be designed and installed properly; must provide cooling to compressor and motor
Semihermetic	May be disassembled for service; no crankshaft seal to leak; good cooling to compressor and motor by suction gas; sold as "made-up" system—easier to install	Difficult (but possible) to open system for service
Hermetic	No crankshaft leakage; requires little assembly; inexpensive	Hard to service; motor-compressor is a throwaway item (i.e., for small residential units)

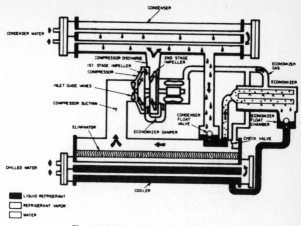

Figure 8-B: Hermetic centrifugal system
Courtesy of Carrier Corporation, Division of United Technologies Corporation

Another classification of vapor-compression systems reflects the type of metering device. (For details on these controls, see Chapter 4, "Controls.")

A *capillary tube* has a small ID, which restricts the flow of refrigerant. Cabinet temperature is controlled by a thermostat in the cabinet. The system is common in small residential and commercial refrigeration and comfort-cooling systems. (See Figure 8-C.)

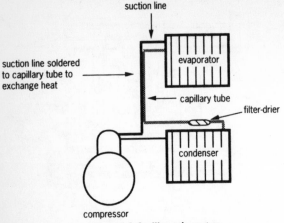

Figure 8-C: Capillary tube system

The motor need not have a high starting torque because high- and low-side pressures equalize during the off cycle. Because the capillary tube has no moving parts, the major hazard is plugging by debris or damage. The refrigerant charge must be measured accurately (a "critical charge") to prevent problems due to low charge or slugs of liquid refrigerant reaching the compressor. To prevent slugging, an accumulator is often installed in the suction line.

An *automatic expansion valve* (AXV or AEV) between the liquid line and the evaporator maintains the desired evaporator pressure. The valve automatically opens when the compressor pulls on the suction line, causing evaporator pressure to drop. The motor thermostat can be clamped to the evaporator near the suction line. When the evaporator is cool enough, the thermostat shuts down the motor. The motor starts again when the cabinet warms up and trips the thermostat. (See Figure 8-D.) An oil separator is not necessary, but the motor usually must be able to start under load. A serious leak in the AXV may allow liquid refrigerant into the evaporator, causing floodback.

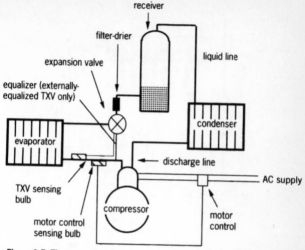

Figure 8-D: Thermostatic- or automatic-expansion valve refrigerant control

A *thermostatic expansion valve* (TXV or TEV) is a common and effective way to control refrigerant flow. The TXV, placed on the evaporator inlet, responds to evaporator pressure *and* suction-line temperature-pressure. The motor can be controlled by a thermostat inside the cabinet. The motor must be able to start under load, as pressures do not balance during the off cycle.

A *low-side float* is a valve inside the evaporator that regulates the liquid level in the evaporator. Because the evaporator always contains some liquid refrigerant, it is said to be "flooded," and it always produces some cooling. A low-side float is often used in large, centrifugal water chillers. Because the system contains liquid refrigerant in both receiver and evaporator, it uses a large charge. The motor must start under load. (See Figure 8-E.) The compressor control powers the motor when suction-line pressure rises (indicating a warm evaporator). Or a thermostat can be mounted on the evaporator (or immersed in the circulating water of a chilled-water system).

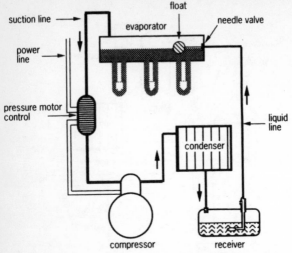

Figure 8-E: Low-side float system

A *high-side float* (HSF) (see Figure 8-F) is a valve inside the receiver that controls the level of liquid refrigerant. The evaporator is always flooded with refrigerant. The compressor pumps refrigerant through the condenser into the receiver. When refrigerant reaches the set level in the float chamber, the float rises and opens the valve, and refrigerant flows to the evaporator.

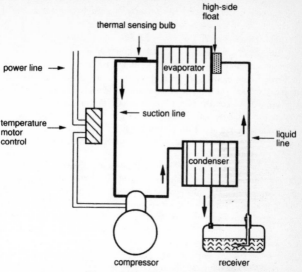

Figure 8-F: High-side float system

> **TIP:** A thermostat in the cabinet, or a pressure sensor on the suction line, may control the compressor motor. Refrigerant charge is critical. With too much refrigerant, the float will open too wide and flood the compressor with liquid refrigerant. But if the charge is too small, the valve will stay closed and the evaporator will starve.

Systems can also be classified by how they combine different compressors or evaporators to create extremely low temperatures, produce a lot of cooling power, or make different temperatures in different cabinets.

A *compound system* has multiple compressors connected in series. The output of the first compressor discharges into the inlet of the second compressor, and so on. Aside from this, the system resembles a conventional vapor-compression system. Multiple compressors produce extremely high vacuum and extremely low temperature. An intercooler may cool the hot vapor between the compressors. The system is regulated by one motor control and a thermostatic expansion valve. Because the pressures do not balance when the compressor is off, the motors have to start under load.

A *cascade system* uses two separate compression systems to achieve temperatures around $-50°F$ ($-46°C$) for industrial processes. The connection between the systems is the evaporator of the primary, or "booster," compressor, which cools the condenser of the secondary compressor. The evaporator of the secondary system cools the load. Both systems use TXVs. A single control regulates both motors according to temperature or pressure in the secondary evaporator. Due to the extremely low temperatures in the secondary system, the refrigerant must be extremely dry. Oil separators are desirable on the liquid lines.

A *modulating system* links several compressors in parallel; the number of compressors in operation depends on the load. The compressors usually all feed one evaporator, but they can have common or separate condensers. A modulating system helps when the load varies greatly during a 24-hour cycle. This is typical in office buildings, where the comfort-cooling load is much greater during the day, and a system that could handle the peak load might not be able to throttle down at night. And if one compressor is shut down for service, some cooling capacity will remain. Capacity controls can also modulate by (1) holding suction valves open or (2) routing compressed refrigerant to the low side without passing through the condenser. (See Chapter 4, "Controls.")

Multiple-evaporator systems have several evaporators in different locations. If these evaporators run at the same temperature, the system can be controlled by a low-side float or a TXV. If temperatures must be different, a two-temperature valve is used to control pressures in the evaporators. A check valve in the suction line of the colder evaporator may prevent refrigerant being sucked from the warmer evaporator to the colder, lower-pressure evaporator during the off cycle.

A *reheat system* reduces humidity by cooling the air to a certain humidity and then warming it enough to be circulated at the design temperature. Part of the heat may come from room air and part from a furnace or the cooling system. A reheat system can control both relative humidity and temperature. If the air delivered is too cool, the reheating element can be shut off. If the air is too damp or warm, check for a problem with the cooling components or controls.

DEFROST SYSTEMS

Frost, the freezing of moisture on a cold surface, can be a problem for any ACR system where the evaporator operates below water's freezing point. Frost is an insulator, and its formation can dehydrate food. On a warmer evaporator, condensation, but not frost, will form on the coil. However, almost any evaporator operating below 30°F will frost and needs either a defrost system or regular manual defrosting.

To defrost, the coils may be allowed to warm during part of the cycle, or they may be heated from inside or outside. Most systems require a drain so melted frost does not cause rot, discoloration, refrosting, and other problems.

Defrost Controls

Three controls are used to regulate defrost in commercial systems:

1. A *timer* is set to defrost for a specific period at set intervals. This system is simple, but it cannot account for varying loads or humidity, and thus will probably run too many defrosting cycles, wasting energy and wearing equipment.

2. A *pressure control* ("LP") measures suction pressure. The control starts a defrost cycle when pressure falls, indicating a fall in evaporator temperature caused by ice forming on the coil. This control must be installed carefully, as it tends to respond to the coldest point in the system, which may not be in the evaporator it is supposed to measure. A fail-safe timer may order a defrost cycle at set intervals if the ΔT control fails.

3. A *temperature sensor* registers a rise in temperature on the suction line, and terminates the defrost cycle at a set temperature, often about 50°F (10°C). Unlike the pressure control, a temperature control is not likely to read temperatures in remote evaporators.

Hot-Gas Defrosting

Hot-gas defrost systems feed hot, discharge gas into the evaporator and can usually melt all frost in about 10 minutes. The condenser and metering device normally play no part in the defrost cycle. Units with multiple evaporators may be set to defrost each evaporator as needed. Solenoid valves operate hot-gas defrost systems. Two basic layouts of hot-gas defrost system are used, with some variations:

1. The system shown in Figure 8-G directs hot gas through a bypass into the evaporator, which is similar to the hot-gas capacity-control system.

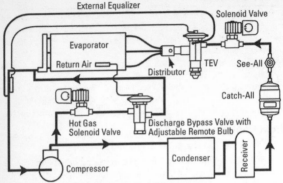

Figure 8-G: Hot-gas defrost system
Courtesy of Sporlan Division of Parker Hannifin, Inc.

This hot-gas defrost system must prevent floodbacks of liquid refrigerant that condenses in the evaporator by:

a. Putting an accumulator in the suction line to trap and vaporize liquid, sometimes with the help of a heater and other floodback preventatives;

b. Warming the suction line with an electric heater;

c. Locating a blower-evaporator in the suction line, set to operate during defrost; or

d. Routing vapor and liquid from the defrosting evaporator to another evaporator, where the liquid vaporizes.

2. A second hot-gas defrost system is shown in Figure 8-H. As before, the compressor pumps hot vapor to the evaporator, but the vapor goes through the suction line instead of the liquid line. After the vapor exits the evaporator, it flows through the liquid line, and ends up in the receiver.

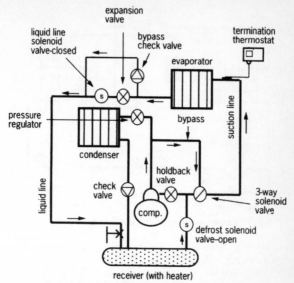

Figure 8-H: Two-pipe defrost system in defrost mode

Reverse-Cycle Defrost

This defrost system (see Figure 8-I) is mainly used with a heat pump and is named because the condenser and evaporator reverse roles during defrost: the heat pump is briefly switched into the summer, cooling mode during winter. An electric duct heater is usually run during defrost to keep cold air from blowing into the house. No defrost is needed during summer because the evaporator runs above freezing temperature.

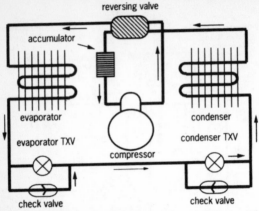

Figure 8-I: Reverse-cycle defrost system (shown in defrost cycle)

The compressor pumps hot gas directly to the evaporator, where the gas condenses, melting the frost. The liquid refrigerant then passes through a check valve (piped parallel to the metering device) and a special TXV to reach the condenser, now serving as an evaporator. Finally, the vapor passes through an accumulator and returns to the compressor. (See Chapter 2, "Energy, Electricity, and Cooling Cycles.")

Electric-Heat Defrost

Electric heaters can defrost evaporators and suction lines. During each defrost cycle, a timer: (a) closes a solenoid valve to close the liquid line, so the compressor pumps out the evaporator, (b) shuts down the compressor, and (c) supplies current to the heating elements and any blowers used to speed defrost. When the evaporator is warm enough (indicating defrost is completed), a thermostat on the evaporator signals the system to resume normal operation. Electric heating elements may be wired into drain pans or floors to help the draining of melted water. If these elements fail, a large sheet of ice might form, so make an inspection part of a service routine.

Nonfreezing Solutions

The nonfreezing solution system uses a tank (usually containing brine), which gradually absorbs heat from discharge gas or an electric heater. After a signal from the defrost timer, the brine is pumped through separate piping to warm the coil.

PUMPDOWN CYCLE

In a pumpdown cycle, the system pumps all refrigerant into a vessel (commonly the receiver or condenser) during the off cycle. Pumpdown prevents refrigerant from migrating to the crankcase, where it can condense and saturate the oil. Without a pumpdown cycle, the crankcase can fill with liquid refrigerant during a long off cycle. At startup, this liquid refrigerant could flood the cylinders and damage the compressor, acting much like a floodback. (Large compressors have check valves on intake and discharge lines to reduce this hazard.)

After the evaporator is cold enough, a solenoid valve closes in the liquid line and the compressor pumps liquid refrigerant into the condenser or receiver, where it remains until the next on cycle. If some refrigerant escapes the vessel, it can be recovered by a recycling-type pumpdown control, which periodically restarts the compressor for a moment to refill the storage vessel. If a recycling control cannot be used, a crankcase heater may keep refrigerant out of the crankcase.

COLD-WEATHER OPERATION

Special precautions are needed to protect an outdoor, air-cooled condenser from low ambient temperatures. The major problem is that the refrigerant will not flow through the metering device without sufficient head pressure. Systems operated in cold conditions require:

- a weatherproof housing;
- a way to prevent short cycling;
- a head-pressure control (if the weather will be colder than the cabinet); and
- a method of preventing oil from being diluted by refrigerant.

Ambient temperatures are a greater problem in areas with high winds, so it is advisable to mount the condenser in a sheltered location, as long as it will get enough air circulation in summer.

Head pressure can be sustained by insulating and heating the receiver, so it does not get cold enough to act as a condenser. If the receiver is mounted above the condenser, static pressure will add to head pressure. A second way to ensure head pressure is to interfere with condenser action by:

1. Slowing the condenser cooling fan (or cycling the fan with a control that responds to condenser temperature).

2. Closing louvers on the condenser to slow air flow.

3. Increasing the charge of liquid refrigerant, leaving less space for vapor to condense in the condenser. One way to do this is to place a condenser pressure-regulator valve (see Figure 8-J) in the liquid line. In cold weather, the pressure regulator raises condenser pressure by closing the condenser outlet, which also keeps more refrigerant in the condenser. The pressure-regulator valve measures ambient temperature and receiver pressure. As ambient temperature cools, the valve reduces the flow through the condenser outlet, increasing head pressure and warming the receiver. (See Chapter 7, "Pipe, Tube, Fittings, and Valves.")

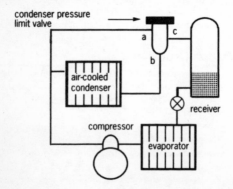

In warm weather, valve *a* is closed. Valves *b* and *c* direct refrigerant through the condenser. In cold weather, valve *a* opens and valve *b* throttles closed. Some discharge gas bypasses the condenser. The condenser is partly filled with refrigerant.

Figure 8-J: Condenser pressure regulator

CHOOSING AND INSTALLING A SYSTEM

System design is the province of engineers, and we will make only a small effort to delve into its devious complexities. Nevertheless, an acquaintance with basic design concepts will help those working in the field.

Cooling Load

Cooling load is the amount of heat that must be removed from the cooled space to maintain design conditions. Calculating cooling load can get complicated, but may need to be performed to size the equipment for a new installation or service a system that seems to be working but is not cooling well.

Cooling load is a function of space heat gain and design temperature and humidity. Space heat gain is the sum of:

- solar heat gain;
- heat conducted through interior and exterior walls, roof, and foundation;
- heat generated by activities in the building, such as people, appliances, equipment, and lighting;
- energy transfers through ventilation and infiltration; and
- other sources of heat.

Buildings can gain both sensible and latent heat. Latent heat gain, carried in humidity, must be condensed from the air by removing the latent heat of condensation.

Cooling load calculations require data on summer and winter temperatures and humidity, and design temperature and humidity. Calculate the temperature difference (ΔT) by subtracting design interior temperature from summer high temperature. Find the heat transmission factor (U) for each material or wall type used in the construction. Then, for each building element with similar construction, calculate:

$U \times \Delta T \times area = heat loss$

Make separate calculations for each area with different construction (exterior and interior walls, floor, ceiling) and total the losses. Then add internal heat gains and infiltration.

Some equipment manufacturers offer worksheets to help calculate cooling loads. Because the result is approximate, it's smart to allow some extra capacity rather than risk installing an undersized system.

Once cooling load has been calculated, the best way to cool that load can be evaluated. Often, the most economical approach is to insulate and weatherstrip first; this reduces both capital and operating costs of the cooling system. Then calculate a new cooling load before choosing the cooling equipment.

Selecting Components

After determining the cooling load and operating conditions, choose the compressor or condensing unit, based on the unit that will offer sufficient cooling at minimum initial, operating, and maintenance costs. Motor voltage and phase, cost, personnel expertise, and other factors all enter into this decision.

The basic rating of compressors is tons of output, at standard condenser and evaporator temperatures. (One ton equals 12,000 BTU/hour or 3,024 kcal/hour.) Manufacturer charts list compressor capacity under various operating conditions. Pay close attention to the specified conditions, such as the amount of superheat or subcooling, when selecting a compressor. Specifications may explain how to adjust capacity for different superheat or subcooling settings. Pressure drop in the system, which represents lost cooling capacity, is another factor in compressor sizing.

The compressor must be matched to the evaporator and condenser. A "condensing unit" is a built-up refrigeration machine with all major components except the evaporator and metering device. The components of a condensing unit are factory-matched to work well together. When selecting components, add a safety margin to allow for pull-down after large loads, unanticipated temperature and pressure losses, and miscalculations.

A condensing unit should be able to:

- run on available electricity (phase and voltage);
- handle the expected maximum load safely and the minimum load without short-cycling;
- create the required evaporator temperature in the number of evaporators that will be used; and
- defrost the system.

The condensing unit should also make optimal use of the cooling medium. Consider:

1. Maximum summer air and water temperatures
2. Cost, quality, and availability of condenser water
3. Location of condensing unit and auxiliary components

Installing the Compressor

Select a location with enough size, ventilation, and support for the compressor or condensing unit. The natural ventilation requirements listed in Table 8-D are figured for a single window; rooms with cross-ventilation may need less window area. Compressor ventilation requirements are much lower with a remote or water-cooled condenser.

Table 8-D: Compressor Ventilation Requirements

For condensing units with water-cooled condensers or compressor units with remote condensers.

Motor H.P.	Natural Ventilation Room Volume Cubic Feet	Forced Ventilation CFM
3	600	300
5	850	500
7½	1100	700
10	1300	900
15	1650	1300
20	2000	1800
25	2250	2200
30	2450	2600
40	2800	3000
50	3100	3400
60	3350	4000
75	3650	5700
100	4000	7000

Courtesy of American Standard

Most compressors are installed on a concrete pad above the floor. If the installation will not rest on a basement floor, use isolator rails to insulate the structure from vibration. Bolt the machine or the isolator rails to the pad, floor, or concrete to prevent movement.

Compressors rock slightly on startup and shutdown. To protect the piping from torqueing, especially if the compressor is affixed to a resilient mounting, install one or more elbows near the compressor, with at least 10 pipe diameters of straight pipe between them. (See Chapter 5, "Components.")

Piping Installation

The piping system may include many "extras," depending on the bid and the cooling situation. A filter-drier in the liquid line, and possibly the suction line, will help prevent burnouts and plugging of the metering device and other components. Insulating the suction line will prevent condensation and save energy.

Installing service valves will save the owner money in the long run, although they are not always essential. The manufacturer or engineer may supply a mechanical drawing using the symbols shown in Table 8-E. Always check to see if the manufacturer provided a key, as symbols may change.

Table 8-E: Mechanical Symbols for Refrigeration Drawings

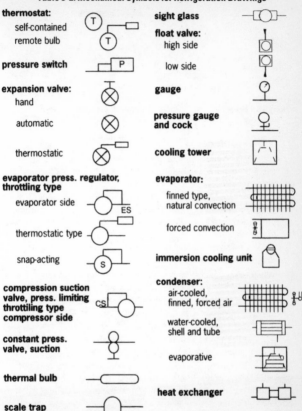

thermostat:

self-contained

remote bulb

pressure switch

expansion valve:

hand

automatic

thermostatic

evaporator press. regulator, throttling type

evaporator side

thermostatic type

snap-acting

compression suction valve, press. limiting throttiling type compressor side

constant press. valve, suction

thermal bulb

scale trap

sight glass

float valve:

high side

low side

gauge

pressure gauge and cock

cooling tower

evaporator:

finned type, natural convection

forced convection

immersion cooling unit

condenser:

air-cooled, finned, forced air

water-cooled, shell and tube

evaporative

heat exchanger

Table 8-E: Mechanical Symbols for Refrigeration Drawings (continued)

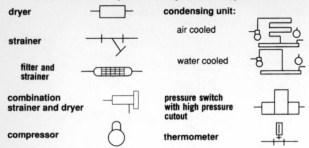

The technique for connecting the compressor depends on too many factors for us to cover, but the following guidelines will help ensure a successful installation:

1. Keep tubing clean and dry before and during installation. Use only sealed ACR-grade tubing. After opening the seals on compressors and filter-driers, work quickly to make connections—about 2 minutes maximum.

2. Slope suction lines 1/2" per 10' (approximately 4 mm per meter) toward the compressor to promote oil return.

3. When using quick-connect fittings, make horizontal coils of extra tubing so oil can flow, especially in the suction line.

4. While brazing, fill the tubing with a non-oxidizing gas, such as dry nitrogen or carbon dioxide, to prevent corrosion.

5. Choose solder and brazing filler metal to withstand the pressure and temperature in the system. Use a minimal amount of soldering or brazing paste or flux.

6. Install vibration absorbers in the proper orientation and position (read the manufacturer's directions). If an absorber is installed perpendicular to the crankshaft, normal compressor shifting will stress it and may break the bellows.

7. Leak test the system before insulating the tubing.

Placing a System into Service

Before running a system for the first time, all control settings and components must be checked. Use the following guidelines:

1. Set the refrigerant and temperature controls according to the designer's specifications. The control differential must be large enough to prevent short cycling.

2. Check interlocks between controls and components to ensure that components that are designed to work together actually do work together.

3. Before starting the compressor, check:

   a. Condenser water shutoff valves: open?

   b. Compressor oil level: above center of the sight glass?

   c. Suction and discharge valves: open?

   d. Refrigerant valves: open?

   e. Liquid-line solenoid: on automatic setting?

   f. Gauges for oil pressure, suction, and discharge pressure: installed?

   g. Tag identifying system refrigerant: in place?

4. Start the system, keeping a close watch on the suction, discharge, and oil pressures.

5. Check superheat if using a thermostatic expansion valve.

6. Check the motor's running amperage and voltage. With a three-phase motor, measure the variation in voltage between the three legs of the circuit. (See Chapter 6, "Motors.")

7. Fill out a log of operating conditions.

8. Run the system for 72 hours, with a technician available if possible. Closely monitor the oil level.

PLANT ___ MACHINE SERIAL NO. ___ MACHINE SIZE ___

1	2	3	4	5	6	7	8	9	10	11	12	13	14	15	16	17	18	19	20	21

COOLER — GPM: Pressure or Vacuum (2), Refrigerant Temperature (3), Refrigerant Level (4); WATER TEMPERATURE: In (5), Out (6)

CONDENSER — GPM: Pressure or Vacuum (7), Condenser Temperature (8); WATER TEMPERATURE: In (9), Out (10)

COMPRESSOR — Vane Position Indicator (11), Main Bearing Temperature (12); OIL: Level (13), Temperature (14), Pressure (15); Motor Amps (16)

THERMAL PURGE — Purge Pressure for Pump Operation: Starts, Stops (17); COMPRESSION PURGE: Suct. Press. (17), Disch. Press. (18); Time Between Pump Starts: I/O, Level (19); Refrig. Level, Relay Level (20); Operator's Initials (21)

Time (1)

REMARKS: Indicate shut-downs on safety controls, repairs, made, oil or refrigerant added or removed, and water drained from purge. Include amounts.

Figure 8-K: Refrigeration system log
Courtesy of Carrier Corporation, Division of United Technologies Corporation

Perform the following at the end of the 72-hour run-in:

1. Check the compressor oil. If it is low, run the compressor for a few hours at full load (to ensure maximum refrigerant velocity, which may return more oil from the piping and components). If crankcase oil is still low, add more.

2. Check for a solid stream of liquid at the liquid-line sight glass. If bubbles are visible, determine if they are due to a restriction in the line or to a low charge. If the charge is low, check for leaks, then add refrigerant as needed.

3. Check the temperature of the liquid line on both sides of the filter-drier. If there is much temperature drop, the drier element is restricted. Remove and replace it.

4. Measure the superheat and adjust if needed.

5. Observe operating pressures. If they do not match specifications, determine the cause and correct it. If correct, backseat the service valves, remove the gauge manifold, and plug or cap the valves. If gauges are permanent parts of the system, close the valves leading to them (continual service will shorten gauge life). Record operating conditions on the log.

6. On an open system, shut off the compressor and check the shaft seal with a leak detector. Also check the alignment of the motor shaft. Lubricate the motor if necessary.

7. Clean all strainers in the condenser circuits.

8. Check and re-tension all fan belts.

9. Check that air filters are clean.

After one week, perform the following services before turning over the system to the owner:

1. Replace the filter-drier element.

2. Tighten the motor-compressor coupling (on an open system).

3. Watch the system cycle once or twice, looking for irregularities.

4. Check:
   - System pressures and temperatures
   - Compressor oil
   - Liquid-line sight glass
   - Condenser operation

After the check-out period, gather the operating specifications, parts lists, and other pertinent information. Make a permanent data sheet for the installation. File one copy and give another to the owner. The sheet should include:

1. Manufacturers, models, and serial or part numbers of compressor, contactor, starter, protection device, and all related electrical components.

2. Electrical diagram, and data for line and control circuits: current, voltage, phase, hertz, wire sizes.

3. Makes, models, sizes, and serial numbers for other equipment: evaporators, condensers, receivers, filter-driers, defrost timer, fans, and pumps.

4. Refrigerant piping diagram.

5. Refrigerant number and initial charge size.

6. Design operating temperature and pressure.

7. Defrost cycle information.

8. Settings on all operating, safety, capacity, and refrigerant controls.

COMFORT COOLING (AIR CONDITIONING)

Properly speaking, air conditioning is the treatment of air to control temperature, humidity, cleanliness, and distribution. Thus, it includes both the heating and the cooling of air. What many call "air conditioning" is divided in the trade into two categories. *Comfort cooling* is cooling used to increase human comfort. *Process conditioning* is cooling used for an industrial process, such as a computer room or a candy factory.

To service comfort-cooling systems, you must be well-versed in heating and air-distribution systems; in many buildings, the same equipment that moves cooled water or air in the summer also handles heated water or air in the winter. And with a heat pump, one mechanical system does both jobs.

Central comfort cooling may use either an air- or a water-cooled condenser. The general practice is to locate the condenser outside and return liquid refrigerant to the evaporator inside the building, but in some cases ducts bring condenser air into the building. The evaporator must be chosen to fit inside the furnace being used.

Residential Central Air Conditioning

Residential central-air systems, like all other cooling systems, must be matched to the load. An undersized system cannot supply enough cooling, while an oversized system will be expensive to install and its operating life will be shortened by short cycling.

To avoid noise problems, locate an outdoor condensing unit away from bedroom windows and neighbors. To promote air circulation, it should be beyond the roof overhang, not in an inside corner of the building, and at least 2' from walls. A 4" concrete slab is often poured to hold the condensing unit. Make sure to provide at least 5' (1.5 m) clearance above the condensing unit fan for air circulation. Allow about 10" (25 cm) on all sides of the unit, with 18" (45 cm) clearance near the access panel.

If the condensing unit is installed above the evaporator, slope the suction line downhill and make a U-bend to aid oil return.

The method of installation will reflect one of three basic configurations. The system can be:

- Built up of *individual components*. This procedure is cumbersome, expensive, and requires a lot of engineering knowledge.

- Ordered *completely assembled*, which requires minimal work at the job site, primarily to uncoil tube, locate the evaporator and condensing units, and connect the power and control circuits.

- Built up from a completely charged *condensing unit and evaporator that are shipped separately* and joined at the job site with sweat or flare fittings, or quick couplings. This technique may offer the best combination of simplicity and ease of assembly.

Place the condensing unit on a concrete pad according to the guidelines above. Install the evaporator in the air ducts, typically in the furnace plenum. Blankoff plates may be needed to force all the air through the coil. Install the evaporator level so condensate can flow out the drainage tube. Feed the drainage into the furnace condensate tube, or route it to a floor drain, sump, or sewer, or pump it the outside. Install and connect the suction and liquid lines, and connect the electrical wiring.

Servicing

A residential central-air system should get some service each year, either from the homeowner or a contractor. Energize the crankcase heater at least 4 hours before startup to drive refrigerant from the oil. Other services should include:

1. Check and balance duct dampers.
2. Inspect and replace filters.
3. Clean condenser and fan.
4. Lubricate motor and fan bearings.
5. Inspect fan belt and replace if cracked or glazed.

As with other cooling systems, occasionally check pressures, operating controls, refrigerant charge, suction-line sweating, voltage, and full-load amperage. Check for condensate drainage inside the furnace; it can cause corrosion if it escapes from the drain pan.

Air Circulation

Air-circulation equipment enables an air conditioning system to deliver the proper amount of cooled, conditioned air where it is wanted. Depending on the system, air may be propelled by a fan located in the furnace, the cooling unit, room units, or ductwork. The ability of a fan to move air depends on its size, speed, and design, and the pressure differential between the intake and output. (See Chapter 5, "Components.")

A good air distribution system will:

1. Mix cooled or heated air and deliver it in a manner that does not expose occupants to drafts or obnoxiously warm or cold air.
2. Limit noise from air flow and equipment.
3. Provide some turbulence in the living area to promote air movement.
4. Operate reliably under all conditions.

Principles of Duct Design and Installation

Although duct design is beyond the scope of this manual, a few principles of design will assist those who must oversee duct installers or install ducts themselves:

1. Air should be delivered as directly as possible, using minimum material, space, power, and money.
2. Avoid noise problems by keeping air flow below recommended maximum velocities.
3. Avoid sharp elbows or turns in the ducts.
4. The angle of divergence in duct enlargements should not exceed 20°. The angle or convergence in contractions should not exceed 60°.

5. Round ducts have the highest capacity per square foot of metal. Square-section ducts have the greatest capacity of any rectangular ducts. The maximum ratio of long side to short side in a rectangular duct should be 6 to 1.

6. Long runs require expansion joints so the metal can expand without buckling.

7. Bracing must be secure enough to prevent movement.

8. Duct insulation prevents heating and cooling losses and also reduces sweating and noise.

9. Each branch needs a damper to balance the system.

10. Ducts should be tight, with laps formed in the direction of flow.

11. If mechanical or electrical apparatus is located in a duct, provide a service opening.

Air flow through a duct can be calculated by multiplying duct size in square feet by air speed in feet per minute (fpm). The "free area," or actual opening, of a grille should be listed in manufacturers' catalogs; it is usually 60 to 85% of the overall size.

Ducts must be sized correctly. The amount of air flow needed to cool a room can be calculated by figuring that each cubic foot of air flow per minute (cfm) will remove about 30 BTUs (1 liter per minute will remove 1,116 joules). Divide the BTU cooling load of a room by 30 to get the approximate cfm needed for cooling. In the SI system, divide the heat load in joules by 1,116 to find the necessary air flow in liters.

Use a manometer to measure pressure in a duct. An inclined-tube manometer is more precise than a U-tube model. The manometer can compare pressure at two places in a duct, or find the pressure drop across a filter, coil, or a long run. It may also be used to measure absolute pressure (the total pressure at one point in the duct), if the current barometric pressure is known. To find absolute pressure, open one manometer tube to the atmosphere and hook the other into a duct.

When connecting a manometer into a duct, do not confuse static pressure with velocity pressure. Static pressure results from the pressure on the fluid, while velocity pressure results from the movement of the fluid. (Static pressure + velocity pressure = total pressure.) Both static and velocity pressures are created when a fan runs, but duct analysis usually depends only on static pressure. To measure only static pressure, use a probe with holes drilled in it and a closed end, instead of an open-end, probe. Be cautious because certain areas of a duct, such as behind obstructions, have eddies that throw off the measurement.

Balancing ductwork is the process of assuring that each room gets the desired amount of conditioned air. Start balancing after the system and controls are working right. First examine the duct setup to see which damper controls which room. Open all dampers, then begin closing those closer to the fan. Continue checking the results and adjusting dampers. Each adjustment will affect the entire system, so the process can take some time.

Water Circulation

Comfort-cooling systems that distribute their cooling with water are called "chiller" systems. As with air-distribution systems, a chiller system can be integrated with the heat distribution system to save capital cost and room in the building. Chilled-water piping can range from simple to complex. Simple systems save initial cost but offer less control and flexibility than more complicated piping.

The most basic water circuit is the *series loop system*, in which chilled water passes through a single loop of pipe and every heat exchanger. All the heat exchangers are connected in series. Slightly more complex is a *one-pipe system*, in which a single pipe circulates all the cooling water and a tee valve diverts some water through a balancing valve to a heat transfer device.

The two versions of the *two-pipe system* (see Figure 8-L) both use a supply main and a return main. In the *direct-return* version, water in the supply and return mains flows in opposite directions. Chilled water can pass through the heat exchanger closest to the chiller and return to the chiller without traveling through the entire piping system. As a result, an adjustable valve in the branch lines to the exchangers should balance out the load. A more sophisticated and more common version of the two-pipe system is the *two-pipe reverse return system*, in which water flows in the same direction in both supply and return mains. This system is easier to control because the distance from the chiller to any unit and back to the chiller is essentially the same.

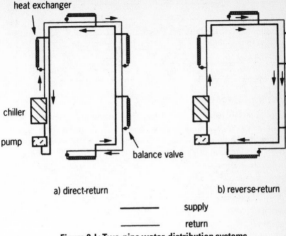

heat exchanger

chiller

pump

balance valve

a) direct-return   b) reverse-return

———— supply

———— return

Figure 8-L: Two-pipe water-distribution systems

Balancing valves are helpful for making fine adjustments in cooling supply. In return for the greater initial cost, this system offers more control and flexibility.

COMMERCIAL REFRIGERATION

Commercial refrigeration systems are generally classified by evaporator temperature according to Table 8-F. Compressors are usually designed for a general range of evaporator temperature, but running the evaporator too warm for a certain refrigerant-compressor combination may not load the compressor enough, causing excess head pressures and other troubles. The main restrictions on reducing the evaporator temperature are motor cooling and overloading. However, refrigerants can be changed to alter the operating temperature of a system. A multistage system is usually required to reach temperatures below −40°F. Two-stage compressors may reach −80°F, and cascade systems can get even colder.

Table 8-F: Commercial Refrigeration Temperature Classification

System class	U.S. units	SI units
High temperature	About 0°F to 50°F	About −17.8°C to 10°C
Medium temperature	−5°F to 25°F	−20.6°C to −3.9°C
Low temperature	−40°F to 0°F	−40°C to −17.8°C
Extra low temperature	−40°F to −20°F	−40°C to −28.9°C

Fixtures and Coolers

The wide variety of commercial refrigerating and freezing fixtures can be categorized as display cases, walk-in coolers, and storage freezers. There is great variation within each category as manufacturers strive to meet new commercial requirements. Fixtures vary according to:

- Condensing unit type
- Metering device
- Evaporator type
- Operating control
- Defrosting method
- Refrigerant

Fixtures can also be classified by the method of transferring heat from the product or atmosphere to the evaporator:

1. *Direct-contact:* Air touches the cooling coil; there is no fan.
2. *Forced-air cooling:* A fan blows air across the coils and through the cooled space.
3. *Indirect-contact:* The coil cools a brine tank, which cools the product. The brine tank minimizes temperature swings.
4. *Combination direct- and indirect-contact:* Part of the evaporator is in a brine tank, and part contacts air in the cooled space.

Open display cases should not be placed in drafts from a duct or window. Display lighting can be a significant cause of warming in refrigerated foods.

Meat display cases need a regular maintenance schedule. A weekly cleaning should begin with the removal of all product and removable shelving. Shut down the machine and clean with a mild soap, mild detergent, or bicarbonate of soda. Avoid ammonia, which will discolor meat. Minimize water use during cleaning to protect electrical components from water damage.

Drains on display cases should be piped so that neither warm air nor sewer gas can enter the case. A trap in the line should be located at least 12" (30.5 cm) from the case outlet.

Air in a display case is usually forced by fans oriented to assist normal convection. The evaporator may be hung from adjustable brackets on the ceiling. Baffles may be used to direct the air flow and help maintain the temperature difference between the evaporator and the product. An adequate ΔT will help ensure heat transfer and minimize the size of evaporator needed. A high ΔT can cause massive dehumidifying and desiccate the product.

Display cases can also be cooled by plate-type evaporators, but this type of evaporator needs good air circulation for thorough cooling. For a list of desired storage temperature for foods, see Tables B and C in Appendix C.

Multiple (Combined) Systems

For many years, the industry has been moving toward operating several evaporators from one large condensing unit, with sophisticated controls. Although these "multiple systems" are undoubtedly more complex to install and service than simple systems, they have the following benefits:

- Equipment and installation costs are reduced.
- Operating and maintenance costs are lowered.
- Fewer components are needed, and larger motors are more efficient.

The chances of trouble increase along with the number of fixtures, and although good design can minimize trouble, it cannot eliminate problems.

Display cases connected to a single condensing unit must produce the desired operating temperature with the same suction pressure and compressor running time. For proper operation, the warmest evaporator (or group of evaporators) should have no more than 40% of the total system load. Temperatures in the various cases can be controlled by evaporator-pressure regulating valves or solenoids in the liquid lines.

The fixtures and condensing unit should be as close together as possible, and the suction lines must be large enough to minimize pressure drops yet still allow oil return. Suction line risers between display cases will help prevent oil from dripping between evaporators, or from an evaporator to the compressor during the off cycle.

Defrost systems must be adapted to conditions in the various cases, and supplemental electric defrost heaters may be needed in areas prone to frosting. A multicircuit time clock can be used to control a variety of defrost cycles on a combined system.

Combined systems may be fed by a refrigeration mechanical center serving the cooling needs of an entire supermarket. These large condensing units may save money and offer the advantage of factory engineering and flexible location. Removing machinery from the display floor saves space for products.

Heat Recovery Systems

Large supermarket cooling systems may have equipment to recover condenser heat for heating the store interior in winter. A lot of heat can be recovered and a lot of energy cost saved, using one of three methods:

1. *Direct air.* In winter, ducts and fans drive air through a housing around the condenser, where it picks up heat. The cost of equipment and operation can be high.

2. *Closed-circuit water.* A three-way valve controls the condenser cooling water. In winter, hot water is routed to indoor heating devices. Otherwise, the water goes to an evaporative cooler. Because the condenser water is not particularly hot, a large radiator is needed for inside heat transfer, and the water pumps can gobble electricity.

3. *Dual condenser.* A second condenser is installed in the air handler, and a three-way valve routes refrigerant to the outside condenser in warm weather and to the inside condenser during cold weather.

Costs are low, and the gas is warm enough that heat transmission to the inside air is quite rapid. Extra refrigerant tubing is needed, but no extra pump is necessary.

ESTIMATING JOBS

Estimating is one of the toughest challenges facing a contractor. Estimate too low, and money can be lost. Estimate too high, and the bid can be rejected. Estimates must be made for both materials and labor.

Formulas given in books on construction estimating can help in estimating labor and material requirements for certain tasks, but they can never be 100% accurate. Estimating books are only helpful if workers meet standard rates of production and local costs are similar to those used by the organization preparing the book.

Contractors also use their own records for estimating jobs, which is a good reason to keep records up to date. Follow these hints for accurate estimating:

1. Keep a record of time requirements and cost for past jobs.

2. Watch out for special situations that will change costs.

3. Explain to the customer the tradeoffs between low first cost and high operating costs. For example, omitting service valves will reduce installation costs but raise service costs in the long run.

9

Refrigerants

At the heart of every cooling system is a fluid that can reliably, and consistently carry a lot of heat without endangering people, equipment, or buildings. These fluids, called refrigerants, can change state and absorb heat in the evaporator and dispose of heat in the condenser. Many chemicals have been used as refrigerants over the years. In the vapor-compression cycle, chlorofluorocarbons and hydrochlorofluorocarbons are being replaced by a new group of ozone-friendly refrigerants. Ammonia is still found in large industrial systems; the absorption cycle uses either water or ammonia.

This chapter covers the ozone question, EPA requirements for refrigerant leaks and technician certification, and refrigerant safety. It also contains pressure-temperature tables for many common refrigerants.

Ideally, refrigerants should:

- work under moderate pressures;
- be stable, nontoxic, nonflammable, non-explosive, non-corrosive, and inexpensive;
- have low viscosity (to allow fast heat transfer without high pumping cost);
- be easy to detect if they leak;
- have a low boiling point and a high latent heat;
- have relatively close condensing and evaporating pressures; and
- not injure the stratospheric ozone layer that protects us from the sun's harmful ultraviolet radiation.

REFRIGERANT SAFETY

The National Refrigeration Safety Code (NRSC) places refrigerants in three categories based on their level of safety. (See Table 9-A.)

Table 9-A: NRSC Refrigerant Safety Classifications

Group	Fire hazard	Includes
I	Safest	R-11 R-12 R-22 R-500 R-502 R-503 R-744 (carbon dioxide)
II	Toxic and somewhat flammable	R-717 (ammonia) R-40 (methyl chloride) R-764 (sulfur dioxide)
III	Flammable	R-600 (butane) R-170 (ethane) R-290 (propane)

Ammonia

Ammonia (NH_3) is often used in industrial vapor-compression (and absorption) systems, but because its fumes are hazardous, it is rarely used in small vapor-compression systems. Ammonia (R-717) is lighter than oil and does not present lubrication problems. Ammonia has a low boiling point and can create below-zero temperatures even when evaporator pressure is above atmospheric pressure; and because it has a high latent heat, systems can be relatively small. Ammonia attacks copper and bronze, so iron or steel tubes and fittings are normally used, connected with welds or threads.

> **CAUTION:** Ammonia is very hazardous to the respiratory system, and can kill at about 5,000 parts per million (ppm). Levels as low 3 to 5 ppm have an obvious odor. Ammonia will cause shortness of breath, eye irritation, and damage to the skin, eyes, and breathing passages. The symptoms depend on the concentration and length of exposure. An air pack, a tight mask, and goggles are excellent safety measures when working on an ammonia system.

Prevent excess pressure in the system. Do not drill or saw into an ammonia system. Stand aside when cracking or opening an ammonia valve, because a quick blast of ammonia could cause blindness and/or a loss of consciousness.

Detect leaks by smell or with a sulfur candle or sulfur spray vapor, which produce a stream of smoky fumes at the leak. (See Chapter 1, "Tools, Equipment, and Materials.") OSHA information on ammonia safety can be found at www.osha.gov/SLTC/ammoniarefrigeration.

WORKING WITH VAPOR-COMPRESSION REFRIGERANTS

Ammonia is used in some large industrial vapor-compression systems, but most vapor-compression cycle cooling systems use halocarbon or a derivative as the refrigerant.

Halocarbons (also called chlorofluorocarbons or CFCs) were introduced to the refrigerant industry in 1930 to replace hazardous ammonia. Halocarbon refrigerants contain halogen atoms (chlorine, fluorine, iodine, and bromine). Halocarbons are stable, noncorrosive, nonflammable, and possess many other desirable refrigerant properties. Halocarbons are heavier than air and will collect in the lowest spot in a room or container. Some halocarbons are commonly called Freon, but this is a trademark and should not be used in place of "halocarbon," "chlorofluorocarbon," "CFC," or the refrigerant number ("CFC-12," for example, is the same as "R-12").

Table 9-B: Pressure-Temperature Table for Ammonia (R-717)

Ammonia (R−717)		Ammonia (R−717)	
Psig (* = inches mercury below 1 atmosphere	Temp °F	Psig (* = inches mercury below 1 atmosphere	Temp °F
5*	−34	5	−17
4*	−33	6	−15
3*	−32	7	−13
2*	−30	8	−12
1*	−29	9	−10
0	−28	10	−8
1	−26	11	−7
2	−23	12	−5
3	−21	13	−4
4	−19	14	−2

Table 9-B: Pressure-Temperature Table for Ammonia (R-717) (continued)

Ammonia (R−717)		Ammonia (R−717)	
Psig (* = inches mercury below 1 atmosphere	Temp °F	Psig (* = inches mercury below 1 atmosphere	Temp °F
15	−1	44	29
16	1	46	31
17	2	48	32
18	3	50	34
19	4	52	35
20	6	54	37
21	7	56	38
22	8	58	40
23	9	60	41
24	11	62	42
25	12	64	44
26	13	66	45
27	14	68	46
28	15	70	47
29	16	72	49
30	17	74	50
31	18	76	51
32	19	78	52
33	19	80	53
34	20	85	56
35	21	90	58
36	22	95	61
37	23	100	63
38	24	105	66
39	25	110	68
40	26	115	70
42	28	120	73

Ammonia (R−717)	
Psig (* = inches mercury below 1 atmosphere	Temp °F
125	75
130	77
135	79
140	81
145	82
150	84
155	86
160	88
165	90
170	91
175	93
180	95
185	96
190	98
195	99

Ammonia (R−717)	
Psig (* = inches mercury below 1 atmosphere	Temp °F
200	101
205	102
210	104
220	107
230	109
240	112
250	115
260	117
275	121
290	124
305	128
320	131
335	134
350	137
365	140

Halocarbons and related refrigerants were designed to be nontoxic, nonflammable, and stable. However, these refrigerants will displace air and can cause asphyxiation, especially in low areas, because the gases are heavier than air.

An emergency medical crew should not administer adrenalin to someone who is overcome by inhalation of R-11, R-12, or other halocarbons, as this can cause ventricular fibrillation (spasm of the heart muscles). A poison control center and a Material Data Safety Sheet (MSDS) on the individual refrigerant are the best sources of information about emergency treatment. Go to www.refrigerants.com.

Observe the following minimum safety guidelines when handling vapor-compression refrigerants:

1. Ventilate the room if a leak is suspected.

2. Keep the system at or below design operating pressure.

3. Do not mix refrigerants.

4. Do not allow flames in an atmosphere containing halocarbon refrigerants, especially near a system that may be leaking—this can create toxic gas. In case of leak, shut off furnaces and pilot lights and allow gas to escape.

5. Wear goggles and gloves, especially when charging or discharging a system.

6. Do not fill a service cylinder more than 80 percent full with refrigerant, as the fluid needs room to expand if temperature increases. A full cylinder is a bomb waiting to explode.

7. Store cylinders in a cool place.

8. Do not refill disposable cylinders.

9. Do not fill cylinders with anything except what is marked on the label. The chemicals are shipped in cylinders labeled with different colors. Read the label; don't rely on color alone to identify a refrigerant.

10. Do not sniff refrigerants—some can be fatal.

11. Do not rely on sense of smell to detect a leak—use an approved method.

12. Liquid refrigerant can quickly freeze the skin. Wash it off immediately with water and treat frostbite if needed.

WORKING WITH ABSORPTION REFRIGERANTS

The two common types of absorption systems are named by the combination of refrigerant and absorber: (1) water as refrigerant and lithium bromide as absorber; and (2) ammonia as refrigerant and water as absorber. Ammonia may also be used in vapor-compression systems; see above for safety information.

In addition to the general qualities needed by all refrigerants, absorption refrigerants should:

- not form a solid phase at operating temperatures, pressures, and chemistry (same for the absorber);
- be more volatile than the absorber at conditions in the generator; and
- have a strong affinity for the refrigerant.

PRIMARY REGRIGERANTS AS A PURE CHEMICAL

Vapor-compression refrigerants are chosen according to the desired evaporator temperature and the type of components in the system. Refrigerants that evaporate at low temperature are used in low-temperature applications;

otherwise the compressor would have to create extremely low suction pressures. The system refrigerant must also have enough specific heat to remove the heat load under the compressor's pumping rate and head pressure.

Refrigerants are described at their pressures at evaporating and condensing temperatures. (See Table 9-C.)

Originally, vapor-compression refrigerants were mainly *primary refrigerants*, meaning they were made of a single chemical. Many refrigerants are now factory-blended into *azeotropes* or *zeotropes*. An azeotrope is a mixture of volatile substances whose equilibrium vapor-phase and liquid-phase compositions are the same at a specific pressure. For that reason, an azeotrope can be treated much like a primary refrigerant. A zeotrope has different components with different volatilities. Even at constant pressure, the composition and saturation temperatures change during evaporation and condensing.

Table 9-C: Refrigerant Specifications and Performance

Based on 5°F evaporation and 86°F condensation

No.	Name	Formula	Boiling Point at One Atmosphere (°F)	Evaporator Pressure (PSIG)	Condensing Pressure (PSIG)	Compressor Ratio	Net Refrigerant Effect (BTU/LB)	Liquid Refrigerant Circulated (LB/Min)	Liquid Refrigerant Circulated (Cu. In./Min)	Specific Volume of Suction Gas (Cu. Ft./LB)	Compressor Displacement (CFM)	Horsepower (Hp)	Coefficient of Performance	Temperature of Compressor Discharge (°F)
11	Trichloromonofluoromethane	CCl_3F	74.8	24.0*	3.6	6.24	67.3	2.97	56.2	12.27	36.48	0.932	5.06	109
12	Dichlorodifluoromethane	CCl_2F_2	-21.6	11.8	93.3	4.08	50.0	4.00	85.7	1.46	5.83	1.002	4.70	101
22	Monochlorodifluoromethane	$CHClF_2$	-41.4	28.2	158.2	4.03	70.0	2.86	67.4	1.24	3.55	1.011	4.66	128
113	Trichlorotrifluoroethane	$CCl_2F \cdot CClF_2$	117.6	27.9*	13.9*	8.02	53.7	3.73	66.5	27.39	102.03	0.973	4.84	86
114	Dichlorotetrafluoroethane	$CClF_2 \cdot CClF_2$	38.4	16.1*	21.6	5.42	43.1	4.64	89.2	4.34	20.14	1.049	4.49	86
500	Azeotrope of r-12 and	CCl_2F_2/CH_3CHF_2	-28.0	16.4	113.4	4.12	61.1	3.27	79.3	1.52	4.97	1.012	4.66	105
502	Azeotrope of r-115 and R-22	$CClF_2CF_3/CHClF_2$	-50.1	36.0	175.1	3.75	45.7	4.38	99.4	0.825	3.61	1.079	4.37	99
717	Ammonia	NH_3	-28.0	19.6	154.5	4.94	474.4	0.422	19.6	8.15	3.44	0.989	4.76	210

† SATURATED SUCTION VAPOR EXCEPT FOR R-113 AND R-114. IN THESE CASES ENOUGH SUCTION SUPERHEAT WAS ASSUMED TO GIVE A SATURATED DISCHARGE VAPOR

* INCHES OF MERCURY VACUUM

Courtesy of Mueller Industries, Inc.

PRESSURE-TEMPERATURE TABLES

Pressure-temperature (P-T) tables have three essential purposes: (a) to set coil pressure to get the right temperature from the refrigerant, (b) to check superheat at the evaporator outlet, and (c) to check subcooling of liquid refrigerant near the condenser outlet. To read a P-T table, one needs to distinguish tables made for primary and azeotropic refrigerants from those for zeotropic refrigerants. Ammonia gets its own P-T table.

Azeotropic Refrigerants

Most technicians are familiar with the azeotropic P-T table. Once a refrigerant's temperature rises to boiling, the refrigerant temperature does not change until it has all boiled Therefore, there is only one boiling-condensing temperature. Looking at Table 9-D, notice that one temperature is opposite each pressure for each refrigerant. To find the evaporator pressure for a given temperature, look at the temperature, and then look across to the evaporator pressure. P-T tables for azeotropic refrigerants appear as Tables 9-D, 9-E, and 9-F.

A one-column (azeotropic) P-T table is used to:

Check superheat: Measure suction-line temperature and pressure. Convert pressure to temperature, and subtract from actual suction-line temperature. The result is superheat.

Example:

1. With R-134A, suction-line temperature is:	40°
2. Suction-line pressure (26 psig) converted to temperature is:	–30°
3. Subtract to get superheat:	10°

For more information, see Chapter 4, "Controls."

Check subcooling: Measure high-side pressure and convert it to temperature. Take the temperature at the liquid line, and then find the difference between the two temperatures. This is subcooling.

Example:

1. With R-134A, the high-side pressure (70 psig) converted to temperature is:	69°
2. High-side temperature is:	–40°
3. Subtract to get subcooling:	29°

Set low-side operating pressure: Read from the desired evaporator temperature, then find the operating pressure from the vapor column.

Example:

1. With R-134A, the evaporator temperature is:	30°
2. Read across to find suction-line pressure:	26 psig

Table 9-D: Azeotropic P-T Table for R-114, R-12, RT-500, R-22, and R-502

PSIG * = below1 atm.	Temperature °F				
	R-114	R-12	R-500	R-22	R-502
10*	20	-38	-44	-57	-65
9*	23	-36	-42	-55	-63
8*	25	-34	-41	-53	-61
7*	27	-33	-39	-52	-60
6*	28	-31	-37	-50	-58
5*	30	-29	-36	-48	-57
4*	32	-28	-34	-47	-55
3*	34	-26	-33	-46	-54
2*	36	-25	-31	-44	-52
1*	37	-33	-30	-43	-51
0	39	-22	-28	-41	-50
1	42	-19	-26	-39	-47
2	45	-16	-23	-36	-45
3	48	-14	-21	-34	-42
4	50	-11	-18	-32	-40
5	52	-9	-16	-30	-38
6	56	-7	-14	-28	-36
7	58	-4	-12	-26	-34
8	60	-2	-10	-24	-32
9	63	0	-8	-22	-30
10	65	2	-6	-20	-29
11	67	4	-4	-19	-27
12	69	5	-2	-17	-25

13	71	7	0	-15	-24
14	73	9	1	-14	-22
15	75	11	3	-12	-20
16	77	12	4	-11	-19
17	78	14	6	-9	-17
18	80	15	8	-9	-17
19	82	17	9	-6	-16
20	83	18	10	-5	-13
21	85	20	12	-4	-12
22	87	21	13	-2	-11
23	88	23	15	-1	-9
24	90	24	16	0	-8
25	91	26	17	1	-7
26	93	27	18	2	-6
27	94	28	20	4	-5
28	96	29	21	5	-3
29	97	31	22	6	-2
30	98	32	23	7	-1
32	101	34	26	9	1
34	104	37	28	11	3
36	106	39	30	13	5
38	109	41	32	15	7
40	111	43	34	17	9
42	113	45	36	19	11
44	116	47	38	21	13
46	118	49	40	23	15
48	120	51	42	24	16
50	122	53	44	26	18
52	124	55	45	28	20
54	126	57	47	29	21
56	128	59	49	31	23
58	130	60	50	32	24

Table 9-D: Azeotropic P-T Table for R-114, R-12, RT-500, R-22, and R-502 (continued)

PSIG * = below 1 atm.	Temperature °F				
	R-114	R-12	R-500	R-22	R-502
60	132	62	52	34	26
62	134	64	54	35	28
64	136	65	55	37	29
66	137	67	57	38	30
68	139	68	58	40	32
70	141	70	60	41	33
75	145	74	63	44	36
80	149	77	66	47	40
85	153	81	70	51	43
90	156	84	73	53	46
95	160	87	76	56	49
100	163	90	79	59	51
105	167	93	82	62	54
110	170	96	84	64	57
115	173	99	87	67	59
120	176	102	90	69	62
125	179	104	92	72	64
130	182	107	95	74	67
135	185	109	97	76	69
140	188	112	99	78	71
145	190	114	102	81	73
150	193	117	104	83	75
155	196	119	106	85	77
160	198	121	108	87	80
165	201	123	110	89	82
170	203	125	112	91	83
175	205	128	114	92	85
180	208	130	116	94	87

185	210	132	118	96	89
190	212	134	120	98	91
195	214	136	122	100	93
200	217	138	124	101	95
210	221	141	128	105	98
220	225	145	131	108	101
230	229	148	134	111	104
240	233	152	138	114	108
250	236	155	140	117	111
260	240	158	144	120	114
270	243	162	147	123	116
280	247	165	150	126	119
290	250	168	153	128	122
300	253	170	156	131	125
310	256	173	158	133	127
320	259	176	160	136	130
330	262	179	163	138	132
340	265	182	166	141	135
350	268	184	168	143	137
360	271	187	171	145	139
370	273	189	173	148	142
380	276	192	175	150	144
390	278	194	178	152	146
400	281	196	180	154	148

Table 9-E: Azeotropic P-T Table for R-11, R-113, and R-503

PSIG * = below1 atm.	Temperature °F			
	R-11	R-113	R-13	R-503
27*	-20	18	-177	-190
26.5*	-15	23	-173	-186
26*	-10	28	-170	-183
25.5*	-6	32	-168	-180
25*	-2	36	-165	-176
24.5*	1	40	-163	-176
24*	5	44	-160	-173
23*	10	50	-157	-170
22*	15	55	-154	-166
21*	20	60	-150	-163
20*	25	65	-148	-160
19*	29	68	-145	-168
18*	32	72	-143	-155
17*	36	76	-141	-153
16*	39	80	-138	-151
15*	42	83	-136	-149
14*	45	86	-134	-147
13*	47	88	-133	-146
12*	50	91	-131	-144
11*	53	94	-129	-142
10*	55	96	-128	-140
9*	57	99	-126	-139
8*	60	101	-124	-138
7*	62	104	-123	-136
6*	64	106	-122	-135
5*	66	108	-121	-134
4*	68	110	-119	-132
3*	70	112	-118	-131

2*	71	114	-117	-130
1*	73	116	-116	-129
0	75	118	-115	-128
1	78	121	-112	-126
2	81	125	-110	-124
3	85	126	-108	-122
4	87	131	-106	-120
5	90	134	-104	-118
6	93	137	-103	-116
7	96	139	-101	-114
8	96	142	-99	-112
9	101	145	-98	-111
10	103	147	-96	-110
11	105	150	-95	-108
12	107	152	-93	-107
13	110	154	-92	-105
14	112	157	-90	-104
15	114	159	-89	-103
16	116	160	-88	-102
17	118	162	-86	-100
18	120	164	-85	-99
19	121	166	-84	-98
20	123	169	-83	-97
21	125	171	-82	-96
22	127	173	-81	-95
23	128	175	-75	-93
24	130	176	-78	-92
25	132	178	-77	-91
26	133	180	-76	-90
27	135	181	-75	-89
28	136	183	-74	-88
29	136	185	-73	-87

Table 9-E: Azeotropic P-T Table for R-11, R-113, and R-503 (continued)

PSIG * = below1 atm.	Temperature °F			
	R-11	R-113	R-13	R-503
30	139	186	-72	-86
32	142	189	-70	-85
34	145	192	-68	-83
36	148	195	-66	-81
38	150	198	-65	-80
40	153	201	-63	-78
42	155	203	-61	-76
44	158	206	-60	-75
46	160	209	-58	-74
48	163	211	-57	-72
50	165	213	-55	-71
52	167	216	-54	-69
54	169	218	-55	-71
56	171	220	-51	-66
58	173	223	-50	-65
60	175	225	-48	-64
62	177	227	-47	-62
64	179	229'	-46	-61
66	181	231	-44	-60
68	183	233	-43	-59
70	185	235	-42	-58
75	189	240	-39	-55
80	194	244	-36	-52
85	198	249	-33	-50
90	202	253	-31	-48
95	206	257	-28	-45
100	209	261	-26	-43
105	213	265	-23	-40

110	216	269	-21	-38
115	220	272	-19	-36
120	223	276	-17	-34
125	226	279	-15	-32
130	229	282	-12	-30
135	232	286	-10	-29
140	235	289	-5	-27
145	238	292	-7	-25
150	241	295	-5	-23
155	243	298	-3	-22
160	246	301	-1	-20
165	249	304	1	-18
170	251	306	3	-17
175	254	309	4	-15
180	256	312	6	-14
185	259	314	7	-12
190	261	317	9	-11
195	263	319	11	-9
200	266	322	12	-8
210	270	327	15	-5
220	275	331	18	-2
230	279	336	21	0
240	283	340	24	3
250	287	344	26	5
260	291	348	29	8
270	294	352	32	10
280	298	356	34	12
290	302	360	37	14
300	305	364	39	17

Table 9-F: Azeotropic P-T Table for R-124, R-134a, and R-507

PSIG * = below1 atm.	Temperature °F		
	R-124	R-134a	AZ50 or R-507
5*	3	-22	-60
4*	4	-21	-58
3*	6	-19	-57
2*	7	-18	-55
1*	9	-16	-54
0	10	-15	-53
1	13	-12	-50
2	16	-10	-48
3	18	-8	-46
4	21	-5	-44
5	23	-3	-41
6	26	-1	-39
7	28	1	-38
8	30	-3	-36
9	32	5	-34
10	34	7	-32
11	36	8	-31
12	38	10	-29
13	40	12	-27
14	41	13	-26
15	43	15	-24
16	45	16	-23
17	46	18	-21
18	48	19	-20
19	49	21	-19
20	51	22	-17
21	52	24	-16
22	54	25	-15
23	55	26	-14
24	57	27	-12
25	58	29	-11
26	59	30	-10
27	61	31	-9
28	62	32	-8
29	63	33	-7
30	65	35	-6
31	66	36	-4
32	67	37	-3
33	68	38	-2

34	69	39	-1
35	71	40	0
36	72	41	1
37	73	42	2
38	74	38	3
39	75	44	4
40	76	45	4
42	78	47	6
44	80	49	8
46	82	51	10
48	84	52	11
50	86	54	13
52	88	56	15
54	90	57	16
56	91	59	18
58	93	60	19
60	95	62	21
62	97	64	22
64	98	65	24
66	100	66	25
68	101	68	26
70	103	69	28
72	104	71	29
74	106	72	30
76	107	73	32
78	109	75	33
80	110	76	34
85	114	79	37
90	117	82	40
95	120	85	43
100	123	88	45
105	126	90	48
110	129	93	51
115	132	96	53
120	135	98	55
125	138	100	58
130	140	103	60
135	143	105	62
140	145	107	64
145	148	109	66
150	150	112	68
155	152	114	70
160	154	116	72
165	157	118	74

Table 9-F: Azeotropic P-T Table for R-124, R-134a, and R-507 (continued)

PSIG * = below1 atm.	Temperature °F		
	R-124	R-134a	AZ50 or R-507
170	159	120	76
175	161	122	78
180	163	123	80
185	165	125	82
190	167	127	83
195	169	129	85
200	171	131	87
205	173	132	88
210	175	134	90
220	178	137	93
230	182	140	96
240	185	143	99
250	188	146	102
260	192	149	105
275	196	153	109
290	201	157	113
305	205	161	117
320	209	165	120
335	213	169	124
350	217	172	127
365	221	176	130

Zeotropic Refrigerants

The *zeotropic refrigerants* are more challenging, because they break the rule about temperature stability during change of state. As these refrigerants start to boil, their temperatures also rise until they hit the superheated region, where boiling is complete. P-T tables for zeotropic refrigerants show two pressures, one for the "bubble point" (where bubbles of vapor form in a warming liquid), and the second for the "dew point" (where dewdrops form in a cooling vapor). The difference between them is called the "glide."

If the bubble and dew points are close together, manufacturers may list only one pressure, but if the glide is at least a few psi, they will list two pressures.

A two-column (zeotropic) P-T table can be used to:

Check superheat: Measure suction-line temperature and temperature, as usual. Now subtract the saturated temperature from the *dew point column* (see Table 9-G) to get superheat.

Example:

1. With R-408A, suction-line temperature is:	0°
2. Suction-line pressure (–19 psig) converted to temperature (dew-point column) is:	–12°
3. Subtract to get superheat:	12°

Check subcooling: Measure pressure of the liquid line and convert to temperature, using the *bubble point column*. Measure temperature at the condenser and subtract from the temperature just measured.

Example:

1. With R-408A, high-side pressure (72 psig) converted to temperature (bubble point column) is:	36°
2. Liquid-line temperature is:	–16°
3. Subtract to get subcooling:	20°

With a two-column P-T table, focus on which state is most important. If saturated vapor is a concern, use the dew (vapor) point. If saturated liquid is a concern, use the bubble (liquid) point.

Table 9-G: Zeotropic Refrigerants Pressure-Temperature Table

D = dew point; B = bubble point

Temperature °F

PSIG * = below 1 atm.	MP39/401K Dew pt.	MP39/401K Bubble pt.	HP80/402 (L) D	HP80/402 (L) B	HP62/404A (S) D	HP62/404A (S) B	KLEA 60/407A D	KLEA 60/407A B	FX-10/408: D	FX-10/408: B	FX-56/409A D	FX-56/409A B
5*	-23		-59		-57		-45		-54		-22	
4*	-23		-58		-56		-43		-52		-20	
3*	-20		-56		-54		-42		-51		-19	
2*	-19		-55		-53		-41		-49		-17	
1*	-17		-54		-52		-39		-48		-16	
0	-16		-53		-50		-38		-47		-15	
1	-13		-50		-48		-36		-44		-12	
2	-11		-48		-46		-33		-42		-9	
3	-9		-45		-43		-31		-39		-7	
4	-6		-43		-41		-29		-37		-5	

PSIG * = below 1 atm.	MP39/401K	HP80/402 (L)		HP62/404A (S)		KLEA 60/407A		FX-10/408:		FX-56/409A	
	Dew pt.	Bubble pt.	D	D	B	D	B	D	B	D	B
5	-4		-41	-39		-27		-35		-2	
6	-2		-39	-37		-25		-33		0	
7	0		-37	-35		-23		-31		2	
8	2		-36	-33		-21		-29		4	
9	4		-34	-22		-20		-27		6	
10	6		-32	-30		-18		-26		8	
11	8		-30	-28		-16		-24		9	
12	9		-29	-27		-15		-22		11	
13	11		-27	-25		-13		-21		13	
14	13		-26	-23		-12		-19		14	
15	14		-24	-22		-10		-18		16	
16	16		-23	-20		-9		-16		17	
17	17		-21	-19		-8		-15		19	

Table 9-G: Zeotropic Refrigerants Pressure-Temperature Table (continued)

PSIG * = below 1 atm.	MP39/401K		HP80/402 (L)		HP62/404A (S)		KLEA 60/407A		FX-10/408:		FX-56/409A	
	Dew pt.	Bubble pt.	D	B	D	B	D	B	D	B	D	B
18	19		-20		-18		-6		-13		20	
19	20		-19		-16		-5		-12		22	
20	21		-17		-15		-4		-11		23	
21	23		-16		-14		-2		-9		25	
22	24		-15		-12		-1		-8		26	
23	25		-14		-11		0		-7		27	
24	27		-12		-10		1		-5		29	
25	28		-11		-9		2		-4		30	
26	29		-10		-8		4		-3		31	
27	30		-9		-7		5		-2		32	
28	32		-8		-5		6		-1		34	
29	33		-7		-4		7		0		35	
30	34		-6		-3		8		1		36	

PSIG * = below 1 atm.	MP39/401K		HP80/402 (L)		HP62/404A (S)		KLEA 60/407A		FX-10/408:		FX-56/409A	
	Dew pt.	Bubble pt.	D	B	D	B	D	B	D	B	D	B
31	35		-5		-2		9		3		37	
32	36		-4		-1		10		4		38	
33	37		-2		0		11		5		39	
34	38		-1		1		12		6		40	
35	39		0		2		13		7		41	
36	40	30	0		3		14		8		43	
37	42	32	1		4		15		9		44	
38	43	32	2		5		16		10		45	30
39	44	33	3		6		17		11		46	31
40	45	34	4		7		18		12		47	32
42	46	36	6		9		19		13		48	34
44	48	38	8		10		21		15		50	36
46	50	40	10		12		23		17			38

Table 9-G: Zeotropic Refrigerants Pressure-Temperature Table (continued)

PSIG * = below 1 atm.	MP39/401K Dew pt.	HP80/402 (L) Bubble pt.	HP80/402 (L) D	HP80/402 (L) B	HP62/404A (S) D	HP62/404A (S) B	KLEA 60/407A D	KLEA 60/407A B	FX-10/408: D	FX-10/408: B	FX-56/409A B	FX-56/409A D	FX-56/409A B
48		42	11		14		24		19		39		
50		44	13		15		26		20		41		
52		45	14		17		28		22		43		
54		47	16		19		29		24		45		
56		49	18		20		31		25		46		
58		50	19		22		32		27		48		
60		52	20		23		33		28		50		
62		53	22		25		35		30		51		
64		55	23		26		36		31	31	53		
66		56	25		27		38		32	32	54		
68		58	26		29		39		34	33	56		
70		59	27		30		40	30	35	34	57		
72		61	29		31	30	41	31	37	36	58		

PSIG * = below 1 atm.	MP39/401K	HP80/402 (L)		HP62/404A (S)		KLEA 60/407A		FX-10/408:		FX-56/409A	
	Dew pt.	Bubble pt.	D	B	D	B	D	B	D	D	B
74		62	30			32	43	37	38		60
76		64	31		33	33	44	38	39		61
78		65	32	30	34	34	45	40	40		63
80		66	34	31	35	35	46	41	42		64
85		69	37	34	36	38	49	44	45		67
90		73	40	37	39	41		47	48		70
95		76	42	40	42	44		50	50		73
100		78	45	43	45	47		52			76
105		81	48	45	48	50		55			79
110		84	50	48	50	52		57			82
115		87		50		55		60			84
120		89		53		57		62			87
125		92		55		59		65			89

Table 9-G: Zeotropic Refrigerants Pressure-Temperature Table (continued)

PSIG * = below 1 atm.	MP39/401K		HP80/402 (L)		HP62/404A (S)		KLEA 60/407A		FX-10/408:		FX-56/409A	
	Dew pt.	Bubble pt.	D	B	D	B	D	B	D	B	D	B
130		94		57		61		62		67		92
135		96		60		64		64		69		94
140		99		62		66		66		71		96
145		101		64		68		68		73		99
150		103		66		70		70		76		101
155		105		66		72		72		78		103
160		108		70		74		74		80		105
165		110		72		76		76		81		107
170		112		74		78		78		83		109
175		114		75		80		80		85		111
180		116		77		81		81		87		113
185		117		79		83		83		89		115
190		119		81		85		85		91		117

PSIG* = below 1 atm.	MP39/401K	HP80/402 (L)	HP62/404A (S)		KLEA 60/407A		FX-10/408:		FX-56/409A		
	Dew pt.	Bubble pt.	D	B	D	B	D	B	D	B	B
195		121		82		87		87		92	119
200		123		84		88		88		94	121
205		125		86		90		90		96	123
210		127		87		92		91		97	124
220		130		91		95		94		100	128
230		133		94		98		97		104	131
240		136		97		101		100		107	134
250		140		99		104		103		109	137
260		143		102		107		106		112	141
275		147		106		111		110		116	145
290		151		110		114		114		120	149
305		155		114		118		117		124	153
320		159		118		122		121		128	157

Table 9-G: Zeotropic Refrigerants Pressure-Temperature Table (continued)

PSIG * = below 1 atm.	MP39/401K		HP80/402 (L)		HP62/404A (S)		KLEA 60/407A		FX-10/408:		FX-56/409A	
	Dew pt.	Bubble pt.	D	B	D	B	D	B	D	B	D	B
335		163		121		125		124		131		161
350		167		125		129		128		135		165
365		170		128		132		131		138		168

THE OZONE PROBLEM

The ACR industry, long dedicated to human comfort and safe food preservation, has been transformed by the environmental impact of halocarbon refrigerants. In 1974, two scientists suggested that CFCs could rise to the upper atmosphere, release halogen atoms, and destroy huge numbers of ozone molecules, which protect Earth's surface from ultraviolet light. They warned that the thinning of the stratospheric ozone layer could spark an epidemic of skin cancer and harm ecosystems, animals, and crops. Although industry ignored the warnings at first, over the next 15 years, it became clear that the same stability that made CFCs good refrigerants was also allowing them to drift to the stratosphere, 8 to 30 miles up, and deliver halogen atoms that destroy ozone.

Ozone is an oxygen molecule with three atoms, unlike the more common (and breathable) oxygen molecule, which has two. Ozone occurs in two places, with quite different health impacts.

Ground-level (tropospheric) ozone occurs up to about 6 miles in the atmosphere. This stuff oxidizes rubber, damages lung tissue, and aggravates diseases like asthma and chronic obstructive pulmonary disease (COPD, or emphysema). Ground-level ozone is produced when sunlight powers chemical reactions between nitrogen oxides and volatile organic compounds. Factories, electric utilities, vehicles, gas stations, and chemical solvents are major sources of nitrogen oxides and volatile organic compounds.

Stratospheric ozone occurs above an altitude of about 10 miles. The stratospheric "ozone layer" contains about 90% of all ozone in the atmosphere. This ozone is essential to life on Earth, because it intercepts incoming ultraviolet-B (UV-B) radiation—powerful radiation that can cause skin cancer and cataracts, suppress the immune system, damage plants and animals, and even penetrate water and harm fish and marine plants. The ozone layer does a lot with a little: all this ozone at sea-level pressure would make a layer just 1/4" thick! Still, we're talking 3 billion tons of ozone.

The basic picture of ozone destruction has changed little since the 1970s: Chlorine and bromine, carried aloft by stable CFCs and other molecules, including the halons used for fire-suppression equipment, rise high into the atmosphere, where they break apart and release chlorine and bromine, which in turn form highly reactive structures that destroy ozone. Each chlorine atom can destroy thousands of ozone molecules, and chlorine may remain in the stratosphere for a century, destroying ozone the whole time. Eventually, chlorine and bromine drop back toward the surface and get removed by snow and rain. In 1999, 23% of ozone-depleting chlorine in the stratosphere came from the venting of R-11, and 32% from R-12, two of the most popular (and damaging) refrigerants.

The Ozone Hole and Montreal Protocol

The ozone threat remained theoretical for a few years. Then, in the mid-1980s, an alarming "ozone hole" appeared above Antarctica, making the first definite sign of ozone depletion. A second, less drastic decline appeared in the Northern Hemisphere. In 1987, representatives of forty-three nations signed the Montreal Protocol, pledging to cut CFC production in half by 1999. But as scientists began measuring ozone, they found alarming declines: between 1997 and 2001, total stratospheric ozone decreased 3%. As other scientific studies documented the damage of individual refrigerants to the ozone layer, the Protocol was tightened five times by 1999. The ACR industry was forced to find alternative refrigerants, to stop venting ozone-damaging refrigerants to the atmosphere, and to start recovering, reconditioning, and recycling existing refrigerants. Table 9-H shows how the Protocol will reduce chlorine levels in the upper atmosphere.

Table 9-H: Effects of the International Treaties on Ozone-Depleting Chemicals

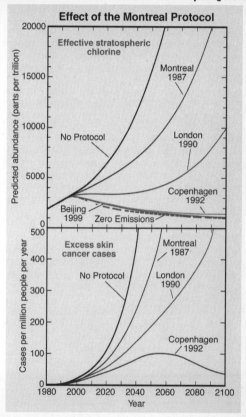

City names and dates indicate amendments that tightened the original Montreal Protocol.

CFCs also feed into the greenhouse effect, which occurs when gases in the atmosphere reflect heat back to Earth. Increases in these gases—including carbon dioxide, methane and CFCs—could raise the average global temperature 10°F in the next century—about as much warming as has occurred since the last ice age, when Canada and the Midwestern United States were under a mile of ice! After a string of record temperatures over the past 15 years, global warming is clearly much more than environmentalist scare tactics.

Although the Montreal Protocol placed heavy responsibility on the ACR industry, industry has responded. Chemical companies have invented many replacement refrigerants that should have little or no impact on the ozone layer. Admittedly, the ozone problem made life more complicated for ACR technicians. With so many new refrigerants on the market, some people feel they are doing "on-the-job testing" for the industry. But the good news is that as people follow the Protocol, the level of ozone-depleters in the atmosphere has begun to drop. If the Protocol continues to be followed, scientists expect the ozone layer to heal by the middle of the twenty-first century. The ozone story is the best example of international cooperation to prevent an environmental disaster, and the response will save lives.

EPA Requirements

In the United States, the Environmental Protection Agency (EPA) governs the recovery and recycling of ozone-depleting compounds from stationary sources under section 608 of the Clean Air Act. Additional details can be found at www.epa.gov/ozone/title6/608/index.html.

In particular, Section 608:

- requires service practices that maximize recycling of ozone-depleting compounds (chlorofluorocarbons [CFCs], hydrochlorofluorocarbons [HCFCs], and blends) during the servicing and disposal of air conditioning and refrigeration equipment;

- sets certification requirements for recycling and recovery equipment, technicians, and reclaimers;

- restricts the sale of refrigerant to certified technicians;

- requires persons servicing or disposing of air conditioning and refrigeration equipment to certify to the EPA that they have acquired recycling or recovery equipment and are complying with the rule;

- requires the repair of substantial leaks in ACR equipment with a charge greater than 50 pounds (Leaks in the commercial and industrial-process refrigeration sectors must be repaired when they would release at least

35% of the charge over a year. Leaks in all other sectors, including comfort-cooling, must be repaired when they would release at least 15% of the charge over a year.); and

• establishes safe-disposal requirements to ensure removal of refrigerants from goods that enter the waste stream with the charge intact (e.g., motor vehicle air conditioners, home refrigerators, and room air conditioners).

Since 1992, the EPA has practically banned venting of halocarbon (CFC and HCFC) refrigerants into the atmosphere during maintenance, service, repair, or disposal of air conditioning or refrigeration equipment. Four types of releases are still permissible:

1. Minimal releases during good-faith attempts to recapture and recycle, or safely dispose of refrigerant (Note the requirements for system evacuation in Table 9-1).

2. Emitted refrigerants in the course of normal operation of air conditioning and refrigeration equipment, such as from mechanical purging and minor leaks

3. Releases of CFCs or HCFCs that are not used as refrigerants, such as mixtures of nitrogen and R-22 being used as holding charges or as gases for leak testing

4. Small releases from refrigerant purging hoses or from connecting or disconnecting hoses to charge or service appliances

Table 9-I: Required System Evacuation Before Service

Type of Appliance	Inches of Mercury Vacuum* Using Equipment Manufactured:	
	Before Nov. 15, 1993	On or after Nov. 15, 1993
HCFC-22 appliance** normally containing less than 200 pounds of refrigerant	0	0
HCFC-22 appliance** normally containing 200 pounds or more of refrigerant	4	10
Other high-pressure appliance** normally containing less than 200 pounds of refrigerant (CFC-12, -500, -502, -114)	4	10
Other high-pressure appliance** normally containing 200 pounds or more of refrigerant (CFC-12, -500, -502, -114)	4	15
Very High Pressure Appliance (CFC-13, -503)	0	0
Low-Pressure Appliance (CFC-11, HCFC-123)	25	25 mm Hg absolute

* Relative to standard atmospheric pressure of 29.9" Hg

** Or isolated component of such an appliance

Source: US EPA, http://www.epa.gov/ozone/title6/608/608evtab.html, last updated March 25, 2005

Technician Certification

The EPA has a certification program for technicians who perform operations that could be expected to release refrigerants into the atmosphere. According to the agency, "technicians":

- attach and detach hoses and gauges to and from an appliance to measure pressure within the appliance;
- add refrigerant to, or remove refrigerant from, an appliance; and
- do any other activity that violates the integrity of appliances that use the vapor-compression cycle.

The EPA has four types of certification:

- Type 1: For servicing small appliances.
- Type 2: For servicing or disposing of high- or very high-pressure appliances, except small appliances and motor vehicle air conditioners.
- Type 3: For servicing or disposing of low-pressure appliances.
- Universal: For servicing all types of equipment.

To become certified under the mandatory program, technicians must pass an EPA-approved test given by an EPA-approved certifying organization. Technicians who work on commercial and industrial cooling systems generally need the universal certification. Apprentices do not need certification if they are closely and continually supervised by a certified technician. Section 608 Technician Certification credentials do not expire.

Technicians servicing appliances that contain at least 50 pounds of refrigerant must provide the owner with an invoice that indicates the amount of refrigerant added to the appliance. Technicians must also keep a copy of their proof of certification at their place of business.

10

Troubleshooting

Troubleshooting is the process of tracing a symptom back to its source. Often, you must analyze several complaints before finding the source or sources of problems. Good troubleshooting does not stop with replacing faulty parts—it also requires finding and correcting whatever condition caused the part to fail.

Although a "try this, replace that" approach is common in the trade, troubleshooting is best done logically. Each technician should develop a method that is comfortable, thorough, and effective. This chapter contains an overall vapor-compression troubleshooting guide that starts from three general problems: (1) the compressor motor fails to start, (2) the system cools but runs erratically, and (3) the system runs without producing enough cooling.

This chapter also contains detailed troubleshooting guides for other components. After isolating the problem, consult these chapters as needed.

- Compressor (Chapter 3)
- Condenser (Chapter 5)
- Expansion valve (Chapter 4)
- High-side float (Chapter 4)
- Low-side float (Chapter 4)
- Oil-control system (Chapter 8)
- Absorption system (Chapter 8)
- Motor (Chapter 6)
- Pump (Chapter 5)

BASIC SYSTEM REQUIREMENTS

To function properly, a cooling system must have:

1. Sufficient liquid refrigerant in the evaporator.
2. Evaporator pressure low enough so refrigerant can boil at the desired temperature.
3. Sufficient contact between the cooled space and the evaporator.
4. Correct temperature and pressure in the condenser.
5. Properly sized condenser.

6. Sufficient heat removal from the condenser.

7. Liquid line large enough and not restricted.

8. Little pressure drop in the suction line; no excessive restriction in filters, driers, valves, or other line components.

9. A control system that can establish and maintain the desired conditions in a safe and economical manner.

TROUBLESHOOTING BASICS

The first step in troubleshooting is to ask the owner or operator about the problem. Then install the gauge manifold. During troubleshooting, keep asking yourself, "Why is this happening?" "What else could cause these symptoms?" "Why does this switch not stay closed?"

If a system is not running, you can take the pressure and check if the circuits are energized. But to learn more, you must get the motor running, so troubleshooting often starts with a look at electrical components.

If the system is operating but not cooling properly, concentrate on the pressure-temperature aspect, especially the operating and capacity controls. If the system is new, the problem is likely to be found in design, wiring, control setting, or the proper rotation of motors. Trouble in established systems may build up for a long while before surfacing. Check for worn parts, plugged filters, or sagging or leaking pipes.

Perhaps vibration has weakened or loosened something, or a change in operating conditions caused the problem. Has the operator recently changed a setting or procedure? Sometimes, several factors can cause the same operating deficits, which can challenge you to sift through the possible sources of trouble and finger the true culprit.

The ability to think through the intricacies of a cooling system is a great asset in troubleshooting. For example, a frosted crankcase does not prove that the compressor is getting enough cooling from the suction line. True, the refrigerant is cold, but it is also less dense, and thus has less ability to remove heat from the compressor. Thus, subnormal suction pressure-temperature can lead, somewhat paradoxically, to overheating.

Your five senses can tell you a lot about a balky system. For example:

- **Look** for vibration, gauge readings, leaks, and broken or loose parts.

- **Listen** for compressor knocks, valves opening or closing, and switches clicking at the right time.

- **Feel** for temperature changes, pipes that are hot when they should be cool, or vice versa.
- **Smell** for burned wire insulation, hot parts, or slipping belts.

VAPOR-COMPRESSION SYSTEMS

The following contains troubleshooting guides to the system, condenser, metering device, high- and low-side floats, and oil-control systems.

If a system will not run, start troubleshooting with *Unit Fails to Start*. Once you get the system running, take gauge pressures and analyze further, with help from suggestions in *Unit Runs Erratically, Unit Runs But Does Not Cool Sufficiently,* or *Compressor Loses Oil.* If you can trace the problem to a certain component, turn to the section on that component.

Table 10-A: Vapor-Compression System Troubleshooting

Major Symptom	Minor Symptom	Problem	Test	Solution
Unit Fails to Start				
No hum	No power at motor, starter, or relay	Open switch or blown fuse	Test across line side of starter to ground with voltmeter	Find out why protector is open and close it; replace fuse
	Power at motor, starter, or relay, but contacts in starter or relay are open	Open motor control—no signal to coil	Test holding coil with voltmeter (relay is normally open); if coil is not powered, test through control circuit with continuity tester or voltmeter	Isolate problem and correct
		Open relay with energized holding coil	Test through holding coil with continuity tester or voltmeter	Replace holding coil
	Contacts closed; no hum	Burned contacts in starter	Check load side of starter with voltmeter; check contacts with ohmmeter for low resistance	Replace faulty starter if resistance is high

		Open windings in motor	Check motor continuity with voltmeter	Replace faulty motor
Contactor closed				
Motor hums	Any motor	Shorts or grounds in winding	Check compressor windings with ohmmeter	Replace motor
	Three-phase motor	Compressor is stuck	Check oil level in crankcase with sight glass or dipstick; attempt to rock compressor manually	If good, reverse any two power wires to reverse rotation; rebuild compressor
	Single-phase, capacitor-start and run	Compressor is stuck or start capacitor is bad	Check oil level in crankcase with sight glass or dipstick; attempt to rock compressor manually; check start and run capacitors	Replace capacitors if needed; try a hard-start kit; rebuild compressor
	Single-phase, permanent-split capacitor	Compressor is stuck	Inspect starting relay visually or test with voltmeter	Replace starting relay
		Open winding	Test with voltmeter	Replace compressor
		Bad capacitor	Test with capacitor checker	Replace capacitor
	Compressor is stuck, motor tests okay	Refrigerant pressure not balancing in off cycle	Check with gauge manifold	Low-pressure cut-out control set too close together; expand differential; check metering device; replace plugged capillary tube or valve to balance pressure

Table 10-A: Vapor-Compression System Troubleshooting (continued)

Major Symptom	Minor Symptom	Problem	Test	Solution
Unit Runs Erratically				
Compressor short-cycles	Control circuit makes and breaks	Faulty control	Use meters to isolate problem control	Repair or replace
	Low-pressure control short-cycles	Leaks; plugged filter-drier in liquid line; low air flow across evaporator; solenoid not closing; control set too close	Use gauge manifold to isolate problem	Repair leaks; adjust or replace components as necessary
		Low evaporator load; low air flow	Examine load situation; check for dirty filter plugging evaporator air flow; check for broken fan belt or motor problem	Repair problem; shut off unused evaporators on multi-evaporator system
	High-pressure control short-cycles	Air-cooled condenser plugged with debris or fan inoperative	Compare condenser inlet- to outlet-air temperature; inspect condenser fan and controls	Repair or replace as indicated

		Water-cooled condenser valve not opening; cooling tower pump not working; strainer plugged; water side of condenser fouled or scaled	Compare inlet-to outlet-water temperatures in condenser; inspect condenser pump, piping, controls, water valve; check for plugged strainers in piping (pull out plug at bottom of strainer and check that water runs out)	Repair or replace valve; clean or replace strainer
		Pump motor faulty	Check relays and capacitor	Replace part or repair motor
	Water leaving condenser too warm	Condenser water pump not pumping enough water	Check holding coil of pump controller; vent condenser	Repair or replace if still needed
		Overcharge of refrigerant or noncondensables in condensor	Check for noncondensables (see condenser procedures); if absent, check charge level	Bleed off noncondensable or excess refrigerant
Compressor runs continuously	Room too cold or product temperature too low	Thermostat not opening; contacts welded on LPCO	Check calibration of thermostat; check action of LPCO	Repair or replace as indicated
Unit Runs But Does Not Cool Sufficiently				
	Room or product warm	Lack of refrigerant	Check for bubbles in sight glass	Repair leak and recharge

Table 10-A: Vapor-Compression System Troubleshooting (continued)

Major Symptom	Minor Symptom	Problem	Test	Solution
	High suction pressure and low head pressure	Leaking valves or blown head gasket	Test pressures with gauge manifold; remove head and check gasket and valves	Pump down, replace faulty parts, reassemble, and recharge
HPCO locks out, will not automatically reset	Water leaving condenser is cool	Fouled or limed condenser tubes; pump inoperative	Compare incoming- and outgoing-water temperature differential—if too small, poor contact between water and refrigerant due to fouling or liming; check pump and valve operation	Clean tubes with brush or acid; repair or replace pump or valve
	Hot-air cooled condenser	Noncondensables (air) in refrigerant tubing	Check for air	Purge air from condenser tubes
	Evaporative condenser	Low air movement; low water flow	Check fan belt and motor; check water pump	Repair or replace faulty parts; acid-clean tubes
	Refrigerant leaving condenser is too hot	Overcharge	Check level of liquid refrigerant in condenser tubes with back of hand: area with liquid refrigerant will be cool, area with vapor will be warm (a high level indicates excess refrigerant)	Remove excess refrigerant

Low head pressure	Water leaving condenser is cold	Water valve stuck open	Check water leaving condenser; temperature should be warm	Repair water valve
	Bubbles in sight glass	Low charge	Check sight glass	Locate leak, repair, and recharge
	Suction pressure rises quickly on shut-down	Discharge valves leaking back	Check valves with gauge manifold; pull head and inspect valves and gasket	Fix problem
	High suction pressure while running	Internal relief open or blown; head gasket blown (high-side to low-side)	Install gauge manifold and try to pump down; if unable, pull head to inspect	Fix problem
High suction pressure	Compressors run continuously	Large load on evaporator	Check if load is abnormally large; system may be too small	This may be a normal reaction to a large cooling load; "if it ain't broke, don't fix it!"
	Suction line too cold	TXV overfeeding or oversized	Check superheat and sensing bulb placement; check valve rating	Adjust superheat; repair or replace valve with proper size; reattach bulb securely
	Noisy compressor	Broken valves	Pull head and check; check for floodback; check temperature of various heads; cooler heads will have broken valves	Repair or replace as indicated; check metering device and superheat to correct floodback before restarting

Table 10-A: Vapor-Compression System Troubleshooting (continued)

Major Symptom	Minor Symptom	Problem	Test	Solution
	Inadequate cooling	Compressor will not pump because unloader is stuck	Check oil pump discharge pressure, unloader oil pressure, electric unloader assembly solenoid, unloader valve filter; compare full-load amps (from nameplate) to actual amp draw	Fix problem
Low suction pressure	Bubbles in sight glass	Lack of refrigerant	Check sight glass	Find leak; repair and recharge
		Unloaders not working due to dirty screen or wrong setting	Check screen and setting	Correct or consult manufacturer's information
	Temperature drop at liquid line filter-drier	Plugged filter-drier	Compare temperature on each side of filter drier	Pump down system, clean, and recharge
	Temperature drop at solenoid valve	Valve not fully open	Compare temperature on each side of valve	Pump down system, dismantle, and clean valve; recharge
	Low flow through TXV	Power element dead; inlet screen partly plugged	Check power element; check superheat; check screen	Pump down, replace power element; clean screen in TXV
Compressor Loses Oil				
	Low oil level in sight glass	Initial oil charge was inadequate	Check at sight glass	Add oil

	Compressor loses oil gradually	Oil settling out in system	Check pitch of suction and hot gas lines for presence of traps; run compressor continuously to bring oil back to compressor	Correct pipe pitch to remove traps and add oil if needed
		Dirty strainers and/or drier	Inspect suspect parts	Clean strainer, replace drier
	Cold crankcase	Refrigerant flooding back and filling crankcase	Check crankcase with continuity meter; check TXV superheat; check contact between suction line and TXV sensing bulb	Fix problem
	Oil leaking outside compressor	Loose fitting and/or gasket; other leak	Inspect entire oil system	Tighten fittings and/or replace gasket or leaking part

Condenser

The major troubles with condensers stem from restrictions in the supply of air or water used to dispose of heat. The refrigerant temperature in an air-cooled condenser should be about 30° to 35°F (16.7° to 19.5°C) above outside ambient temperature. In a water-cooled condenser, refrigerant temperature should be about 10° to 15°F (5.6° to 8.3°C) above ambient temperature. Add this temperature to the ambient and convert to pressure to find the correct head pressure. If the system is operating at a significantly different pressure, troubleshoot the problem.

A thin film of dirt can significantly slow heat transfer. Clean a dirty air-cooled condenser with high-pressure air or water-detergent solution. Use a pressure washer or a garden hose with a cleaning attachment.

A leaking air-cooled condenser may be repaired, but a leaking water-cooled unit is usually replaced. Straighten fins with a fin comb, a plastic device that fits one or two sizes of fins. (See Chapter 11, "Standard ACR Procedures.")

Testing the Condenser for Air

Air in the condenser can cause excess head pressure, sometimes high enough to trip limits. Air cuts efficiency because it does not condense at system pressures, so it robs valuable condenser room.

Use the following steps to check for noncondensable gas (mainly air) in a condenser:

1. If a purge valve is present, shut the compressor off and allow its fan or water pump to run for 15 minutes. During this time the air will gather at the top of the condenser and liquid refrigerant at the bottom.

2. Compare head pressure with pressure for ambient-temperature air (or condenser water for a water-cooled condenser). If the difference is greater than about 15 psi, there probably is noncondensable gas in the system.

3. Briefly open the purge valve. Again compare head pressure to the equivalent pressure for condenser air or water. Purge again if the pressure differential is still above 15 psi.

4. Purging is limited by EPA regulations. (See Chapter 9, "Refrigerants.") One may need to evacuate and recharge to remove a great deal of air.

Do not purge a water-cooled condenser so fast that the temperature falls below freezing, as this could burst the condenser. Eyeball the pressure gauge while purging.

Scale, the buildup of minerals inside condenser water tubes, can be a major problem with water-cooled condensers, as it can seriously slow heat transfer. Remove scale with an acid solution.

A "scale free" system has been developed to reduce the deposition of scale. An electrolyte rod is placed in the condenser water and grounded to the equipment. The system can even cause existing scale to enter solution for removal.

Air-Cooled Condenser

Table 10-B: Air-Cooled Condenser Troubleshooting

Symptom	Problem	Solution
Undercooling by system	Fan operating incorrectly	Check motor, belts, fan speed, and operating controls; repair as necessary.
		Check operation of variable- or multiple-stage fans and repair as needed
	Fins plugged	Clean and straighten if needed
Head pressure excessive	Noncondensable air robbing condenser of space	Purge air through valve on top of condenser (see above)
	System overcharged	Bleed off excess charge
	Condenser cooling blocked	Inspect and remove blockage; check for worn fan belt, damaged fan blades, or dirty, corroded, or bent fins; repair as needed
Head pressure too low	System undercharged	Add refrigerant until charge is correct

Water-Cooled Condenser

Table 10-C: Water-Cooled Condenser Troubleshooting

Symptom	Problem	Solution
Unit does not cool sufficiently	Incoming condenser water too warm	Correct problem at cooling tower or wherever heat is removed.
Condenser tubes plugged	Scales on tubes interfering with water flow and heat transfer	Clean with acid and begin a program to control scale if the problem is severe. Handle acids carefully.
Condenser pressure and temperature higher than expected, liquid line warm; other system parameters working	Corrosion from improper cleaning.	Replace condenser.
System erratic	Excess oil in condenser	Install better oil control system.

Metering Device

The metering device has one basic job—to control the flow of refrigerant into the evaporator under all load conditions. If the evaporator gets too little refrigerant, the superheat will be too high and the motor may overheat. If the evaporator gets too much refrigerant, superheat will be too low, and there is a danger of floodback.

The troubleshooting guide (see Table 10-D) describes the basic complaints, possible causes, and corrective actions on both automatic expansion (AXV) and thermostatic expansion (TXV) valves. The information applies to both devices unless otherwise stated. To check the capillary tube as a metering device, see Chapter 4, "Controls."

Table 10-D: Metering Device Troubleshooting

Symptom	Problem	Solution
Low suction pressure with high superheat—inlet pressure (head pressure) too low	Excessive vertical lift of refrigerant; inadequate head pressure; condensing temperature low	Replace liquid line with correct size; increase head pressure
	Flash gas in liquid line; insufficient charge; noncondensable gas in system	Depends on cause of flash gas; to ensure a solid stream of liquid at the metering device, add refrigerant; purge noncondensible gases; clean strainers and filter-driers; check size of lines; increase head pressure; add heat exchanger in liquid line
	Orifice plugged by moisture, dirt, or wax	Moisture and dirt: install new filter-drier; wax: replace rise oil
	Excessive pressure drop; evaporator causes false evaporator pressure reading at TXV body	Install external equalizer
	Superheat adjusted too high	Readjust according to manufacturer's instructions
	Diaphragm or bellows ruptured	Replace valve
	Valve power assembly (remote sensing bulb) has lost charge	Replace bulb or entire valve
	Restriction elsewhere in system, caused by undersized or plugged component	Usually marked by frost; repair replace problem component
Low suction pressure with low superheat (usually indicates poor distribution or unequal evaporator loading)	If distribution is poor, refrigerant will take the easiest path back to the compressor	Install a proper distributor and balance loads on the evaporators
	Compressor oversized or running too fast	Install capacity control on compressor; change pulleys to slow compressor

Table 10-D: Metering Device Troubleshooting (continued)

Symptom	Problem	Solution
	Inadequate air flow due to plugged filters or balky fan motor	Clean filters; check and repair or replace motor
	Evaporator too small (shows excessive icing)	Replace with the proper sized evaporator
High suction pressure with high superheat	System out of balance; compressor too small; evaporator too large; load too great	Balance the system by replacing components; test system and compare operating conditions with temperature-pressure charts
	Compressor valves leaking	Test compressor; repair or replace if needed
High suction pressure with low superheat	Compressor undersized	Replace with proper unit
	Superheat setting too low	Measure suction pressure and evaporator outlet temperature to determine present superheat setting; readjust if needed
	Valve held open due to foreign matter	Clean valve; repair or replace filter-drier
	External equalizer line plugged or capped	Replace equalizer line
Fluctuating suction pressure	Superheat adjustment incorrect	Adjust superheat
	External equalizer linked to several TXVs	Install a separate equalizer for each TXV
	Liquid refrigerant flooding back due to poor distributor or uneven evaporator loading	Install proper distributor; ensure that air flow across evaporator is balanced
	Excessive blower speed or frequent blower cycling causes large pressure differences	Check coils, thermostat overloads, and other controls; repair or replace as needed
	Oversized metering device hunting	Replace with correct size

High- and Low-Side Floats

The high-side float (HSF) and the low-side float (LSF) are relatively free from operating problems, and since they are rather inaccessible, this is just as well. The following conditions may arise with these controls.

Table 10-E: High-Side Float Troubleshooting

Symptom	Problem	Solution
No cooling—no refrigerant flow	Float stuck closed	Tap housing with soft hammer to dislodge
	Float full of liquid or collapsed	Pump down system and replace float
Suction line frosting	Float valve open	Tap housing with soft hammer to dislodge
	Overcharge	Remove some refrigerant
	Float disconnected	Reconnect float

Table 10-F: Low-Side Float Troubleshooting

Symptom	Problem	Solution
Lack of cooling—no refrigerant flow	Screen ahead of seat plugged	Pump down and clean or replace screen
	Float stuck closed	Tap housing with soft hammer
	Float bound with oil (also lack of oil in crankcase)—oil return hole inside float is plugged	Pump down and dismantle float; clean out oil return hole
Excessive refrigerant in evaporator—possibly cold crankcase	Float disconnected; possible floodbacks	Reconnect float
Suction line frosting	Float full of liquid or stuck open	Pump down and disassemble; replace float and clean float leakage

OIL CONTROL SYSTEMS

Table 10-G: Oil Control Troubleshooting

Individual Regulator Problems

Symptom	Problem	Solution
Oil regulator maintains a high level; oil feed line cool	Oil regulator level set too high	Replace oil regulator
Oil regulator maintains a high level; oil feedline hot	Leaking oil regulator valve	Replace oil regulator
Oil regulator maintains a low level or feeds slowly; oil feedlines cool	Oil feedline or float valve clogged with foreign material	Blow high pressure gas into feedline or inlet fitting to remove foreign material
	Low reservoir pressure or gravity feed may be a problem	Remove oil regulator from compressor and flush out; install oil line filter
		Increase reservoir pressure; replace oil regulator

System Problems

Symptom	Problem	Solution
Oil regulator maintains a low oil level and/or foaming observed in regulator and reservoir; oil feedline hot; oil failure switch may trip out	Pressure differential between oil reservoir and crankcase over 5 pounds	Replace reservoir pressure valve or change spring in valve to 5-pound spring
	Oil separator float stuck open or leaking	Clean or replace float assembly or replace oil separator
	Oil separator not precharged with oil before installation	Add oil until level is between sight glasses of oil reservoir
	Not enough oil in system	Replace or repair compressor

	Worn compressor; excessive oil being pumped	Locate and repair leak
	Loss of oil from system; system leak	Locate and repair leak
Oil regulator maintains a low oil level; an oil level cannot be maintained in oil reservoir; oil feedline cool; oil failure switch may trip out	Oil separator float assembly clogged; undersized oil separator; oil blowing by oil separator into system with discharge gas; small amount of oil being fed to oil reservoir	Clean or replace float assembly or replace oil separator; install larger oil separator
Oil regulator maintains a high oil level; reservoir full; oil feedline hot	System oil logged: (A) Oil separator feeding oil reservoir continuously	Remove excess oil from system (See note below).
	(B) oil entering crankcase via suction line	
Oil regulators maintain a high oil level; an oil level is maintained in oil reservoir; oil feed lines cool	Liquid refrigerant buildup in crankcase of compressors (oil boils at startup)	Check for overcharged system; install suction line accumulator

NOTE: Oil can be added to or removed from the oil control system with valves on the oil reservoir. The top valve is for adding oil, the bottom valve is for removing oil. To quickly remove excess oil from an oil-logged system, remove the oil-return line between the oil separator and the oil reservoir. Attach a testing manifold or small valve to the line to control the flow of oil from the oil separator, discharge the excess oil into a drum until the oil separator shuts off. Most of the excess oil will be removed and the system and oil level regulators should be stabilized. Reattach the oil discharge line to the oil reservoir.

ABSORPTION SYSTEM

Table 10-H: Absorption System Troubleshooting

Symptom	Problem	Solution
Low capacity	Improper capacity control valve setting	Reset valve to design temperature by resetting control point adjuster
	Solution in generator below design concentration at full load	Raise steam pressure to design; check strainers, traps, and condensate system
	Machine needs octyl alcohol	Add octyl alcohol
	Insufficient condensing water or temperature too high	Check operation of tower flow fans; check strainer and valves
	Tubes are fouled (poor heat transfer)	Clean tubes; determine if water treatment is necessary
	High absorber loss (noncondensables in machine)	See High Absorber Loss below
	Malfunction of Cycle-Guard™ (low concentration)	
	Malfunction of absorber valve (solution bypass)	Check refrigerant charge, thermo-switch calibration, and transfer-valve operation
Machine shuts down on safety control	Condensing water pump or chilled-water pump overloads or flow switches trip out	Reset; determine reason for failure; adjust control-point setting or chilled-water controller to maintain design leaving-chilled-water temperature; check capacity control valve adjustment and closure
	Refrigerant or solution pump overloads trip out; shutdown on low-temperature cut-out	

Crystallization at startup or during machine operation	Malfunction of Cycle-Guard™ (over-concentration)	Check refrigerant charge, thermo-switch calibration, and transfer-valve operation
Crystallization during shutdown	Insufficient dilution	Check dilution float switch (SW-7); weak solution should dilute to 56% or less during shutdown
High absorber loss	Leakage in vacuum side of machine	Determine noncondensible accumulation rate; have solution analyzed for indication of air leak; leak-test; repair if necessary
	Purge malfunctions	See Failure to Keep Machine Purged below
	Inhibitor depleted	Have solution analyzed to determine extent of depletion
Vacuum loss at shutdown	Leakage in vacuum side of machine	Leak test the machine and repair if necessary
Failure to keep machine purged	Noncondensable accumulation rate above pumping rate of the purge	Determine noncondensable accumulation rate; have solution sample analyzed for indication of leak or inhibitor depletion; leak test; repair if necessary
	Purge valves not positioned correctly	Check valve positions
	Purge crystallized	Decrystallize
	Lack of solution flow from solution pump to purge	Contact your Carrier representative

Courtesy of Carrier Corporation, Division of United Technologies Corporation

> NOTE: Table is specific to Carrier Model 16JB010-068 but gives an
> overview of absorption system troubleshooting.)

MOTORS

Compressor motors are a common trouble spot, but the actual problem often
resides outside the motor, as shown in Table 10-I. Motor failure often results
from a problem in lubrication, compressor mechanics, or external controls.

Table 10-I: Hermetic Motor Troubleshooting

Symptom	Problem and Solution
Uniform Burn	Check and correct: low or unbalanced voltage, rapid cycling, poor motor cooling
Single-Phase Burn (in three-phase motor, the unburned phase is not getting enough current, so the other two phases are overloaded and burned)	Check and correct: blown fuses or circuit breakers, contactor, connections at compressor, balance of voltage on the phases
Primary Single-Phase Burn (one phase burned on three-phase motor)	Check and correct: loss of one phase in delta to wye, or wye to delta, transformer; input and output voltage at transformer
Single-Phase Burn, Half-Winding (part-wind motor, two-contactor system)	Check and correct: both contactors, timer delay
Burned Start-Winding (single-phase motor)	Check and correct: C, S, R wiring; starting capacitor or relay; overloading of compressor
Burned Run-Winding (single-phase motor)	Check and correct: relay, run capacitor

PUMPS

Table 10-J: Pump Troubleshooting

Symptom	Problem
No output	Not primed; excess suction lift; rotation direction incorrect
Inadequate output	Leaks or obstructions in suction line; running too slow; excess suction lift; air pockets in lines; pump damaged: impeller worn, shaft bent, packing damaged or otherwise defective
Intermittent output	Leaks in suction line; pump damaged by abrasives in water; excess suction lift; air or grease in water
Excess power draw	Running too fast; lines obstructed; mechanical problem in pump: shaft bent, parts dragging, misaligned pipe connection, misaligned flexible coupling

11

Standard ACR Procedures

All cooling-system technicians should know the procedures for maintaining and repairing air conditioning and refrigeration equipment. These procedures concern the compressor, condenser, pump, operating controls, refrigerants, and periodic maintenance.

COMPRESSOR PROCEDURES

Use great care in installing and adjusting a compressor, and make sure all safety devices are working properly. The following procedures all start with the installation of the gauge manifold.

Gauge Manifold Installation

To connect the gauge manifold to a system:

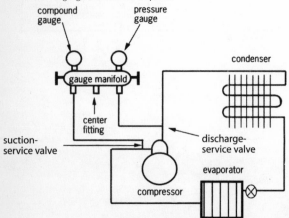

Figure 11-A: Gauge manifold installation

1. Carefully remove the pipe plugs from the suction- and discharge-service valves and backseat them (screw them all the way out).

2. Screw an adaptor in each valve and fasten a charging hose to it.

3. Connect the compound gauge to the port of the suction-service valve. Connect the pressure gauge to the port of the discharge-service valve.

4. Turn each valve one-quarter turn.

5. Once readings are established in both gauges, proceed with troubleshooting, charging, and so on.

Oil, Draining and Adding

Two methods can be used to add oil, depending on system size and design.

Method 1: System without service or drain valves This method does not require suction- and discharge-service valves, nor even an oil drain valve. Recover refrigerant from the system before installing the Schraeder valves, then add refrigerant after refilling the oil. (See Figure 11-B.)

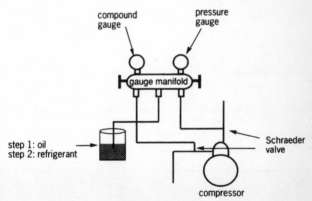

Figure 11-B: Adding oil

1. Recover refrigerant from the system by opening a line or installing a hermetic service kit.

2. Solder Schraeder valves in the suction and discharge lines for the gauge manifold connection.

3. Attach the gauge manifold (with both manifold valves closed) to the Schraeder valves.

4. Pour some refrigerant oil in a small, clean container.

5. Flare a piece of 1/4" OD soft refrigerant tube and attach one end to the gauge manifold center fitting. Place the other end in the oil container.

6. Run the compressor briefly to pull a vacuum. Shut off the compressor.

> **CAUTION:**   Running without refrigerant for a long time will burn out a compressor.

7. Open the suction valve on the manifold and allow the system vacuum to pull in the desired amount of oil. If there is a sight glass, use it to check the oil level. In many cases a cupful is enough. Keep the bottom of the 1/4" tube immersed in the oil can, or air will be sucked into the system.

8. Recharge the unit:

   a. Attach the middle manifold hose to the refrigerant drum.

   b. With the compressor running, open the low-side gauge manifold valve.

   c. Pull in the proper charge.

   d. Close the low-side manifold valve.

   e. Disconnect the refrigerant drum from the middle manifold hose.

Method 2: Drain and fill system with oil drain valve This method is used on larger reciprocating compressors (hermetic, semihermetic, or open) with a sight glass welded to the side and an oil drain valve on the bottom.

1. Drain the oil. (See Figure 11-C.)

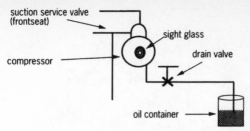

suction service valve
(frontseat)

sight glass

drain valve

compressor

oil container

Figure 11-C: Draining oil

   a. Frontseat the suction service valve.

   b. Pump down the compressor crankcase to 1- or 2-lb. psig (117 kPa). The closer to 0 lb. (101.34 kPa), the easier this procedure will be. Make sure to maintain a positive pressure and do not run very long in this condition as the compressor can overheat.

   c. Disconnect electric power to the compressor.

   d. Disconnect any oil heaters (they must be immersed in oil to work properly).

   e. Hook a hose or piece of tube from the drain valve to a large container to hold the oil. (No matter how well the system has been pumped down, the oil will foam when it reaches atmospheric pressure. A large container will prevent spills.)

   f. Open the drain valve, taking care that the crankcase is not under vacuum, which would suck in air. Drain the oil until it stops flowing, then close the drain valve. Remove the drain tube (unless it will be used to add oil).

2. Hook an intake tube to an oil pump. Place the other end of the tube in a can with new, clean oil. (See Figure 11-D.) Connect the pump discharge to the oil drain line.

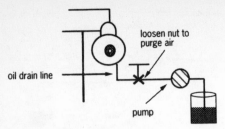

Figure 11-D: Adding oil

3. Loosen the nut connecting the pump discharge tube to the drain valve and operate the pump until all air is purged from the discharge tube. Tighten the nut.

4. Open the drain valve and start the pump to transfer oil from the can to the crankcase. Make sure no air gets in. (The crankcase should still be near 0 psig (101.34 kPa). Crankcase pressure will resist pumping in the oil.)

5. Pump in the desired amount of oil, usually to 1/4 to 1/2 of the sight glass.

6. Close the drain valve and remove the oil pump. Open the suction valve, reconnect the crankcase heater, switch on power to the compressor, and start the unit.

Cleanup After a Hermetic System Burnout

With the exception of total compressor failure, a motor burnout in a hermetic system is about the worst trouble in a refrigeration system, because it will contaminate the refrigerant. A short-circuit in the motor windings will suddenly raise its temperature and burn the rest of the insulation in the windings. Obviously, the windings must be replaced. But the big problem is the carbon deposit from the burning insulation. Unless this carbon is removed from the entire system before resuming operation, it will cause repeated burnouts.

When a motor refuses to respond, first check out the power supply; then look at the motor, the safety and operating controls, and the capacitors. Check the winding continuity. If a burnout is suspected, check the insulation of the windings with an ohmmeter or megohmmeter. Then, if a burnout is still suspected, look for carbon and acid in the refrigerant. Carbon darkens oil. Detect the acid with an oil test kit. (See Chapter 6, "Motors.")

A thorough cleanup takes a lot of work, but if shortcuts are taken, the restored system may fail.

> CAUTION: When a burned-out system is opened, air can combine with refrigerant and carbon to form hydrochloric or hydrofluoric acid. The acidity is nothing to laugh about—it can blind someone and burn the skin. Use standard precautions for working with acid, such as goggles, rubber gloves, and a rubber apron. Make sure not to spill the acid. If acid does get on someone's hands or eyes, wash it off with a great deal of water and neutralize the acid with baking soda. Seek medical help if appropriate.

Assessing the Contamination

If it has been determined that the motor has definitely burned out, make a complete inspection to see how far the carbon has moved. The extent of contamination depends on several factors. If a reciprocating compressor motor burned out before it began turning quickly, the head valves and pistons might have protected the high side from contamination. If the discharge port is clean, the high side is probably clean.

Head valves and pistons will not protect the low side, and contamination likely will be found some distance up the suction line. To check, recover the refrigerant and cut the suction line a few feet from the compressor, preferably beyond the first elbow. If that part of the tube is clean, replace the tube between the cut and the compressor, and recharge the system. If that part is dirty, replace as much tube as necessary.

Reciprocating compressors are the only ones with valves and pistons to protect the high side, so contamination may be more widespread with other compressors.

Cleanup Methods

Either of two methods can be used to clean up, based on system size. If it is easy to change the oil in the replacement compressor, do so soon after startup. Otherwise, use extra care to clean the system before installing the new compressor, using plenty of filter-driers.

1. On small systems (under 25 tons), recover the refrigerant and replace the compressor. Install a new liquid-line filter-drier. After a few hours' operation, check:

   a. The condition of the filter-drier elements. Replace if needed.

   b. Pressure drop through the filter-driers. If excessive, replace the filter element.

   c. The oil acidity (by odor, color, or test). If excessive, drain and replace the oil and change the filter-drier.

   d. After two days, check oil acidity again and continue replacing filter-drier elements until a test kit reads "no acid."

2. For larger chiller systems, replace the stator (which is the only part that burns) and clean the rest of the compressor. Use this procedure:

   a. Shut off the compressor from the system and recover the refrigerant through service valves.

   b. Coat parts with compressor oil. (To prevent corrosion, never allow compressor parts to be exposed to air for longer than necessary.)

   c. Remove the old stator and get it rebuilt at the manufacturer.

   d. Slide the new or rebuilt stator into position and reassemble the compressor.

   e. Add a new charge of oil to the crankcase.

   f. Run the compressor dry (without refrigerant) for a few seconds to check that all the pieces work properly. During this period, watch the oil pressure and keep the dry run brief, because the compressor is not getting any coolant.

   g. Evacuate the compressor. Break the vacuum with the refrigerant that will be used in the system.

   h. Install a new filter-drier in the liquid line and, if possible, a new suction-line filter-drier.

   i. Charge the system. (See "Refrigerant Procedures" in this chapter.)

   j. Operate for one hour and drain the oil. If possible, wipe out the crankcase. Then add new oil.

   k. Return the system to service.

   l. After one day, test the oil for acid. Change the oil and the drier elements until the oil tests clean.

CONDENSER PROCEDURES

To remove heat, condensers must be clean and supplied with the proper amount and quality of air or water. The requirements for air- and water-cooled types are similar:

- Cooling fins must be clean and straight.

- The fan or pump must operate correctly under all load conditions. Fans and pumps are switched by various control devices. (On smaller units the compressor control signals the fan to begin running.) The control on a variable-speed fan or pump must operate through the whole range of speeds and load conditions.

- A thermocouple that controls the fan or pump should be attached to a return bend in the condenser.

- Belts must be in good condition, with the proper tension.

- Fan, pump, and motor bearings must be adequately lubricated.

- Dampers in air-cooled systems must be operating correctly. Dampers usually are moved by head pressure in a cylinder on the damper. When the compressor starts, head pressure rises and opens the damper. When the compressor stops, the spring closes the damper.

- Valve controls in water-cooled units should be operating correctly.

Repairing an Air-Cooled Condenser

Use good ventilation because heat may convert leftover refrigerant in the condenser into toxic gas. To repair a leaking air-cooled condenser:

1. Isolate the leak with a leak detector. Mark the leak clearly.

2. Recover refrigerant from the system into a recovery apparatus. (Do not pump down to the receiver because this will increase the amount of leaking.)

3. Remove the condenser if necessary to reach the leak.

4. If the leak is at a brazed joint, heat it and take it apart.

5. Clean both mating surfaces and braze them back together. (See Chapter 1, "Tools, Equipment, and Material.")

6. If leak is not at a joint, clean the area thoroughly and patch it with hard solder. Use a coupling if the hole is too large to be patched.

7. Remove flux.

8. Test the condenser by pressurizing it with nitrogen overnight. Test-pressure can be found on the equipment nameplate.

9. Replace the condenser and restore the system to service.

Cleaning a Water-Cooled Condenser

Scale, microbes, and fouling can all interfere with heat transfer and water flow in water-cooled condensers. (See Chapter 5, "Components.") The intensity of the problem depends greatly on the quality and hardness of the cooling water, the water flow rate, and the use of water softening or other water treatments. Scale, microbes, and fouling can be removed by brushing and/or chemical treatment.

In some systems, the degree of scaling, fouling, or microbe growth in condensers can be seen. In other types, primarily tube-within-a-tube and tube-and-coil, an indirect diagnosis must be made. Compare records of temperature difference between entering and leaving water from periods with roughly equal loads. A change in ΔT indicates problems with heat transfer. A pump failure or a partly closed cooling-water valve will increase ΔT, while insulation caused by scale or fouling will reduce it. If other problems have been ruled out, it is possible to conclude that scaling or fouling is what is clogging a condenser.

If some of the offending coating can be brushed or scraped away, that's a logical first step. Then decide which form of chemical treatment is best for removing the remaining material.

Acid treatment is most effective for scale, if done with care. Analyze the system and look for possible leaks (acid will attack metal as well as scale). Remind the customer that acid treatment may create leaks. Check for air pockets that may trap acid fumes; they will not be thoroughly cleaned by the acid. Water flow may be able to be reversed to treat all parts of the system, or vents may have to be installed in the air pockets. (See Figure 11-E.)

Cleaning-chemical manufacturers are a good resource for solving problems with scale and fouling, but make sure to follow the acid manufacturer's instructions closely.

The following acid treatment uses an acid pump to circulate cleaning solution through the condenser:

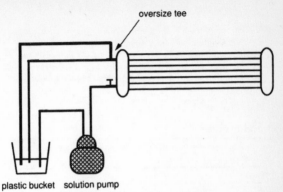

Figure 11-E: Acid washing a condenser

Circulate solution into water side of condenser to move gases through the system. An oversized tee on the outlet allows gas to exit one hose and liquid another.

1. Add acid slowly to a plastic pail and dilute as directed by the solution manufacturer. Leave plenty of room in the pail in case pressure in the condenser forces solution back into it.

2. Turn on the pump and monitor system pH with treated paper. If the solution gets too strong, it can coat the scale and make it harder to clean.

3. Monitor the pH. When the pH holds steady for 1 or 2 hours, the acid is no longer being neutralized by the scale. Either the acid is spent or the scale is gone. Make a visual check. If scale is still present, add more acid and continue.

4. Neutralize the acid while it is still circulating. Add soda ash or the chemical recommended by the chemical manufacturer. When the solution measures neutral (pH 7), drain the spent solution and discard it.

> CAUTION: Acid safety: Observe safety precautions when using acid. Dilute the acid to the proper strength by adding acid to water—not water to acid. Use a face shield and long rubber gloves. Use rubber or plastic buckets. Avoid breathing fumes and use with adequate ventilation.

PUMP PROCEDURES

The following inspections will improve operation of centrifugal and reciprocating pumps for water or brine.

Pump part	Inspect and check
Motor and pump shaft	Alignment; impeller for abnormal wear
Foot valve	Opening should be at least as large as the suction pipe
Units	Must have a level and sturdy base
Pump speed	Should match pump nameplate
Pressure gauge on discharge	Must meet specifications
Suction line	Should slope gradually to prevent formation of air pockets
Suction lift	Generally should not exceed 15' (4.6 meters), including friction losses

REFRIGERANT PROCEDURES

Many of the standard ACR procedures concern refrigerant, including leaks and removing, replacing, and pumping down refrigerant before servicing the system.

Detecting Leaks

After a system is assembled, it must be tested for leaks. Read the compressor's installation instructions to determine the testing procedure. Manufacturers may specify that a certain pressure be sustained for a specific period before considering a system leak-tight. Read the instructions for the specific leak detector, noting especially whether it must be balanced to the atmosphere before each use (some detectors do this automatically). While making these tests, remember that excess system pressure can damage some components.

New System

To test a new system for leaks:

1. Install the gauge manifold and pressurize both sides of the system with nitrogen. Consult the manufacturer's specifications for the proper pressure. Generally, water-cooled equipment should be tested at 250 psi (1,724 kPa), and air-cooled equipment at 350 psi (2,413 kPa). Make sure to uniformly pressurize the entire system.

2. Watch for a drop in pressure that would indicate a leak.

3. If the system passes this test, pressurize to 150 psi (1,035 kPa) with dry nitrogen and test with soapsuds.

4. If the system is still tight, blow out the nitrogen and add refrigerant to 30 psi (207 kPa). Pressurize the refrigerant to 150 psi (1,035 kPa) by adding nitrogen. Test for leaks with a halide torch. Nitrogen with trace gas can be vented to the atmosphere.

5. If the system still checks out, use an electronic leak detector to make the final check. Electronic detectors are so sensitive that they will read "positive" several feet from a big leak—too far to tell the exact source of the leak.

Old System

If a leak is causing system trouble, search for it before disassembly. Otherwise, the atmosphere may become contaminated with refrigerant and the leak will be hard to find. Some leaks will leave a smear of oil, but a good test with a leak detector is the surest means of finding a leak.

When testing for leaks on a running system, briefly increase discharge pressure by blocking the air or water flow to the condenser. (Remember: This can damage the system if run too long.) It is difficult to raise the pressure in the suction line. An electronic leak detector is quite handy for these tests. Red dye may be used to find a sneaky leak; the dye should not contaminate the refrigerant. Or wrap a suspect area with household plastic wrap and wait a few hours. If the joint is bulging, the leak has been isolated.

Repairing a Leaking Joint

To repair a leaking solder joint, disassemble and resolder it. Although it is tempting to just heat the joint and add solder, this will fail for the same reason the first one failed: oxide inside the joint that is not accepting solder or brazing.

If the joint leaked when the system was running, it needs to be cleaned out of oil. Use the following procedure:

1. If the area contains refrigerant, pump down or recover the refrigerant.
2. Saw through the leaking fitting and drain the remaining refrigerant from it.
3. Heat the leaking joint and quickly pull it apart.
4. Inspect the inside of the joint to determine the cause of the leak, such as an unclean spot or a deformed fitting. Then solder or braze with the normal procedure.

Removing Refrigerant

In systems without a receiver, generally, refrigerant must be removed before working on any component between the high-side service valve and the king valve (on the condenser outlet). To remove refrigerant, either pump down to the receiver or use a recovery apparatus.

Pumping Down to a Receiver

A complete pumpdown to the receiver allows for service to the liquid line, evaporator, or suction line in a reciprocating compressor. This is different from the partial pumpdown used in some normal operating cycles. For a complete pumpdown, the receiver and condenser combined must be large enough to hold the complete system charge, and there must be a shutoff valve in the liquid line (the compressor discharge valves shut off the other end in a reciprocating compressor). Some condensers are large enough to hold the charge by themselves, but as a rule, tube-within-a-tube models are not.

Use the following procedure to pump down to a receiver:

1. Install the gauge manifold.
2. Temporarily disable the low-pressure cutout. To do this, you may (a) connect a jumper cable with a toggle switch across the cutout terminals; or (b) hold the switch in the "made" position. (If the

cut-out is in an electronic control circuit, consult the manufacturer's recommendations to avoid damage.)

3. Close the king valve and run the compressor until the suction pressure falls to about 10" Hg vacuum (66.6 kPa). Remember that the suction gas is becoming less dense, so hermetic motors are in danger of overheating. Do not run the compressor indefinitely in this condition.

4. Stop the compressor and let the low-side pressure build up. If it reaches 20 psig (241 kPa), repeat until the pressure settles at about 2 to 3 psig (117 to 124 kPa). (Never open a system if it has a vacuum, because air and moisture will be sucked in. The only exception to this rule is an ammonia system, which should have a slight vacuum when it is opened to prevent escape of ammonia.)

5. With the system pumped down, try to lock the main disconnect switch open. If this is impossible, place a tag on the switch explaining that the compressor is down for service.

6. Frontseat the discharge service valve. Do not depend on compressor head valves to hold the pressure during a service pump-down.

Do not fill any cylinder holding liquid refrigerant more than 80% full (this allows for expansion). In semihermetic and hermetic systems, watch for motor overheating, as the amount of refrigerant available to cool the motor will be steadily reduced. The head-pressure reading on the gauge manifold will always be slightly below actual head pressure. The internal relief valve will bypass discharge gas to the suction side of the compressor. These valves do not always reseat automatically, and this can overheat the compressor.

Recovery

Identify the refrigerant first to minimize contamination of the recovery apparatus with different refrigerants. Use an in-line filter to keep the recovery equipment clean. If the recovery tank has an automatic shutoff, connect the recovery unit to the float switch on the recovery cylinder. Otherwise, fill the cylinder to 80% of capacity, by weight. Connect the apparatus according to the manufacturer's directions. (See Figure 11-F.)

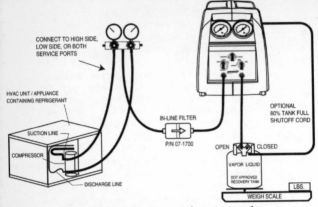

Figure 11-F: Typical recovery-equipment connection
Courtesy of Bacharach, Inc.

Time is money when recovering refrigerant. The following suggestions can be useful:

- Use short hoses; long hoses cause too much friction.
- Keep restrictions out of hoses. Hoses with ball valves will recover faster than self-sealing hoses.
- Pump out liquid first, then the vapor that remains.

With large systems, liquid push-pull (see Figure 11-G) is three times faster than normal liquid recovery. Try to recover from the high- and low-side service ports.

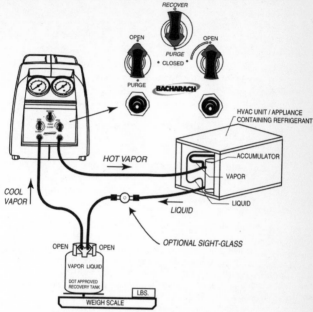

Figure 11-G: "Push-pull" refrigerant recovery hookup
Courtesy of Bacharach, Inc.

Drying (Evacuating) a System

Moisture in the refrigerant is an enemy of vapor-compression systems. Moisture can attack motor windings, freeze and plug a line or metering device, combine with halocarbons to form acids, and impair the lubrication value of oil. Moisture can enter a system through: (1) mistakes in the factory or field, (2) wet oil or refrigerant, (3) low-side leaks, or (4) a burst water-cooled condenser.

Drying, or evacuating, eliminates moisture and air before a new or repaired system is charged. Evacuating and charging are not necessary for factory-sealed and charged systems. Evacuating removes air and creates a vacuum, causing water to boil in the system so the water vapor can be removed with a vacuum pump.

Observe the following guidelines before starting the evacuation:

1. If a liquid-line drier is present, be sure to remove its element.

2. If a great deal of refrigerant has mixed with the oil, the evacuation will be slow because the vacuum pump must boil the refrigerant from the oil.

3. On systems with a great deal of water, blow out the lines with nitrogen before pulling the vacuum. This will save a lot of pump wear and speed the evacuation. Place a moisture trap (available from vacuum pump manufacturers) in the line from the pump to the system to prevent most of the water from reaching the pump. After evacuating, reinstall the drier.

4. In relatively dry systems, the vacuum-pump stage can be omitted in favor of a liquid-line drier. The drier elements may need to be replaced several times before all the moisture is removed.

Single-Evacuation

The single-evacuation method requires a high-vacuum pump and a method of reading a deep vacuum, and can only be used in a hermetic or semihermetic system that can sustain a high vacuum. (An open system cannot withstand a high vacuum and must be evacuated with the triple method.) This method can dry a system if the ambient temperature is at least 70°F (21°C). At this temperature, water will boil out when system pressure is no higher than 2,000 microns psia. If ambient temperature is below about 70°, use triple-evacuation.

Even though the compound gauge on a gauge manifold will read 30 inches of vacuum (near 0 kPa), it is not accurate enough for single-evacuation. Instead, read the pressure with a wet-bulb thermometer, an electronic high-vacuum gauge, or a mercury manometer.

Make the connections shown in Figure 11-H with special vacuum-pump hoses or copper tubing instead of gauge-manifold hoses.

1. Run a recovery apparatus to empty the system of refrigerant.

2. Hook the vacuum-pump line to a tee so it can be connected to a wet-bulb thermometer, a mercury manometer, a micron gauge, or an electronic vacuum gauge.

3. Connect this tee to a second tee linked to the discharge- and suction-service valves, so the vacuum pump can be connected to both sides of the metering device. (If the vacuum lines cannot be attached

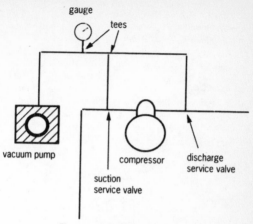

Figure 11-H: System evacuation

to the compressor through service valves, plan how to remove the lines because they will be under vacuum or pressure when finished. Generally, valves will need to be installed where the tubes connect to the system.)

4. Check that all valves are open. Open the solenoids in the system either manually or by applying electric power.

5. Shut off power to the compressor motor and crankcase heaters. Keep the power off while the vacuum pump operates or the windings can be damaged.

6. Start the vacuum pump and run it until a deep enough vacuum is maintained to vaporize the water in the system. Most vacuum gauges read direct. When a wet-bulb thermometer measures and holds 15°F (−9.5°C), there is a vacuum of 29.84" Hg. This vacuum is the same as 2,500 microns Hg on an electronic micron gauge; or 2.5 mm Hg on a mercury manometer.

7. Close both service valves and shut off the pump.

8. Watch the vacuum gauge for 30 to 45 minutes. A rise indicates either a leak or that water is boiling inside the system. With a leak, pressure will rise all the way up to atmospheric pressure. The warmer the

ambient temperature, the faster water will vaporize at any given vacuum. If water is boiling, pressure will eventually level off. If there are cold spots, that's where moisture is probably evaporating. To speed drying, warm these spots with a heat lamp.

9. Continue evacuating until a deep vacuum can be held for the period specified by the manufacturer.

Triple-Evacuation

During cool conditions, below about 70°F (21.1°C), the best way to completely dry a system is with "triple evacuation" using nitrogen. Note that the exact procedure can vary from that listed below. Some manufacturers suggest that the first two evacuations reach 1,500 microns, that the final evacuation reach 500 microns, and that the vacuum be broken with 2 psig (117.2 kPa) of system refrigerant.

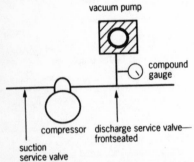

Figure 11-I: Evacuating an open compressor, compressor isolated

1. Run a recovery apparatus to empty the system of refrigerant.

2. Install the apparatus as shown in Figure 11-I and pull a vacuum of about 25" Hg (16.7 kPa) with a vacuum pump.

3. Charge the system with nitrogen to about 5 psig, measured at the compressor. (This charge breaks the surface tension so moisture can evaporate during the next evacuation.)

4. Release the nitrogen to the atmosphere.

5. Repeat the procedure twice more and then pull the required vacuum to make the final charge. A different number of evacuations may have to be made to reach the desired vacuum conditions.

Isolating and Evacuating an Open Compressor

With an open, or some semihermetic systems, it may be easiest to evacuate the compressor, not the rest of the system. When evacuating an open system, take care not to pull air in through the crankshaft seal.

Although this will not cause permanent damage, it will prevent the sustaining of a vacuum. Look over the system to find the best way of isolating the piping from the compressor.

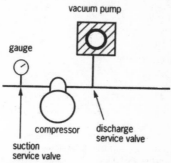

Figure 11-J: Evacuating an open compressor, compressor not isolated

1. Frontseat the suction- and discharge-service valves and connect the vacuum pump. Evacuate the compressor to a deep vacuum, just enough to vaporize the water inside it. (See Figure 11-J.)

2. Connect a vacuum pump to the discharge service valve and a compound gauge to the suction service valve.

3. Run the vacuum pumpdown to the vacuum specified by the compressor manufacturer. Single evacuation usually works, but a triple-evacuation may be required to remove air.

4. Backseat the discharge service valve. Shut off and remove the vacuum pump.

5. Recharge the system or install a holding charge (enough refrigerant to raise the pressure to about 2 psig).

6. Backseat the suction-service valve and remove the gauge.

7. Replace and tighten plugs in the valve ports.

Checking the Charge

A cooling system relies on a proper refrigerant charge. Some systems, particularly those with a receiver, are less sensitive to charge level than "critical-charge" systems, which typically have a flooded evaporator or use a capillary tube as the metering device. These systems require close control of refrigerant level.

If a low charge is found, it is probably due to a leak that must be repaired before recharging. However, systems that have performed poorly after recent service may have gotten the wrong charge.

1. Assuming all components of the system are in good condition and operating properly, the charge should be checked by examining head pressure.
   a. Find the design condenser temperature from the specifications.
   b. Convert that temperature to pressure.
   c. Charge to that head pressure while the compressor is running. Pressure should be 30°F higher than ambient on low-efficiency compressors, and 20° above ambient on high-efficiency compressors.

2. If a sight glass is in the liquid line, bubbles indicate (but do not prove) a low charge. Use a clamp-on sight glass to "listen" electronically for bubbles. A restriction in the line ahead of the sight glass may cause foaming and be mistaken for a low charge. Lack of bubbles does not prove a full charge, however, and another method, such as measuring superheat, may be chosen to complement the sight glass.

3. A receiver may be fitted with two petcocks, one above the other. When the charge is correct, the upper petcock will emit vapor, and the lower petcock will emit liquid.

4. In systems with a water-cooled condenser, hot vapor will be above cool liquid. Use a hand to feel the liquid level.

5. In cap-tube systems, measure the superheat. Superheat decreases as the charge increases, because the evaporator becomes increasingly full of refrigerant. Select a safe superheat, perhaps 12°F to 20°F (6.7°C to 11.4°C), and adjust to that figure by adding or removing refrigerant.

> CAUTION: Other methods for checking the charge in cap-tube systems, such as measuring full-load motor current draw, or looking at the frost line or sweat line, are not accurate.

Charging a System

Six methods can be used to charge refrigerant to a system: by sight glass, by charging chart, by weight, by frost line, by liquid-charging a flooded evaporator, and by using the charging cylinder. The chosen method should be selected based on system size, component configuration, and the presence or absence of service valves and sight glasses. Refrigerant can be added as either a gas (for small systems) or a liquid (for large systems). Gas charging is more accurate but liquid charging is faster. Never put liquid into the suction line—this can destroy a compressor.

The first step in all these methods is to purge air from the gauge manifold hoses, using refrigerant from a tank, and install the gauges.

> TIP: Older refrigerant cylinders have a single valve. To get a gas charge, leave the cylinder upright; for a liquid charge, invert the cylinder. Newer cylinders have valves at the top and the bottom.

By Sight Glass

Ideally, the sight glass should be installed just ahead of the metering device, because this is where a solid stream of liquid should be visible.

Gas

Add gas charges into the suction line near the compressor. The transfer can be sped up by putting the charging cylinder in a pail of warm water. Never use a flame to speed the transfer. (See Figure 11-K.)

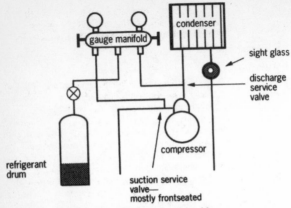

Figure 11-K: Sight-glass charging with gas

1. Install the gauge manifold and run the unit until it stabilizes.

2. Attach the refrigerant cylinder to the center hose of the gauge manifold.

3. Frontseat the suction-service valve almost all the way so the compressor pulls crankcase pressure below the cylinder pressure.

4. Open the suction valve on the manifold and pull gas from the cylinder into the crankcase.

5. After a period of transfer, backseat the suction-service valve. Run the unit normally and look for foaming in the sight glass. With a full charge, no bubbles will be visible.

6. Backseat both service valves and remove the gauge manifold.

Liquid

Use this method on large units with (1) a charging valve on a tee in the liquid line, and (2) a king valve at the condenser outlet. Use caution as a charge can transfer rather fast. Experience will help to transfer the proper charge without overcharging. (See Figure 11-L.)

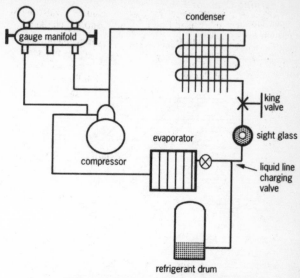

Figure 11-L: Sight-glass charging with liquid

1. Install the gauge manifold as shown. Connect the refrigerant cylinder to the liquid-line charging valve. Make sure the drum outlet is flooded by liquid.

2. Start the compressor and close the king valve to stop the flow of refrigerant.

3. Run the unit until the suction pressure is below refrigerant cylinder pressure. (If the cylinder is at room temperature, use a pressure-temperature chart to find its pressure.)

4. With the compressor still running, open the charging valve to draw liquid into the system.

5. After a period of time, shut the charging valve and open the king valve.

6. Operate the system and check the charge in the sight glass. Repeat if needed.

By a Charging Chart or Table

Get a charging chart (or table) from the compressor manufacturer, showing the relation between ambient air temperature, suction-line pressure, and suction-line temperature Charts are written for specific machines with a specific refrigerant. You can also look for the chart on the inside of the control panel door.

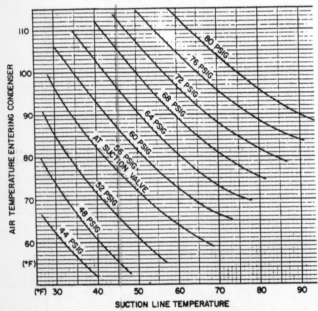

Figure 11-M: Manufacturer's charging chart
Courtesy of Carrier Corporation, Division of United Technologies Corporation

1. Install the gauge manifold and run the unit until it stabilizes. Note the pressure and temperature of the suction line.

2. Measure the entering-air temperature (ambient temperature) at the condenser.

3. Find the curved line on the chart for the actual suction pressure. Find the ambient temperature on the left-hand scale and read across to the intersection with the suction-pressure line.

4. Read down from the intersection to find the proper suction-line temperature. For example, in Figure 11-M, if the suction-line pressure is 60 psi and entering air temperature is 80°, the suction-line temperature should be about 53°F.

5. If measurements do not agree with the chart, the charge is probably wrong. In the example shown, refrigerant would be added if the suction line were much warmer than 53°F, and bled if it was much colder than 53°F.

By Weight

This method can only be used to install a full charge, using either the gas- or the liquid-charging method.

1. Find the proper charge from the manufacturer's literature.

2. Install the gauge manifold.

3. Put the refrigerant cylinder on a scale.

4. Subtract the desired charge from the cylinder weight to find the target weight.

5. Start the unit and charge until the scale reaches the target weight.

6. Disconnect the charging hose.

By Frost Line

This method can install a full or partial charge, but only in small systems with a capillary-tube metering device. Charge with gas only. Use special care to get an accurate charge, especially if the suction line is short.

1. Install the gauge manifold and run the unit.

2. Add refrigerant to the system until frost is noticeable on the suction line.

3. Stop when the frost is visible just outside the evaporator. The frost shows that the evaporator is being fully used but no liquid is flooding back.

4. Check the superheat (see Chapter 9, "Refrigerants") to ensure that the charge is accurate.

By Liquid-Charging a Flooded Evaporator

TIP: While charging, never let the evaporator pressure drop below the freezing point of water because liquid refrigerant added in these conditions may freeze the water pipes. To prevent freezing and rupturing the evaporator:
   a. Keep the chilled water circulating by manually controlling the chilled-water pump; or
   b. Drain the chilled-water circuit; or
   c. Charge the refrigerant as a gas until the pressure exceeds the freezing point of water. Then charge the remaining refrigerant as a liquid, keeping the pressure above the freezing point.

To liquid-charge a flooded evaporator:

1. Connect the refrigerant drum to the liquid-charging valve. Keep the drum outlet flooded with liquid.
2. Start the compressor and open the liquid-charging valve to start the flow of refrigerant into the system.
3. After a period of time, shut the charging valve.
4. Operate the system and check the liquid level in the sight glass. Repeat if needed.

By Using a Charging Cylinder

A charging cylinder can conveniently measure a full charge, but **never fill a refrigerant cylinder to the top**—this may cause an explosion. The columns on the cylinder safety shroud are graduated in pounds and ounces for the various refrigerants. Rotate the shroud to line up the sight tube with the column for the refrigerant being changed. Read the level of refrigerant before starting. If the charging cylinder has a digital readout, follow the manufacturer's directions. (See Figure 11-N.)

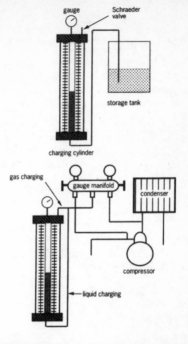

Figure 11-N: Charging with a charging cylinder

First, fill the charging cylinder with the amount of refrigerant to be added to the system.

1. Depress the Schraeder valve on the top of the charging cylinder to bleed excess pressure, and close the valve.

2. Connect the charging cylinder to the storage tank on the truck with a charging hose.

3. Open the liquid refrigerant valve on the storage tank. (Invert a small, one-valve storage tank to make sure the outlet is flooded.)

4. Open the valve on the bottom of the charging cylinder to start the refrigerant flowing.

5. When the cylinder has the received the correct charge, close the valves on the storage tank and the charging cylinder and disconnect.

Then transfer refrigerant from the charging cylinder to the system:

1. Install the gauge manifold to Schraeder fittings or service valves on the suction and discharge lines. Crack the service valves (Schraeder valves will open automatically).

2. Connect the hose from the gauge manifold center fitting to the charging cylinder. For a liquid charge, connect to the lower fitting on the cylinder (the one that was used to fill the cylinder). For a gas charge, attach to the upper cylinder fitting. (If an electric heater is being used in the cylinder, be sure it has a thermostat shutoff and the charging cylinder has a pressure relief.)

3. Run the compressor and open the gauge-manifold suction valve. Use the compressor to pull refrigerant from the cylinder into the system. Open the suction valve very carefully when installing a liquid charge so the compressor is not slugged. Plug in the heater to force the liquid refrigerant to flash to a gas in the line to the suction-service valve.

4. Monitor the amount of refrigerant being transferred from the column on the cylinder or the digital readout. Shut down the compressor when the correct amount is transferred.

5. Close the valve on the cylinder. Close the manifold suction valve and backseat the service valves. Remove the cylinder and the gauge manifold from the system.

Maintenance Procedures

It's a good idea to establish a periodic maintenance schedule for cooling-system equipment.

Weekly

1. Check compressor oil level. Low readings may occur because oil is trapped in the system. Run the compressor at full load for a few hours and check again. Add oil if the level is still low.

2. Check oil pressure differential. Oil pressure should be 20 to 35 psi (138 to 241.5 kPa) above crankcase pressure.

3. Inspect any air filters and air-handling equipment.

4. Check all important operating conditions, especially sight glasses, system pressures, and temperatures. List operating conditions on the maintenance log. Investigate significant departures from past conditions.

5. **Open systems only:** inspect crankshaft seal for leaks.

Monthly

Perform weekly maintenance plus:

1. Lube motor and fan bearings (follow the manufacturer's directions—do not overlube).

2. Check tension and alignment of V-belts. If sheaves are loose, realign before tightening.

3. Condensers: check fan, control, dampers, and cleanliness of air-cooled models; check water condition of water-cooled condensers and treat if microbes, fouling, or scale are present.

Annually

If the system will be run year-round, perform these procedures at least once a year. See below for system shutdown and startup techniques. The system must be shut down to carry out these procedures.

1. Perform weekly and monthly maintenance.

2. Flush all pipes of water-cooled condenser. Inspect condenser tubes and clean if needed. Clean air-cooled condenser.

3. Flush pumps and sump tank of cooling tower or evaporative condenser. Check for corrosion. Paint as needed.

4. Replace worn V-belts.

5. Inspect all bearings for wear and proper end-play.

6. Clean all water strainers and inspect or replace filter-driers.

7. Inspect contacts in motor starters and repair or replace as indicated.

Seasonal Shutdown

Traditionally, all systems were pumped down into the condenser or receiver in the winter to prevent loss of refrigerant through the crankshaft seal and low-side. The procedure is not used as often because hermetic systems have no crankshaft seal.

Hermetic System

Follow this procedure if a pumpdown is desired:

1. Close the liquid line shutoff and start the compressor. The compressor will run until the low-pressure cut-out shuts it down and most refrigerant is in the high side.

2. Open the compressor disconnect and frontseat the discharge- and suction-service valves. Close liquid-line service (king) valve. See additional procedures for all systems below.

Open System

Pump down the system with these steps:

1. Install the gauge manifold.

2. Close the king valve and manually open any liquid-line solenoid valves. If the solenoid cannot be opened manually, adjust its control setting so it will stay open during the pumpdown.

3. Place a jumper wire across the LPCO to run the suction pressure below its cut-out setting.

4. Run the compressor until the suction gauge reads 2 psig (117.2 kPa). Open the compressor disconnect. (A deeper vacuum could draw contaminants into the system through the crankshaft seal.)

5. Backseat both service valves. Remove the gauge manifold and replace the caps.

6. Frontseat both service valves. Replace the valve caps.

7. Remove the jumper on the LPCO. See additional procedures below.

All Systems

Do the following additional work:

1. Check the condenser and receiver for leaks with an electronic detector.

2. Check that the condenser is full of water, and close all water valves leading to it. (A full condenser will rust less than an empty one.) Replace water with antifreeze if the condenser will be subject to freezing conditions.

3. Drain the cooling tower or evaporative condenser, if used. Inspect the condition of metal, and paint it if needed.

4. Lock the master disconnect in the open position.

5. Leave a warning near the safety switch, explaining which valves must be moved before the compressor is started up. Do not assume that the person performing the startup will know much about ACR.

Seasonal Startup

Use the following schedule to place a system into service at the beginning of the year:

1. Drain the antifreeze if it was used in a water-cooled condenser. Energize the crankcase heaters.

2. Perform the annual maintenance specified by the manufacturers of motors, fans, drives, compressor, air-handling equipment, and pumps.

3. Fill the water sump on a cooling tower or an evaporative condenser to the correct level and add water treatments if needed to control scaling, fouling, or microbes.

4. Open shutoff valves to water-cooled condenser.

5. Check all pumps and fans for proper rotation and action. Check the water spray in a cooling tower or evaporative condenser.

6. Check that all solenoid valves are set on automatic control.

7. Open the liquid-line shutoff valve and backseat the compressor suction and discharge valves.

8. Install the gauge manifold.

9. Unlock and close the master disconnect.

10. Check the compressor safety controls using the procedures in Chapter 4, "Controls."

11. Start the system.

12. Adjust the bleed-off valve to the position that is recommended by the supplier of the water treatment used in the evaporative condenser or cooling tower.

13. After about 15 minutes of running, check oil level, oil pressure, and refrigerant level. Monitor system pressures and temperatures and write them down in the operating log. Adjust the thermostat to the desired setting.

A

Apprenticeship Program

Apprenticeship is a system for training new workers for technical occupations, like air conditioning and refrigeration installation and repair, that require a broad range of knowledge and skills. The training combines planned, supervised work experience with classroom study of topics relevant to the trade.

An apprenticeship program is based on a written agreement between an employee and an employer describing the terms and conditions for the apprentice's training and employment. The National Apprenticeship Act gives the Bureau of Apprenticeship Training (B.A.T.) in the U.S. Department of Labor responsibility for servicing and assisting apprenticeship programs. States that operate under federal law are known as B.A.T. states. States with their own standards are known as S.A.C. (State Apprenticeship Committee) states. S.A.C. states use federal law as a minimum; their standards generally exceed federal law.

Committees with an equal number of labor and management representatives are established to oversee the various areas of instruction in S.A.C. states. All apprenticeship programs must meet U.S. Department of Labor equal-employment opportunity standards. Information is available from the Bureau of Apprenticeship Training (www.doleta.gov/atels_bat/bat.cfm), state apprenticeship agencies and employment service offices, labor unions, employers, and school guidance counselors.

INDUSTRY CONTACTS

Many groups are established to serve the industry with education, certification, promotion, research, and information.

Air Conditioning Contractors of America (ACCA)
2800 Shirlington Road, Suite 300
Arlington, VA 22206
Phone: 703-575-4477
E-mail: info@acca.org
Web site: www.acca.org

Air Conditioning and Refrigeration Institute (ARI)
4100 North Fairfax Drive, Suite 200
Arlington, VA 22203
Phone: 703-524-8800
Web site: www.ari.org

The American Society of Heating,
Refrigeration and Air Conditioning
Engineers (ASHRAE)
1791 Tullie Circle, N.E.
Atlanta, GA 30329
Phone: 404-636-840
Web site: www.ashrae.org

American Society for Mechanical
Engineers (ASME)
22 Law Drive
P.O. Box 2900
Fairfield, NJ 07007-2900
Phone: 973-882-1170
Web site: www.asme.org

Copper Development Association,
Inc. (CDA)
260 Madison Avenue
New York, NY 10016
Phone: 212-251-7200
E-mail: questions@cda.copper.org
Web site: www.copper.org

Mechanical Contractors
Association of American (MCCA)
1385 Piccard Drive
Rockville, MD 20850
Phone: 301-869-5800
Web site: www.mcaa.org

National Safety Council (NSC)
1121 Spring Lake Drive
Itasca, IL 60143-3201
Phone: 630-285-1121
E-mail: info@nsc.org
Web site: www.nsc.org

Occupational Safety and Health
Administration (OSHA)
U.S. Department of Labor
200 Constitution Avenue N.W.
Washington, D.C. 20210
Web site: www.osha.gov

Refrigeration Engineers and
Technicians Association (RETA)
(Ammonia Systems)
30 East San Joaquin Street,
Suite 102
Salinas, CA 93901
Phone: 831-455-8783
Web site: www.reta.com

Refrigeration Service Engineers
Society (RSES)
1666 Rand Road
Des Plaines, IL 60016
Phone: 800-297-5660
Web site: www.rses.org

B

Mathematics and Measurements

AMERICAN AND SI (METRIC) MEASURES

Mathematics plays an important role in several areas of cooling-system work: for planning system capacity and choosing components, for installing piping and components, and for troubleshooting. Measuring is needed to translate figures on blueprints into structures that mirror the blueprints. The mathematical skills required to work with feet and inches, fractions, decimals, angles, area, the perimeter and volume of shapes, and the various systems of measurement are described below.

The United States is the only major country still using feet and inches, which should now be called the American system. Scientists and the rest of the world use the Standard International (SI, or metric system). Many of the measurements needed in air conditioning and refrigeration work are commonly given in both measuring systems. Some, such as high vacuum pressures, are more convenient in microns (one-millionth of a meter) than in fractions of inches.

Although American measurements now predominate in the American industry, in the long run, SI will probably gain importance. One of its major advantages is the exclusive use of decimals instead of fractions, simplifying the use of a hand calculator. Another advantage is the simplicity of converting between units. The international predominance of SI will make the system more important as imported equipment becomes more common.

The basic unit of length in the metric system is the meter (39.37"). The basic unit of weight is the kilogram (2.2 lb). While some parts of the SI system are baffling to people trained in feet and inches, SI units are already used for such important measures as sound (decibel, or dB), acidity (pH), and electricity (all units).

The metric system uses prefixes to indicate multiples and decimals of the basic units. The important prefixes are:

micro	=	.000001
milli	=	.001
centi	=	.01
kilo	=	1000
mega	=	1 million

Thus, 1 centimeter equals 0.01 meter, and 1 kilometer equals 1,000 meters. To convert measurements, just shift the decimal place. Thus, 2.566 meters is the same as 2 meters 566 millimeters, 256.6 centimeters, or 2566 millimeters.

SI uses the Celsius (formerly centigrade) degree for temperature (1°C equals 1.8°F). Boiling is 100°C and freezing is 0°C. The Kelvin scale uses the Celsius unit, but starts at absolute zero, –273°C.

Table A: Measurement Conversions

American		SI
1 inch	=	2.54 centimeters
1 foot	=	30.4 centimeters
1 yard	=	91.4 centimeters
0.032 foot	=	1 centimeter
3.28 feet	=	1 meter
1.093 yards	=	1 meter
1 square foot	=	0.092 square meter (m^2)
1 square yard	=	0.836 square meter
0.155 square inch	=	1 square centimeter (cm^2)
10.763 square feet	=	1 square meter
1.195 square yards	=	1 square meter
1 cubic inch	=	16.387 cubic centimeters
1 cubic foot	=	0.028 cubic meter (m^3)
1 cubic yard	=	0.764 cubic meter
0.061 cubic inch	=	1 cubic centimeter (cm^3)
35.314 cubic feet	=	1 cubic meter
1.307 cubic yards	=	1 cubic meter

Table B: Area And Volume Conversions

1 sq. in.	=	1/144 sq. ft.
1 sq. ft.	=	144 sq. in.
1 sq. yard	=	1,296 sq. in.
1 sq. ft.	=	1/9 sq. yard
1,728 cu. in.	=	1 cu. ft.
1 cu. in.	=	1/1728 (0.00057) cu. ft.
1 cu. ft.	=	1/27 (0.037) cu. yd.
1 cu. yd.	=	27 cu. ft.

Table C: Fraction/Decimal/Millimeter Conversion Table for One Inch

Fraction	Decimal	Millimeter	Fraction	Decimal	Millimeter
1/32	.03125	0.794	17/32	.53125	13.494
1/16	.0625	1.588	9/16	.5625	14.288
3/32	.09375	2.381	19/32	.59375	15.081
1/8	.125	3.175	5/8	.625	15.875
5/32	.15625	3.969	21/32	.65625	16.669
3/16	.1875	4.763	11/16	.6875	17.463
7/32	.21875	5.556	23/32	.71875	18.256
1/4	.250	6.350	3/4	.750	19.050
9/32	.28125	7.144	25/32	.78125	19.844
5/16	.3125	7.938	13/16	.8125	20.638
11/32	.34375	8.731	27/32	.84375	21.431
3/8	.375	9.525	7/8	.875	22.225
13/32	.40625	10.319	29/32	.90625	23.019
7/16	.4375	11.113	15/16	.9375	23.813
15/32	.46875	11.906	31/32	.96875	24.606
1/2	.500	12.700	1	1.000	25.400

DECIMALS

Decimal systems use a system based on 10, in which digits represent groups of 1, 10, 100, and so on. For example, 324 equals 3 hundreds, 2 tens, and 4 ones. The same relationship holds to the right of the decimal point. For example, 3.24 equals 3 ones, 2 tenths, and 4 hundredths.

U.S. money uses the decimal system, with each dollar divided into 10 dimes or 100 cents. Thus, $1.25 equals 1 dollar and 25 cents. Decimal calculations are much simpler than fraction calculations, especially with an electronic calculator. Decimals are exclusively used in SI.

To multiply by 10, just move the decimal place to the right.
   EXAMPLE: $1.25 \times 10 = 12.5$

To divide by 10, move the decimal place to the left.
   EXAMPLE: $1.25 \div 10 = .125$

> **NOTE:** This is often written as 0.125 to make the decimal point more obvious.

Rounding

Calculations may result in an answer with more numbers, called "decimals," to the right of the decimal place than are necessary. You can round off these numbers for simplicity. In working with pipes and setting up equipment, for example, you will rarely need to deal with measurements more exact than tenths of an inch or hundredths of a foot. Some calculators can round off automatically.

Round digits 5 and up to the next higher number.
   EXAMPLE: 3.45 rounds to 3.5.

Round digits below 5 to the next lower number.
   EXAMPLE: 3.44 rounds to 3.4.

When rounding, ignore all decimals except the one to the right of the digit you will keep. Thus, 3.47 rounds to 3.5 (look at the 7 hundredths) if you want to retain tenths. But it rounds to 3 (look at the 4 tenths) if you want to wind up with an integer.

ANGLES, PERIMETER, AREA, AND VOLUME

Angles are measured with a system of degrees. 360 degrees (360°) equals one full circle, and 90° is a right angle. Degrees are broken into 60 minutes (60'). Each minute is broken into 60 seconds (60").
   Angles less than 90° are acute angles. Angles between 90° and 180° are obtuse angles.

Perimeter is the length of the outside of a two-dimensional shape. Perimeter is useful for calculating the material needs of entire structures.

Area is the amount of space occupied by a two-dimensional shape. Area calculations may be needed for estimating cooling loads.

Volume is the three-dimensional space occupied by a structure. Volume is also used to estimate cooling load.

Shape	Area	Perimeter
Triangle	base × height ÷ 2	AB + CB + AC
Rectangle	length × width	2 × (l + w)
Circle	$\pi \times r^2$	$\pi \times d$
Sphere	$4/3 \times \pi \times r^2$	$4/3 \times \pi \times r^3$
Cylinder	$(2\,\pi \times r^2) + (\pi \times d \times h)$	$\pi \times r^2 \times h$

NOTE: (1) Circumference is the term for the perimeter of a circle. (2) r^2 means "radius squared." To square a number, multiply it by itself. (3) π, or pi (pronounced "pie") is the ratio of circumference to diameter, about 3.14. (4) diameter = radius × 2; radius = diameter ÷ 2.

ENERGY

Table D: Energy Equivalents in the American System

Heat to mechanical:	1 BTU/hr = 0.000393 hp
Heat to electrical:	1 BTU/hr = 0.293 watt (W)
Mechanical to heat:	1 hp = 2,546 BTU/hr
	778 ft. lb. = 1 BTU
Mechanical to electrical:	1 hp = 746 W
Electrical to mechanical:	746 watt = 1 hp
Electrical to heat:	1 watt = 3.412 BTU/hr
	1 kilowatt (kW) = 3,412 BTU/hr

Table E: Energy Conversions

Tons of refrigeration to BTUs:	tons × 12,000 = BTUs
Tons to hp:	tons × 4.716 = hp
hp to BTU/min:	hp × 42.44 = BTU/min
hp to kilocalories/min:	hp × 10.7 = kilocalories/min

Table F: Equivalents Between American and SI Systems

1 J = 1 Nm = 0.737 ft. lb.	1 ft. lb. = 1.3558 J = 1.356 Nm
1 W = 0.7376 ft. lb./s	1 ft. lb./s = 1.3558 W
1 kW = 1.34 hp = 3,412 BTU/hr	1 hp = 0.746 kW

The joule (J) measures three forms of energy in SI. The kilowatt-hour also measures electrical power.

Table G: Pressure Conversions

atmospheres ×	1.013	=	bars
	29.92	=	inches of mercury
	1.033	=	kilograms/sq. centimeter
	14.7	=	pounds per square inch
	104.4	=	kilopascals
pounds per square inch ×	068	=	atmospheres
	2.036	=	inches of mercury pressure
inches of mercury vacuum		=	29.9 — inches of mercury absolute pressure
inches of mercury absolute pressure + inches of mercury vacuum		=	29.2

BTU FORMULAS

BTU/Hour and Water Flow

You can calculate cooling rates in a water-cooled condenser. The relationship between the volume of cooling water through the condenser, the temperature rise in that water, and the compressor's output in BTU/hour is:

BTU/h	=	$500 \times$ gpm $\times \Delta T \times$ SG
gpm	=	gallons per minute
ΔT	=	temperature difference between entering and leaving water
SG	=	specific gravity of cooling water (Should equal 1 unless additives are used.)

NOTE: Multiplying by 500 (above) converts gpm to lb./hour: 8.3 lb./gallon $\times$ 60 min/hour)

To find ΔT from the other factors: $\Delta T = $ (BTU/hour)$/(500 \times$ gpm $\times$ SG)

Pressure drop in water-cooled condenser:

If you know specification gpm, actual pressure drop, and rated pressure drop, you can find the actual gpm for a condenser.

$$gpm_{actual} = gpm_{specs} * \sqrt{\frac{P_s}{P_a}}$$

P_s = specification pressure drop
P_a = pressure drop measured at outlet
Thus, a condenser with a pressure drop above specifications will have a slower flow than specified, and one with a lower pressure drop will have a faster flow.

Tons and BTU/Day

One ton of refrigeration is the cooling power that would be achieved from melting 1 ton of ice per day:

1 ton = 12,000 BTU/hour = 288,000 BTU/day.

Condenser Heat Dispersal

Heat dispersed by the condenser in BTU/hour = $1.25 \times 12,000 \times$ tonnage rating (motor not cooled by condenser).

Air-cooled: Entering air + 30° to 35°F (16.7° to 19.4°C) = pressure inside coil (head pressure)

Water-cooled: Entering water + 15° to 20°F (8.3° to 11.1°C) = pressure inside coil

Cooling tower: Entering water should be 7° to 11°F (3.9° to 6.1°C) cooler than leaving water.

C

Charts and Tables

Table A: Pressure Settings for Fixtures

APPLICATION	R-12 Out	R-12 In	R-22 Out	R-22 In	R-502 Out	R-502 In	R-717 Out	R-717 In
Ice Cube Maker—Dry Type Coil	4	17	16	37	22	45	—	—
Sweet Water Bath—Soda Fountain	21	29	43	56	52	66	33	45
Beer, Water, Milk Cooler, Wet Type	19	29	40	56	48	66	—	—
Ice Cream Trucks, Hardening Rooms	2	15	13	34	18	41	5	24
Electric Plates, Ice Cream Truck	1	4	11	16	16	22	4	8
Walk In, Defrost Cycle	14	34	32	64	40	75	23	55
Reach In, Defrost Cycle	19	36	40	68	48	78	30	57
Vegetable Display, Defrost Cycle	13	35	30	66	38	77	—	—
Vegetable Display Case—Open Type	16	42	35	77	44	89	—	—
Beverage Cooler, Blower Dry Type	15	34	34	64	42	75	24	55
Retail Florist—Blower Coil	28	42	55	77	65	89	44	67
Meat Display Case, Defrost Cycle	17	35	37	66	45	77	—	—

Table A: Pressure Settings for Fixtures (continued)

Meat Display Case—Open Type	11	27	27	53	35	63	—	—	—	—	—
Dairy Case—Open Type	10	35	26	66	33	77	—	—	—	—	—
Frozen Food—Open Type	-7	5	4	17	8	24	—	—	—	—	—
Frozen Food—Open Type—Thermostat	2°	10°	—	—	—	—	—	—	—	—	—
Frozen Food—Closed Type:	1	8	11	22	16	29	—	—	—	—	—

Courtesy of Sporlan Division of Parker Hannifin, Inc.

Table B: Storage Data for Fruits and Vegetables

Numbers in ( ) refer to the footnotes at the end of the table.

Commodity	Temperature °F	Relative humidity percent	Approximate length of storage period	Average freezing point[1] °F
Fresh fruits:				
Apples	(2)	85 to 90	(3)	28.4
Apricots	31 to 32	85 to 90	1 to 2 weeks	28.1
Avocados	(2)	85 to 90	(2)	27.2
Bananas	(2)	(2)	(2)	(4)
Blackberries	31 to 32	85 to 90	5 to 7 days[2]	28.9
Cherries	31 to 32	85 to 90	10 to 14 days	(5)
Coconuts	32 to 35	80 to 85	1 to 2 months	25.5
Cranberries	36 to 40	85 to 90	1 to 3 months	27.2
Dates	(2)	(2)	(2)	-4.1
Dewberries	31 to 32	85 to 90	5 to 7 days[2]	
Figs, fresh	31 to 32	85 to 90	10 days	27.1
Grapefruit	(2)	85 to 90	(2)	28.4

Commodity	Temperature °F	Relative humidity percent	Approximate length of storage period	Average freezing point[1] °F
Grapes				
Vinifera	30 to 31	85 to 90	3 to 6 months	24.9
American	31 to 32	85 to 90	3 to 4 weeks[2]	27.5
Lemons	(2)	85 to 90	1 to 4 months	28.1
Limes	48 to 50	85 to 90	6 to 8 weeks	29.3
Logan Blackberries	31 to 32	85 to 90	5 to 7 days[2]	29.5
Mangoes	50	85 to 90	15 to 20 days	29.8
Olives, fresh	45 to 50	85 to 90	4 to 6 weeks	28.5
Oranges	(2)	85 to 90	(2)	(6)
Papayas, firm ripe	45	85 to 90	7 to 21 days	30.1
Peaches and nectarines	31 to 32	85 to 90	2 to 4 weeks	29.4
Pears				
Bartlett	30 to 31	90 to 95	(2)	28.5
Fall and winter varieties	30 to 31	90 to 95	(2)	(7)

Table B: Storage Data for Fruits and Vegetables (continued)

Commodity	Temperature °F	Relative humidity percent	Approximate length of storage period	Average freezing point[1] °F
Persimmons, Japanese	30	85 to 90	2 months	28.3
Pineapples				
Mature-green	50 to 60	85 to 90	2 to 3 weeks	29.1
Ripe	40 to 45	85 to 90	2 to 4 weeks	29.9
Plums, including prunes	31 to 32	85 to 90	3 to 4 weeks[2]	28.0
Pomegranates	34 to 35	85 to 90	2 to 4 months	
Quinces	31 to 32	85 to 90	2 to 3 months	28.1
Raspberries	31 to 32	85 to 90	5 to 7 days[2]	29.9
Strawberries	31 to 32	85 to 90	7 to 10 days[2]	29.9
Tangerines	31 to 38	90 to 95	2 to 4 weeks	28
Dried fruits	(2)	(2)	(2)	
Frozen fruits	(2)	(2)	(2)	
Nuts	(2)	65 to 75	8 to 12 months	(8)

Commodity	Temperature °F	Relative humidity percent	Approximate length of storage period	Average freezing point[1] °F
Fresh vegetables:				
Artichokes				
Globe	32	90 to 95	30 days	29.1
Jerusalem	31 to 32	90 to 95	2 to 5 months	27.5
Asparagus	32	85 to 90	3 to 4 weeks	29.8
Beans				
Green, or snap	45 to 50	85 to 90	8 to 10 days	29.7
Lima				
Shelled	32	85 to 90	15 days	
	40	85 to 90	4 days	30.1
Unshelled	40	85 to 90	10 to 14 days	
Beets				
Topped	32	90 to 95	1 to 3 months	26.9
Bunched	32	90 to 95	10 to 14 days	

Table B: Storage Data for Fruits and Vegetables (continued)

Commodity	Temperature °F	Relative humidity percent	Approximate length of storage period	Average freezing point[1] °F
Broccoli (Italian, or sprouting)	32	90 to 95	7 to 10 days	29.2
Brussels sprouts	32	90 to 95	3 to 4 weeks	
Cabbage				
Early	32	90 to 95	3 to 6 weeks	31.2
Late	32	90 to 95	3 to 4 months	
Carrots				
Topped	32	90 to 95	4 to 5 months	29.6
Bunched	32	90 to 95	10 to 14 days	
Cauliflower	32	85 to 90	2 to 3 weeks	30.1
Celeriac	32	90 to 95	3 to 4 months	
Celery	31 to 32	90 to 95	2 to 4 months	29.7
Corn, sweet	31 to 32	85 to 90	(2)	28.9
Cucumbers	45 to 50	85 to 90	2 to 3 weeks	30.5
Eggplants	45 to 50	85 to 90	10 days	30.4
Endive, or escarole	32	90 to 95	2 to 3 weeks	30.9

Commodity	Temperature °F	Relative humidity percent	Approximate length of storage period	Average freezing point[1] °F
Garlic, dry	32	70 to 75	6 to 8 months	25.4
Horseradish	30 to 32	90 to 95	10 to 12 months	26.4
Kohlrabi	32	90 to 95	2 to 4 weeks	30.0
Leeks, green	32	90 to 95	1 to 3 months	29.2
Lettuce	32	90 to 95	2 to 3 weeks	31.2
Melons				
Watermelons	36 to 40	85 to 90		[10]28.8
Cantaloupes				
Full-slip	40 to 45	85 to 90	4 to 8 days	29.0
Half-slip	45 to 50	85 to 90	1 to 2 weeks	[10]28.4
Honey Dew	45 to 50	85 to 90	2 to 3 weeks	[9]29.2
Casaba	45 to 50	85 to 90	3 to 6 weeks	[10]28.8
Crenshaw and Persian	45 to 50	85 to 90	1 to 2 weeks	

Table B: Storage Data for Fruits and Vegetables (continued)

Commodity	Temperature °F	Relative humidity percent	Approximate length of storage period	Average freezing point[1] °F
Mushrooms cultivated	32	85 to 90	3 to 5 days	30.2
Okra	50	85 to 95	2 weeks	30.1
Onions	32	70 to 75	6 to 8 months	30.1
Onion sets	32	70 to 75		29.5
Parsnips	32	90 to 95	2 to 4 months	30.0
Peas, green	32	85 to 90	1 to 2 weeks	30.0
Peppers				
Chili, dry	(2)	65 to 70	6 to 9 months	
Sweet	45 to 50	85 to 90	8 to 10 days	30.1
Potatoes				
Early-crop	(2)	85 to 90	(2)	
Late-crop	(2)	85 to 90	(2)	28.9
Pumpkins	50 to 55	70 to 75	2 to 6 months[2]	30.1

Commodity	Temperature °F	Relative humidity percent	Approximate length of storage period	Average freezing point[1] °F
Radishes				
Spring, bunched	32	90 to 95	10 to 14 days	29.5
Winter	32	90 to 95	2 to 4 months	
Rhubarb	32	90 to 95	2 to 3 weeks	28.4
Rutabagas	32	90 to 95	2 to 4 months	29.5
Salsify	32	90 to 95		28.4
Spinach	32	90 to 95	10 to 14 days	30.3
Squashes				
Summer	32 to 40	85 to 95		29.0
Winter	50 to 55	70 to 75	4 to 6 months	29.3
Sweet potatoes	55 to 60	85 to 90		28.5
Tomatoes				
Ripe	50	85 to 90	8 to 12 days	30.4
Mature-green	55 to 70	85 to 90	2 to 6 weeks[2]	30.4

Table B: Storage Data for Fruits and Vegetables (continued)

Commodity	Temperature °F	Relative humidity percent	Approximate length of storage period	Average freezing point[1] °F
Turnips	32	90 to 95	4 to 5 months	30.5
Vegetable seeds	32 to 50	50 to 65	(2)	
Dried vegetables	(2)	70	1 year	
Frozen vegetables	(2)	(2)		

[1] These figures, except for summer squash, represent actual commodity temperatures recorded when freezing occured in tests.

[2] See Departement of Agriculture Handbook 66.

[3] See Departement of Agriculture Handbook 66, Table 4.

[4] Green: Flesh, 30.2°; Peel, 29.8°. Ripe: Flesh, 26.0°; Peel, 29.4°.

[5] Eastern Sour, 28.0°; Eastern Sweet, 24.7°; California Sweet, 24.2°.

[6] Flesh, 28.0°; Peel 27.4°.

[7] Winter Nelis, 27.2°; Anjou, 26.9°.

[8] Persian (English) Walnuts, 20.0°; Pecans, 19.6°; Chestnuts (Italian) 23.8°; Peanuts, 13.4°; Filberts, 14.1°.

[9] Flesh.

[10] Rind.

Table C: Storage Data for Dairy and Meat

Commodity	Temperature	Relative humidity percent	Approximate length of storage period
Dairy			
Butter	32 to 40	80	2 months
Butter, frozen	–10 to 0	80	1 year
Cheese	30 to 40	65	Varies
Eggs, fresh	29 to 31	80	6 to 9 months
Eggs, frozen	0 or below		1 year or more
Milk, fluid	33		7 days
Milk, sweetened, condensed	40		Few months
Fish and meat			
Bacon, frozen	–10 to 0	90	4 months
Bacon, packer style	34 to 40	85	2 to 4 weeks
Beef, fresh	33	88 to 90	1 to 5 weeks

Table C: Storage Data for Dairy and Meat (continued)

Commodity	Temperature	Relative humidity percent	Approximate length of storage period
Beef, frozen	-10 to 0	90	9 to 10 months
Fish, fresh	33–35	90	5 to 15 days
Fish, frozen	-10 to 0	90	8 months
Fish, smoked	45	55	6 months
Lamb, fresh	33	85	6 to 12 days
Lamb, frozen	-10 to 0	90	8 months
Livers, frozen	-10 to 0	90	3 months
Shellfish, fresh	33	90	3 to 7 days
Shellfish, frozen	-20 to 0	90	3 to 8 months
Veal	33	90	5 to 8 days

Abbreviations

A	ampere, or amp	CSR	Capacitor start, induction run motor
A	area	cu. ft.	cubic foot = ft³
A.N.S.I.	American National Standards Institute	cu. in.	cubic inch = in³
A.S.M.E.	American Society of Mechanical Engineers	D	diameter of circle
		DA	direct acting
AC	alternating current	DBV	discharge bypass valve
AEV or AXV	automatic expansion valve	DC	direct current
ASC	auxiliary side connection	deci	one-tenth (SI system)
ASHRAE	American Society of Heating, Refrigeration, and Air Conditioning Engineers	deka	10 (SI system)
		dm	decimeter
		dp	double-pole (switch)
ASTM	American Society for Testing and Materials	DR	discharge regulating
		dt	double-throw (switch)
BTU	British thermal unit	EER	energy efficiency ratio
BTU/h	British thermal unit per hour	emf	electromotive force
		EPR	evaporator pressure regulator
C	capacitance		
cal	calorie	f or fd	farad
CDA	close on decrease of ambient	FPT	female pipe thread
		FS	flow switch
centi	one-hundredth (SI system)	ft.	foot, feet
CFC	chlorofluorocarbon	ft. lb.	foot pound
cfm	cubic feet per minute	g	gram
cm	centimeter	gpm	gallons per minute
Cp	specific heat at constant pressure	gr	grain
		h	enthalpy per unit mass
Cv	specific heat at constant volume	h	hours
		hecto	100 (SI system)
CPR	crankcase pressure regulator	hp	horsepower
CRO	close on rise of outlet (pressure)	HPCO	high-pressure cut-out
		HSF	high-side float
CROT	close on rise of outlet temperature	hz	hertz (cycle per second)
		I	impedance (in ohms)
CSIR	Capacitor start, induction run	ID	inside diameter

in. Hg	inch of mercury vacuum	**ORI**	open on rise of inlet (pressure)
J	joule		
kcal or Kcal	kilocalorie	**OROA**	open on rise of outlet (pressure)
kg	kilogram		
kilo	1,000 (SI system)	**OTC**	oil-temperature control
kJ	kilojoule	**P**	pressure
kPa	kilopascal	**Pa**	pascal
kV	kilovolt	**pcb**	polychlorinated biphenyl
kVA	kilovolt-ampere	**PE**	pneumatic-electric (switch)
kW	kilowatt	**ppm**	parts per million
kwh	kilowatt hour	**PSC**	permanent split capacitor motor
L	liter		
lb.	pound	**psi**	pound per square inch = lb./sq. in.
lb./cu. ft.	pound per cubic foot		
LPCO	low-pressure cut-out	**psia**	pounds per square inch atmospheric
LSF	low-side float		
M	mass	**psig**	pounds per square inch gauge
m	meter		
mA	milliamp	**qt**	quart
mega	one million (SI system)	**R**	gas constant
mfd	microfarad	**r**	radius of circle
micro	one-millionth (SI system)	**RA**	reverse acting
milli	one-thousandth (SI system)	**RH%**	relative humidity
mm	millimeter	**RMS**	root-mean-squared (the effective voltage of an AC current)
MOP	maximum operating pressure		
MOPD	maximum operating pressure differential		
		SAE	Society of Automotive Engineers
MPT	male pipe thread		
MTC	motor temperature control	**sec**	seconds
mV	millivolt	**SORIT**	solenoid open on rise in temperature
MW	megawatt		
N	newton	**sp**	single-pole (switch)
NC	normally closed	**sq. ft.**	square foot = ft^2
NO	normally open	**sq. in.**	square inch = in^2
OA	outdoor air	**st**	single-throw (switch)
OD	outside diameter	**TD or ΔT**	temperature difference
ODF	outside diameter female	**TDR**	time-delay relay
ODM	outside diameter male	**TDS**	time-delay switch
OPCO	oil pressure cut-out	**ton**	ton of refrigeration effect
ORD	open on rise of differential	**Tr**	reference temperature
		TXV or TEV	thermostatic expansion valve

UV	ultraviolet light	**°F**	degree Fahrenheit
V Max	maximum voltage in AC cycle	**°K**	degree Kelvin
		°R	degree Rankine
V	volt	**Ω**	ohm
v	volume	**π**	pi (3.1416)
VA	volt-ampere	**1Φ**	single-phase current
W	watt	**3Φ**	3-phase current
°C	degree Celsius		

Glossary

A

Accumulator: Storage tank at the evaporator exit or suction line used to prevent floodbacks to the compressor.

AC: Alternating current; the form of electricity generated and distributed through power lines.

ACR tube (air conditioning and refrigeration) tube: Copper tube (usually hard-drawn) sold cleaned and sealed with nitrogen inside to prevent oxidation. Identified by actual OD.

Ambient temperature: Temperature of the fluid (usually air) that surrounds the object under discussion.

Ampere (amp): Unit of electric current equal to 1 coulomb of electrons flowing past a point each second.

Anneal: To heat metal to reduce work hardening before more bending, etc.

Anode: Positive terminal in an electric cell.

Automatic expansion valve (AEV or AXV): Valve that controls flow of refrigerant into the evaporator, depending only on evaporator pressure.

Azeotropic mixture: Mix of refrigerants. At constant pressure, temperature does not change during evaporation and condensing. On a P-T chart, it's like a primary refrigerant.

B

Back pressure: Pressure on system low side; also called suction, evaporator, or low-side pressure.

Bellows: Accordion-like container used to detect changes in pressure.

Bimetal strip (bimetallic strip): Strip made of two metals that have different rates of expansion. Used to measure temperature.

Bleed: To reduce pressure by slightly opening a valve; to remove unwanted fluids, such as air, from a system.

Booster: The first-stage compressor in a cascade system.

Bourdon tube: Tube of elastic metal bent into circular shape that is found inside a pressure gauge.

British thermal unit (BTU): The amount of heat needed to warm 1 pound of water by 1°F.

C

Calorie: SI unit of heat. One small calorie (cal) will warm 1 cubic centimeter of water 1°C. One large calorie (kcal) will warm 1 kilogram of water 1°C.

Capacitance: The ability of a material to hold electric energy on oppositely charged plates. Measured in farads.

Capacitor: Device with the ability to store electricity as capacitance; used to start motors, among other purposes.

Cascade system: A refrigeration system with multiple compressors and evaporators. The evaporator of the first compressor cools the condenser of the second compressor. Can reach very cold temperatures.

Cathode: Negative terminal, the source of electrons in an electric cell.

Celsius scale (°C): Temperature scale in SI. Water freezes at 0°C and boils at 100°C.

Change of state (change of phase): A change of the condition of a substance from one state to another, accompanied by a gain or loss of latent heat.

Chiller: An air-conditioning system that circulates cooled water to the conditioned space; an evaporator that cools the water in a chiller system.

Clearance space: The volume in a reciprocating compressor cylinder when the piston is at top dead center = $\pi \times r^2 \times h$

Coil, holding: Electromagnetic coil in a motor starter used to hold the contacts closed.

Compound system: A system in which the first compressor feeds refrigerant to the second compressor. Capable of high suction and low temperatures.

Compression ratio: Total cylinder volume divided by clearance space. *See Pumping ratio.*

Compressor displacement: Compressor volume in cubic inches is found by multiplying the piston area by the stroke by the number of cylinders. 1,728 cubic inches = 1 cu. ft., so displacement in cubic feet per minute =

$$\frac{\pi \times r^2 \times L \times rpm \times n}{1728}.$$

Condense: To change from gas to liquid by removing the latent heat of condensation.

Condenser limiter: *See Condenser pressure regulator.*

Condenser pressure regulator: A valve that maintains high-side pressure so that adequate pressure drop will occur at the metering device.

Conditioned space: The room, cabinet, or other area being cooled or heated by an air conditioning system.

Constant-temperature valve: *See Evaporator pressure regulator.*

Convection: Movement of heat in a fluid, propelled by a difference in density.

Cooling load: Amount of heat that must be removed from a conditioned space in 24 hours to maintain design conditions.

Critical charge: An exact charge of refrigerant; commonly found in a system using a flooded evaporator or a capillary tube.

Cross-charged: A fluid used in a TXV sensing bulb that contains a different refrigerant from what's in the system.

Cut-in: The temperature or pressure at which a control device signals a piece of equipment to operate.

Cut-out: The temperature or pressure at which a control device signals a piece of equipment to stop operating.

Cycling, short: *See Hunt (cycle).*

D

Dalton's law: Total vapor pressure in a vessel equals the sum of the vapor pressures of the individual gases.

DC: Direct current; the form of electricity produced by batteries.

Dehumidification: The process of removing water vapor from air.

Desiccation: Removal of moisture from a substance.

Design pressure: The highest or lowest expected pressure in a system.

Desuperheater, liquid: Valve that allows a small amount of liquid refrigerant to enter the low side to cool the suction gas.

Dew point: The temperature at which water vapor in a mass of air will begin to condense; the temperature at which relative humidity would reach 100%. Equal to saturation temperature.

Differential: A valve that opens at one pressure and closes at another. Allows a system to adjust itself with a minimum of over-correction.

Differential, control: The difference between the cut-in and cut-out settings.

Direct-expansion evaporator: An evaporator in which an AXV or TXV is the metering device.

Discharge gas: Hot, high-pressure vapor refrigerant that has just left the compressor.

Discharge line: The line from the compressor to the condenser; contains discharge gas.

Dry-bulb temperature: The actual temperature of air as measured on an ordinary thermometer. *See Wet-bulb temperature.*

E

Electromechanical: A device in which electricity creates a motion, or a motion affects the electrical properties of the device.

Electromotive force (EMF): Potential, measured in volts.

Energy efficiency ratio (EER): The ratio found by dividing rated cooling capacity in BTU/hour by watts of electricity consumed.

Enthalpy: The total heat content of a substance, compared to a standard value (32°F [0°C] for water vapor, –40°F [–40°C] for refrigerant).

Evaporation (boiling): Process of taking up latent heat and changing from liquid to a gas.

Evaporator pressure regulator: A valve to maintain a high pressure in warmer evaporators in systems with several evaporators.

Evaporator temperature: The temperature of the refrigerant boiling in the evaporator.

External equalizer: The tube from the body of a TXV to the suction line; used to register an accurate suction-line pressure at the valve.

F

Farad (f): The unit of electrical capacitance. One farad can store 1 coulomb of electrons across a potential of 1 volt.

Flash gas: An unwanted phenomenon in which some refrigerant vaporizes (flashes) just ahead of the metering device. Interferes with the metering device and reduces capacity.

Floodback (slugging): A return of liquid refrigerant to the compressor via the suction line. Likely to cause compressor damage.

Flooded system: System in which the evaporator is nearly filled with liquid refrigerant.

Frost back: Frosting of suction line due to entry of liquid refrigerant.

Fusible plug: Safety device designed to release pressure from a vessel in a fire or malfunction. Made of metal that melts at a low temperature.

G

Galvanic action: Corrosion of two metals that touch each other, caused by electric currents created between them.

Gas, noncondensable: A gas (usually air) that is unable to condense at the temperature and pressures in the condenser. Robs the system of capacity.

Gauge manifold: Device with three outlets and two gauges used for diagnostic and service procedures.

Ground wire: Safety wire used to conduct electricity from a component to the ground in case of malfunction.

H

Halogen: An element from the halogen group: chlorine, fluorine, bromine, and iodine. Two halogens are present in chlorofluorocarbon refrigerants. Halogens can destroy stratospheric ozone.

Head pressure control: *See Condenser pressure regulator.*

Head pressure (high-side pressure): Pressure in the condenser.

Heat: Form of energy that increases the motion of molecules and may raise the temperature of a substance.

Heat of compression: Heat added to a system by the work of the compressor.

Heat of condensation: *See Latent heat of condensation.*

Heat of fusion: *See Latent heat of fusion (freezing).*

Heat of vaporization: *See Latent heat of vaporization (boiling).*

Heat, latent: The amount of heat required to change the state of a substance without changing temperature.

Heat, sensible: Heat that can be detected with a dry thermometer.

Hermetic compressor or system: A sealed unit containing a motor and a compressor.

Hertz (hz): Correct name for cycles per second.

Hg (mercury): Metal that is liquid at room temperature; used to measure pressure in some manometers and to make contact in a mercury switch or relay.

High side: Segment of a system between the compressor and the metering device; under high-side pressure.

Holdback valve: *See Condenser pressure regulator.*

Horsepower: Unit of power equal to 746 watts. *See Power.*

Hot-gas bypass: System allowing refrigerant to bypass the condenser; used to control cooling capacity.

Hot-gas defrost: System that pumps discharge gas directly to the evaporator for defrosting.

Humidification: The process of adding water vapor to air.

Humidity (absolute): The mass of water vapor in a given quantity of air. Expressed as grains per pound (7,000 grain = 1 lb.).

Humidity (relative): Proportion of actual moisture in a volume of air compared to the maximum the air could hold at that temperature.

Hunt (cycle): To cycle erratically because the control cannot hold the desired conditions.

Hygrometer: Instrument used to measure moisture in the air.

I

Impedance: Opposition to flow of current in an AC circuit; similar to resistance in a DC circuit. Measured in ohms.

J

Joule: One newton operating through 1 meter. An SI unit of heat and energy.

K

Kelvin scale: Absolute SI temperature scale; 0°K is absolute zero. Ice thaws at 273°K.

King valve: A valve at the condenser outlet used during service work.

L

Latent heat of condensation: Amount of latent heat that must be removed so a substance will condense without changing temperature.

Latent heat of fusion (freezing): Amount of heat that must be removed to freeze or crystallize a substance with no change in temperature.

Latent heat of vaporization (boiling): Amount of heat that must be added to boil a substance without change in temperature.

Limit: A safety device that prevents unsafe system conditions; may measure pressure or temperature.

Limitizer: *See Condenser pressure regulator.*

Low pressure cut-out (LPCO): Control that shuts down the compressor if suction pressure drops below a safe level.

Low side: Portion of system between metering device and compressor. Entire area is at evaporating, or low-side, pressure.

Low-side pressure: Pressure in the low side.

M

Manifold: A chamber connecting several ducts, tubes, or components, usually all at the same pressure.

Manifold, gauge: *See Gauge manifold.*

Manometer: Device for reading pressure by measuring its effect on a fluid, usually water or mercury.

Megohm: One million ohms.

Megohmmeter: Instrument capable of reading resistances in the million-ohm range; used to test motor insulation.

Micron gauge: Meter capable of measuring vacuums close to absolute; reads in microns of mercury.

Modulating system: A refrigeration system that can match capacity to demand. In a compound system, the number of compressors operating at any time depends on the demand. A single compressor may modulate capacity with unloading devices.

Motor, induction: A motor in which electromagnetism is induced in the rotor by the field magnets. No electrical connection to the rotor is needed.

Multiple system: Several evaporators are connected to a single condensing unit.

N

Newton: The SI unit of force; will accelerate 1 kilogram by 1 m/sec2.

Nominal size tubing: Plumbing tube with actual OD about ⅛-inch larger than the nominal size; includes water tube, drainage tube, but not ACR tube.

O

Ohm (Ω): The unit of resistance in a DC circuit.

Oil binding: A layer of oil on top of refrigerant that prevents normal evaporation in the evaporator; also jamming of a mechanism with excess oil.

Oil-pressure cut-out: Limit switch that shuts down the compressor if oil pressure drops to near crankcase pressure.

Overload protector: Device to shut down an overloaded compressor motor. May detect overload by measuring current, pressure, or temperature.

Ozone: A molecule of oxygen with three atoms (O_3). A pollutant in the lower atmosphere but an essential barrier to ultraviolet light in the upper atmosphere. Ozone in the upper atmosphere is destroyed by released halocarbon refrigerants.

P

Package unit: A complete system, including compressor, condenser, and evaporator in one unit.

Partial pressure: The pressure of a single gas in a mixture of gases.

Ph: Scale for measuring acidity and alkalinity: 7 is neutral; lower numbers are acidic and higher numbers are alkaline (basic).

Phase (Φ): The number of waves of AC flowing in a single circuit. *See State.*

Pipe: Steel, iron, or other cylindrical material used to convey fluids.

Plenum chamber: An equalizing or mixing chamber to which several supply ducts are connected.

Pound of air: Generally means a pound of dry air.

Power: The rate at which work is done; measured in horsepower or watts.

Power factor: Ratio to describe actual capacity for work of an AC circuit. Measures the amount of coincidence between current and voltage waves.

Pressure, absolute: Total pressure in pounds per square inch absolute (psia) or kilopascals (kPa); equal to gauge pressure plus atmospheric pressure.

Pressure drop: Difference in pressure between two points in a system.

Pressure, gauge: Pressure in pounds per square inch gauge (psig). Zero gauge pressure equals atmospheric pressure at sea level. Not used in SI.

Pressure motor control: Control that operates a motor by measuring low-side pressure.

Pressure-reducer valve: *See Evaporator pressure regulator.*

Pressure regulator, evaporator: Device to keep evaporator pressure above a setting. Used to prevent abnormally low temperature.

psi: Pressure in pounds per square inch.

psia: Absolute pressure in psi.

psig: Gauge (measured) pressure in psi.

Psychrometer (wet-bulb hygrometer): Device for measuring relative humidity.

Psychrometric chart: A chart listing absolute humidity, temperature (dry bulb and wet bulb), dew point, vapor pressure, total heat (enthalpy), and relative humidity of air.

Pump down: To use the system compressor to pump most refrigerant into the condenser or receiver before storage or service.

Pump, fixed displacement: A pump that moves a given amount of fluid with each stroke.

Pumping ratio: The ratio of absolute discharge pressure to absolute suction pressure. *See Compression ratio.*

Q

Quick-connect: A connector used to join components of a precharged system without needing evacuation.

R

Recover: To remove refrigerant from a system and store it in a tank.

Recycle: To remove moisture and other contaminants from recovered refrigerant prior to reuse.

Reed valve: Flat metal element that comprises intake and discharge valves in the head of a reciprocating compressor.

Refrigerant, primary: A refrigerant containing a pure chemical. *See Azeotropic mixture.*

Relative humidity: *See Humidity (relative).*

Relay: Electromagnetic switch operated by control circuit voltage that switches line voltage.

Relay, current: Relay that responds to current in a circuit.

Relay, potential: Relay that measures voltage of a circuit.

Relay, thermal (hot-wire relay): Control device that uses a hot wire to convert electricity to heat. When the current rises above the setting, it creates too much heat, forcing a contact to bend and break the circuit.

Remote system: Cooling system in which the evaporator is far from the condensing unit.

Resistance: The opposition to flow. Electrical resistance is measured in ohms.

Riser, suction: Vertical piece of suction line.

Riser valve: Valve in vertical piping used to control flow.

Rotor (armature): Part of motor or other device that rotates.

Running time: Number of hours a machine operates in each 24-hour day.

S

Safety control (limit): Control designed to prevent unsafe operating conditions.

Saturated air: Air holding the maximum possible water vapor (100% relative humidity) at its temperature and pressure.

Saturated gas: A gas in equilibrium with its liquid phase; the amount of evaporation equals the amount of condensation.

Saturation pressure-temperature: Condition in which both liquid and vapor phases are present and the temperature is constant. Found inside an evaporator. The rate of boiling may not equal the rate of condensation.

Schraeder valve: Valve that permits flow in one direction if pressure exceeds a setting, and in the other direction if a pin is depressed.

Sensor: Device that detects a change in conditions and creates a signal for another device.

SI system (SI): International Standard measurement system (metric system).

Sine wave: Type of wave characteristic of AC. Current and voltage go above and below 0 once per cycle.

Slugging: *See Floodback (slugging).*

Solenoid: Electromagnetic device used to move a valve or switch.

Specific gravity: Density of fluid compared to water, which has a specific gravity of 1.0.

Specific heat capacity: The amount of sensible heat needed to change the temperature of a substance 1°F in the English system and 1°C in SI. Measured in BTU/lb. per °F and joule per kilogram kelvin, or J/(kg·K).

Split-phase motor: Motor with two stators; one only for starting, the other for starting and running.

State: The phase (solid, liquid, gas, or plasma) of matter.

Static pressure: Pressure exerted by a gas against all the walls of its container. *Compare Velocity pressure.*

Stator (field): Part of a motor that is stationary; contains field windings.

Sublimate: Change directly from solid to gas, as with dry ice.

Suction pressure regulator: *See Evaporator pressure regulator.*

Superheat: Increase in temperature above boiling point for a given pressure; increase in temperature of suction-line gas over the evaporator.

Sweat: (1) Water that condenses on a surface. (2) To join with soldering or brazing.

T

Temperature, absolute: Temperature measured using absolute zero as the starting point. Uses the Rankine or Kelvin scale.

Therm: Amount of heat equal to 100,000 BTUs.

Thermistor: An electronic sensor in which resistance is proportional to the temperature sensed.

Thermocouple: A temperature-sensing device having two metals in contact with each other; creates a current proportional to temperature.

Thermostatic expansion valve (TEV or TXV): Valve used to control entry of refrigerant into an evaporator, based on suction-line temperature and evaporator pressure.

Three-phase (3Φ) power: Electric supply with three phases flowing simultaneously. Each current is 120° out of phase with the other two.

Throttle (modulate): To close or open gradually in response to a manual or automatic adjustment.

Ton of refrigeration: Cooling capacity equal to melting 1 ton of ice in 24 hours. Equals 12,000 BTU/hour or 288,000 BTU/day.

Torque, starting: Amount of turning force developed by a resting motor when current first enters it.

Two-temperature valve: *See Evaporator pressure regulator.*

U

Universal motor: Motor that can operate on AC or DC.

Unloader: (1) A device to reduce compressor capacity or starting load. (2) A valve that temporarily prevents a compressor cylinder from pulling in and compressing refrigerant.

V

Valve, backseating: Valve that in normal position has no fluid pressure on the packing. Used in suction- and discharge-service valves.

Vapor: The gaseous phase of a material.

Vapor, saturated: Vapor held in pressure-temperature condition where any cooling will cause condensation.

Vaporization: Change from liquid to vapor state with the addition of the latent heat of vaporization.

Velocity pressure: Pressure due to the movement of fluid. *See Static pressure.*

Viscosity: The resistance to flow of a fluid (commonly refers to oil).

Volt: The unit of electrical pressure.

Volumetric efficiency: Ratio of actual pumping of a compressor or vacuum pump to its theoretical maximum.

W

Watt (W): Unit of electric power equal to 1 J/sec. One kilowatt/hour is the equivalent to 1,000 W operating for 1 hour.

Wet-bulb depression: The difference between wet-bulb temperature and dry-bulb temperature; used to find relative humidity with a psychrometric chart.

Wet-bulb temperature: The temperature of air as indicated on a thermometer where evaporation can take place. Cooling due to evaporation reduces the temperature below dry-bulb temperature.

Z

Zeotropic refrigerant (zeotrope): A refrigerant with several components with different volatilities. Even at a constant pressure, the composition and saturation temperatures change during evaporation and condensing.

INDEX